Arthur
MILLER

a reference guide

A
Reference
Publication
in
Literature

Ronald Gottesman
Editor

Arthur
MILLER

a reference guide

JOHN H. FERRES

G.K.HALL&CO.
70 LINCOLN STREET, BOSTON, MASS.

Distributed in the United Kingdom and Europe
by George Prior Associated Publishers, Ltd.,
37-41 Bedford Row, London WC1R 4JH, Englard
ISBN (U.K.) 0-86043-174-6

Library of Congress Cataloging in Publication Data

Ferres, John H
   Arthur Miller, a reference guide.

   (A Reference publication in literature)
   Includes index.
   1. Miller, Arthur, 1915-   — Bibliography.
I. Title.   II. Series.
Z8574.88.F47 [PS3525.I5156]   812'.5'2   79-10121
ISBN 0-8161-7822-4

Contents

Introduction

As major playwright, public person and private individual, Arthur Miller has been an important figure on the American scene for more than three decades. He is a leading twentieth-century American playwright; Eugene O'Neill and Tennessee Williams are perhaps the only others whose achievements are comparable. Willy Loman, the protagonist of Miller's best play, Death of a Salesman, is part of the American idiom; more so perhaps than Blanche Dubois of Williams' A Streetcar Named Desire. As a public person, too, Miller has been a leader, asserting his views on public questions and issues of the day. An early novel, Focus (1945), was an indictment of anti-Semitism. As conscience of the liberal intellectual establishment in the McCarthyite 1950's, he became a culture hero when he read the House Un-American Activities Committee a lesson on the sanctity of human and artistic rights in a free society and eventually won acquittal in court of contempt of Congress charges. (In the court of public opinion, Miller was clearly innocent of un-American activities. What could be less un-American than marrying Marilyn Monroe?) Later, during the Vietnam War, Miller bore persistent and eloquent testimony to the morally devasting effects of the war on American society. Now, his public roles apparently behind him, Miller is "one of those rare celebrity writers who has gracefully made the transition from the limelight back to the desk lamp."[1] He seems content to mellow on his rural Connecticut farm, his instinctive liberalism stirring occasionally to endorse Jewish causes or to cosign protest statements concerning the treatment of dissident intellectuals and artists behind the Iron Curtain.

Miller's adolescence coincided with the Great Depression, a fact which accounts in part for the dominant theme of social and individual responsibility in his plays. In his early unpublished work and radio plays, and in All My Sons, Death of a Salesman and The Price, Miller's criticism of the American economic system and social values, and the conflicts these produce in families and individuals, stems from his own family's Depression experiences. With the collapse of his father's garment manufacturing business during the Depression, Miller's family was forced to move to a smaller house in Brooklyn, one probably similar to the Loman home in Death of a Salesman. For the next two and a half years, and for an additional five years after graduation from college, Miller worked as common laborer, farmhand, warehouse clerk, waiter, factory worker, longshoreman, seaman, truck driver, and assistant pipe fitter. The sense of actuality in many of his plays is attributable in large measure to his wide experience as a wage earner.

Miller's apprenticeship in the school of hard knocks succeeded in bringing about an intellectual awakening where high school had failed. He began to read Dostoyevsky and to wonder about the forces responsible for the economic conditions of the 1930's. After 1929, Miller could not believe "in the reality I saw with my eyes." He was filled with the same yearning he found in The Brothers Karamazov for some connection with the "invisible world of cause and effect, mysterious, full of surprises, implacable in its course."[2] Like many Americans, Miller began to examine alternatives to a literally bankrupt economic and social order, was impressed by the indictments of that system by Clifford Odets, John Steinbeck and others; and, in the inquisitorial 1950's, found himself accused of past Communist heresies by reigning superpatriots like Senator Joseph McCarthy and Congressman Francis Walter, Chairman of the House Un-American Activities Committee. Miller's experiences during this period were analogous to those of The Crucible's John Proctor, a seventeenth century martyr for freedom of speech and thought, and to the anguished self-justifications of Quentin, the leftist-intellectual protagonist of After the Fall.

Miller's typical heroes are men whose unquestioning acceptance of the integrity and sanity of their society is suddenly and rudely jolted. Realizing they have been living an absurd lie, they resolve henceforth to live and die authentically. If the Miller hero's recognition of his responsibility to self and society has a born-again quality, the religion of the plays is, notwithstanding, one of secular humanism. It is a religion based on love, on the compassionate acceptance of the universal bond that defines our humanity. Daring to love, we learn how to live. Though it may be argued that human, especially family, relationships in his early plays are disastrous, Miller is indirectly emphasizing the need for love through its absence or perversion. If this seems simplistic, it is nonetheless the time-honored message of most religions. City bred, Miller's values have always been country oriented. They are the values mythically associated with the American agrarian utopia—honesty, hope, responsibility, simplicity, integrity, pride, courage, honor, and compassion.

It will no doubt occur to the reader perusing this bibliography that, although Miller's achievement is still regarded by audiences and many newspaper reviewers as the equal of that of O'Neill or Williams, the academic or "serious" drama critics do not now hold him in such high esteem. When a critic does acknowledge Miller as a leading contemporary American playwright, he is likely to grant the accolade by default. Though his career has not sustained the early promise of Death of a Salesman and The Crucible, the argument goes, no younger playwright has yet matched his limited achievement. Harold Clurman is perhaps the only important critic who is consistently sympathetic toward the later plays. One may speculate on reasons for the disparity between Miller's popular and academic reputations.

The conventional form of the plays and the author's earnest moralizing about the continuing relevance and salutariness of his utopian values, and the possibility of realizing them if we will sincerely try, now seem passé in some quarters. There is no theater of violence, silence, or cruelty in Miller; no total, living, or porno theater. For his own part, Miller accuses the present generation of playwrights of theatrical journalism, or plays that exploit mere sensationalism and dramaturgical gimmickry. And yet to the extent that existentialism is still a force in the contemporary theater, Miller's anxious, questioning heroes are very much of their time.[3] He remains the "significant American dramatist of alienation," a universal condition in the twentieth century.[4] Perhaps Miller's critics are indeed complaining not so much about his themes as his somewhat didactic expression of them. The post-realist distrust of overblown rhetoric, philosophizing, and anything smacking of moralizing in the theater has rendered suspect any playwright who seeks to go beyond disillusionment with the world as it exists to find solutions to its problems. Moreover, before the philosopher-comic Gregory Solomon of The Price (1968) Miller's characters were always relentlessly serious, even when they were not preaching. It has taken him a long time to realize, with Mark Twain, that man's only adequate defense against despair is laughter.

With regard to dramatic form, there is in fact considerable stylistic and structural experimentation in the plays, despite the fact that as a social dramatist of ideas Miller might not be expected to be preoccupied with form. The alternation between expressionism, realism, and stream-of-consciousness flashbacks in Salesman, the conversion of seventeenth century speech into an eloquent medium for modern thought in The Crucible, the attempt to write a modern classical tragedy in A View From the Bridge, and the location of the entire action of After the Fall in the consciousness of the central character prove that, far from shunning innovation or experimentation, Miller's attempts to wed dramatic form with content place him in the mainstream of twentieth-century drama. The nineteenth-century influence of Henrik Ibsen on dramatic form and situation in the early plays has perhaps obscured the originality of Miller's methods.

Another possible reason for Miller's low standing among the critics is the élitist suspicion that a popular playwright and sometime celebrity is unworthy of a place in the playwrights' pantheon alongside Sophocles, Shakespeare and Molière--who also, it might be noted, appealed strongly to popular audiences. After the initial enthusiasm, critics such as Eric Bentley, Mary McCarthy, Susan Sontag, and Robert Brustein have discovered a responsibility to cut Miller

down to size. Perhaps because of his involvement with politics,
Marilyn Monroe, and show business, these critics find praising Miller
as distasteful as praising a preacher who keeps carelessly getting
himself arrested in bordellos. Miller's reputation today is higher
abroad than at home. This could be explained by the fact that
European critics were less ecstatic than their American counterparts
about the early plays, and more tolerant of Miller's personal and
public life; thus they feel no need for sober, face-saving revalu-
ation.

Perhaps contemporary American drama critics have fallen victim
to the dread cultural cringe or inferiority complex about American
versus European culture. William Faulkner's genius was recognized
in France twenty years before he gained critical recognition and
reader acceptance in this country. And Robert Frost's first volume
of poetry, rejected by American publishers, had to be published in
England. Or perhaps the reason for Miller's devaluation is that, in
the absence of a strong theatre tradition in this country, our strength
has lain in other literary forms. Some American critics may be uncon-
sciously programmed to measure Miller against a William Faulkner or
Earnest Hemingway, a Robert Frost or Robert Lowell. Furthermore,
critics often focus on similarities rather than differences between
Miller's early and later plays, concluding that his talent is exhausted.
Thus Miller is seen in The Price as reverting, for lack of new inspir-
ation, to the Depression themes and family conflicts of Death of a
Salesman, written twenty years earlier. In After the Fall he is found
guilty of a compulsive gnawing at the ossified memory of political
involvements of the 1940's and 1950's. Foreign critics, however, less
encumbered by familiarity with the early plays, are able to point out
new themes and dramatic techniques in the later ones. And a new generation of American critics is discovering the mythic intent and
archetypal echoes of the plays.[5]

The critics also discern a certain ambiguity of theme, even in
the most widely acclaimed Miller plays. If Death of a Salesman is an
indictment of a materialistic, dehumanizing social order, why are
Bernard and Ben, who thrive in that order, presented so sympathet-
ically? Who or what is to blame for the destruction of Willy Loman?
Is The Crucible a universal warning never to surrender private conscience to the state, is it special pleading and self-justification
growing out of Miller's own confrontations with the House Un-American
Activities Committee, or is it simply a play about a love triangle,
one of the most popular and universal themes of all? Time has sorted
things out in the case of The Crucible. Ten years after McCarthy's
downfall, a revival of the play was viewed as a universal drama of
conscience rather than a propaganda tract employing specious historical parallels. But fourteen years after it opened, and sixteen
years after the death of Marilyn Monroe, After the Fall is still written off as a voyeuristic mea culpa by the Miller-like hero for his
treatment of the Monroe-like heroine and of leftist friends undergoing

the ordeal of a House Un-American Activities investigation. Though
the memory of Monroe will undoubtedly linger longer than McCarthy's,
the time may come when the theme of <u>After the Fall</u> will be accepted
as the destructiveness at the core of the human heart, and the universal need to prey on the things we love.

Perhaps some of the puzzlement regarding Miller's meaning is his
own fault. Eric Mottram argues that Miller is "caught between a
belief in a fixed 'human nature' and a desire to see it change," and
that his "obsession with 'good name,' law and authority, self and
society, the Unpardonable Sin and the inevitability of suicide in
extreme situations overwhelm his arguments into simplified analyses,
confusions, and a final paralysis of desperate warnings."[6] Though
these criticisms are harsh, it is undeniable that when Miller's subjectivity is not completely transmuted or objectified into art, his
plays reflect the flux of the experiential now. He is in fact an
autobiographical writer whose plays form a continuous whole. A reader
familiar with Miller's life can see parallels with characters such as
Chris Keller in <u>All My Sons</u>, Biff Loman in <u>Death of a Salesman</u>, Quentin
in <u>After the Fall</u>, and Walter Franz in <u>The Price</u>. And in his colorful
<u>Marilyn Monroe</u>, Maurice Zolotow even speculates that the one-man, two-
women triangles in <u>The Crucible</u> and <u>A View from the Bridge</u> (especially
the revised version) are Miller's subconscious attempts to rationalize
guilt feelings arising from his attraction to Marilyn Monroe while
still married to his first wife.[7]

Miller is always interested in tensions, the dialectic of reality.
At least two critics, however, view the dialectic as a contradiction
between idea and feeling in the plays, one that Miller regards as
inherent in a genre he has come to mistrust.[8]

Finally, it is argued that in the attempt to use language such as
men do use, Miller's dialogue is often banal, awkward, and repetitious.
Admittedly, his characters are often inarticulate, prosaic types;
this is one reason why audiences can identify with them. With the
possible exception of John Proctor in <u>The Crucible</u> and Eddie Carbone
in <u>A View from the Bridge</u>, however, the Miller hero lacks even the
rough eloquence and poetry needed to lend dignity and significance
to his ordeal.

Why then, despite their shortcomings, do Miller's plays continue
to appeal to both American and international audiences, whether on
stage, film, or television? First, because they reach an audience
quickly and surely with the shock of recognition that Miller is writing about familiar people, situations, and conflicts. The plays hook
themselves into the fabric of the mind and stay there. They have a
universality that enables them to transcend their period, their pre-
dominately New York Jewish milieu, and their roots in Miller's personal life. At the same time they take a responsible view of life in
American society, a view that Harold Clurman has called Miller's

"humanistic jurisprudence."[9] Together with his fiction and essays,
they are a testimony to his involvement in the life of this country
for the past thirty years. They appeal also precisely because they
do use the banal and repetitious language and rhythms of common
speech; because they are not intellectually intimidating or pretentious in the manner of Edward Albee, for example; and because they
eschew the trendy sickness and self-indulgent escapism of many contemporary playwrights. In a dark age their humanism remains intact.
Finally, they appeal because Miller is an excellent as well as a
rather traditional craftsman of the theater. At his best he has a
sure hand with conflict, pacing, suspense, and climax--with all the
elements in fact that evoke intense audience involvement.

This bibliography includes the major writings of Arthur Miller,
virtually every item of criticism listed in previous bibliographies,
as well as interviews, biographical sketches, and accounts--mostly in
the New York Times--of his considerable involvement in public affairs.
Books, pamphlets, dissertations, reviews, and articles dealing wholly
or in part with Miller are included, whether published in the United
States or abroad. Foreign language items are excluded, unless translated into English, as are the very brief treatments in standard
reference works.

The entries are arranged chronologically from 1944 to 1978, but
numerically and alphabetically by author's name within each year.
Where authorship is unknown, the item is included under "Anon." Cita-
tions are complete for all entries, with the exception of a few original page references for reviews in New York Theater Critics' Reviews,
which omits this information. An asterisk preceding a citation
denotes inaccessibility of the item for annotation.

I am indebted to Michigan State University for an All-University
Research Grant that paid for typing costs, and to Walter Burinski,
Interlibrary Loan Librarian at Michigan State University, for unflag-
ging diligence in obtaining items otherwise unavailable. Compiling
this bibliography was made easier by the existence of previous Miller
bibliographies, notably Tetsumaro Hayashi's An Index to Arthur Miller
Criticism (Metuchen, N. J.: Scarecrow Press, 1969, 1976), and Harriett
Ungar's "The Writings of and about Arthur Miller: A Check List, 1936-
1967," New York Public Library Bulletin, 74 (February 1970), 107-34.
My compilation differs from the others in its updated comprehensive-
ness, its inclusion of summary abstracts of each item, its chrono-
logical arrangement of materials, and its limitation of primary
sources to major works.

---

1.   Josh Greenfield, "Writing Plays is Absolutely Senseless, Arthur
     Miller Says, 'But I Love It. I Just Love It,'" New York Times
     Magazine (February 13, 1972), p. 16.

Introduction

2. Arthur Miller, "The Shadows of the Gods: A Critical View of the American Theater," Harper's, 217 (August 1958), 34–43.

3. For a discussion of the parallels between After the Fall and Albert Camus' The Fall, see Albert Cismaru, "Before and After the Fall," Forum (Houston), 11 (Summer-Fall 1973), 67–71. Lawrence D. Lowenthal discusses parallels between Jean Paul Sartre's The Victors and Miller's A View from the Bridge and Incident at Vichy in his "Arthur Miller's Incident at Vichy: A Sartrean Interpretation," Modern Drama, 18 (March 1975), 29–41.

4. Eric Mottram, "Arthur Miller: Development of a Political Dramatist in America," in Robert W. Corrigan, ed., Arthur Miller: A Collection of Critical Essays (Englewood Cliffs, N.J.: Prentice-Hall, Inc., 1969), p. 51.

5. See, for example, Helen M. McMahon, "Arthur Miller's Common Man: the Problem of the Realistic and the Mythic," Dissertation Abstracts International, 34 (July 1973), 326A–27A, and John M. Roderick, "Arthur Miller and American Mythology," Dissertation Abstracts International, 35 (May 1975), 7324A.

6. Eric Mottram, "Arthur Miller: Development of a Political Dramatist in America," in Robert Corrigan, ed., Arthur Miller: A Collection of Critical Essays, pp. 56–57.

7. Marilyn Monroe (New York: Bantam Books, 1961), pp. 260–70.

8. Ronald Hayman, Arthur Miller (New York: Frederick Ungar Publishing Company, 1972), pp. 121–22, and Orm Överland, "The Action and Its Significance: Arthur Miller's Struggle with Dramatic Form," Modern Drama, 18 (March 1975), 1–14.

9. Harold Clurman, "Theatre: Attention!" New Republic, 120 (February 28, 1949), 28.

Arthur Miller's Major Works

PLAYS
(date of first production in parentheses)

The Man Who Had All the Luck (1944), in Cross-Section. Edited by
   Edwin Seaver. New York: L. B. Fischer, 1944.

All My Sons (1947). New York: Reynal and Hitchcock, 1947.

Death of a Salesman (1949). New York: Viking, 1949.

An Enemy of the People (1950). New York: Viking, 1951. (Adaptation
   of Henrik Ibsen Play.)

The Crucible (1953). New York: Viking, 1953.

A Memory of Two Mondays (1955). New York: Viking, 1955. (With
   A View from the Bridge.)

A View from the Bridge (1955). New York: Viking, 1955. (With
   A Memory of Two Mondays.)

Collected Plays. New York: Viking, 1957.

After the Fall (1964). New York: Viking, 1964.

Incident at Vichy (1964). New York: Viking, 1965.

The Price (1968). New York: Viking, 1968.

The Creation of the World and Other Business (1972). New York:
   Viking, 1973.

FICTION

Focus. New York: Reynal and Hitchcock, 1945.

Arthur Miller's Major Works

The Misfits. New York: Viking, 1961.

I Don't Need You Any More: Stories. New York: Viking, 1967.

ESSAYS AND REPORTAGE

Situation Normal. New York: Reynal and Hitchcock, 1944.

In Russia (with Inge Morath). New York: Viking, 1969.

In the Country (with Inge Morath). New York: Viking, 1977.

The Theater Essays of Arthur Miller. New York: Viking, 1978.

Writings About Arthur Miller, 1944-1977

1   ANON. "Focus." <u>Kirkus</u>, 12 (September 15), 345-46.
     Miller's "telling" first novel uses a mechanical device
to make its point but is "interesting and has a certain
challenge."

2   ANON., ed. "The Man Who Had All the Luck." <u>New York Theatre</u>
<u>Critics' Reviews</u>, 5 (November 27), 73-74.
     Reprints New York critics' reviews: Barnes (1944.3);
Chapman (1944.5); Kronenberger (1944.6); Morehouse (1944.9);
Nichols (1944.10); Rascoe (1944.12); Waldorf (1944.13).

3   BARNES, HOWARD. "P.S.--He Needed It." <u>New York Herald Tribune</u>
(November 24), p. 22.
     Review of <u>The Man Who Had All the Luck</u>. The play is mar-
red by "turbid writing" and "stuttering execution." If
there is a "kernel of philosophic truth" in the play, Miller
has "picked the wrong medium to reveal it." Reprinted:
1944.2.

4   BASSECHES, MAURICE. "'Tenshun!" <u>Saturday Review of Literature</u>,
27 (December 2), 64, 66.
     <u>Situation Normal</u> is "one of the most important books
about America and the war" yet published. It is marked by
"a fresh eye, a keen mind, and an uncommon writing talent."

5   CHAPMAN, JOHN. "The Man Who Had All the Luck a Good Try, But
Is Out of Luck." <u>New York Daily News</u> (November 24).
     Review. The play is marred by many plot elements that
do not cohere. Had Miller taken one part of the plot--that
about the ballplayers--and made three acts of it, he would
have had a better play. Miller does, however, have a "sense
of theatre and a real, if undeveloped, way of making stage
characters talk and act human." Reprinted: 1944.2.

6   KRONENBERGER, LOUIS. "A Big Problem, a Small Play." <u>PM</u> (New
York) (November 24).

1944

> Review of <u>The Man Who Had All the Luck</u>. The story-approach is not banal, several scenes have force and piquancy, but the play is neither very compelling as theater nor very significant as drama. Philosophically, it is too old fashioned and contrived, and Miller's didactic treatment does not improve matters. Reprinted: 1944.2.

7   KUPFERBERG, HERBERT. "Touring Training Camps." <u>New York Herald Tribune Weekly Book Review</u> (December 17), p. 8.
> Review of <u>Situation Normal</u>. Miller is an excellent reporter of what goes on from draft board to port of embarkation in terms of an average soldier's thoughts and feelings.

8   MALONEY, RUSSELL. "Jottings for a Movie." <u>New York Times Book Review</u> (December 24), p. 3.
> <u>Situation Normal</u> is at its best when it describes happenings rather than stalking ideas or impressions. The excitement and bewilderments of basic training have never been better recorded.

9   MOREHOUSE, WARD. "<u>The Man Who Had All the Luck</u> is Folksy, Philosophical and Tiresome." <u>New York Sun</u> (November 24).
> Review. Miller's purpose is sincere, and his play has some engaging moments and several likeable characters, but it sermonizes too much and is burdened by languid, rambling playwriting. Reprinted: 1944.2.

10 NICHOLS, LEWIS. "The Philosophy of Work Against Chance Makes Up <u>The Man Who Had All the Luck</u>." <u>New York Times</u> (November 24), p. 18.
> Review. Some good performances and careful staging do not compensate for the confusion of the script, nor the jumbled philosophies of <u>The Man Who Had All the Luck</u>. Possibly Miller has been reading William Saroyan, but the latter handles similar characters and situations better. Reprinted: 1944.2.

11 PETERSON, RALPH. "'Snafu' and the Facts of G. I. Lives." <u>Chicago Sun Book Week</u> (December 17), p. 3.
> <u>Situation Normal</u> is a "fine book that does a lot to erase all the Technicolor impressions of men at war and bring them into the daylight of actuality."

12 RASCOE, BURTON. "Good Luck at the Forrest." <u>New York World Telegram</u> (November 24).
> Review of <u>The Man Who Had All the Luck</u>. A "fine drama" with a "challenging, new idea," Miller's first play shows

vigor and dramatic skill in attacking a prevalent human
superstition, that all the good things that happen in one's
life will be balanced by an equal number of bad. This is
Emerson's theme in his essay "On Compensation"; hence Miller
has tackled a man-size job. He does so in a "faultlessly
convincing manner." Reprinted: 1944.2.

13   WALDORF, WILELLA. "The Man Who Had All the Luck." New York
     Post (November 24).
          Review. The play is an "earnest but muddled attempt to
     state [Miller's] idea of the American Credo," though after
     seeing the play it is still hard to say what this is.
     Reprinted: 1944.2.

1945

1   ANON. "Situation Normal." Booklist, 41 (January 1), 133-34.
         Brief description of this documentary of the "authentic
    G. I. reaction to the war" by one of "Hollywood's ablest
    reporters."

2   ANON. "Focus." New Yorker, 21 (November 3), 102.
         A pertinent idea for satire, but we get the point "long
    before Mr. Miller has finished belaboring it."

3   ANON. "Focus." Booklist, 42 (December 1), 111.
         Racial intolerance is portrayed artistically, dramatic-
    ally and uncompromisingly.

4   BARRY, IRIS. "Look through This Glass." New York Herald
    Tribune Weekly Book Review (November 18), p. 4.
         Compares Focus with propaganda novels of Charles Reade
    and Harriett Beecher Stowe. It is a "courageous plea on
    the part of a novelist with an urgent message."

5   BUTTERFIELD, ALFRED. "Focus." New York Times Book Review
    (November 18), p. 15.
         As the case history of a strange human experience Focus
    has merit, but as a work of substantial meaning it does
    not. Though Miller handles his explosive materials skill-
    fully, the book reads like an unsubtle, melodramatic tract
    because of its basically implausible plot.

6   DUFFIELD, MARCUS. "Whys and Wherefores." Nation, 160
    (January 13), 50.
         Brief notice of Situation Normal. A "provacative piece
    of work" that exposes the gap between official attempts at

1945

indoctrination of servicemen and their ignorance of what
they were fighting for.

7   KEEFE, EDWARD FRANCIS. "Focus." Commonweal, 43 (December 7),
    219-20.
        Brief, largely unfavorable review of Focus. The suspense
    and dramatic situations are obvious, unconvincing, colorless
    and artificial.

8   KENNEDY, LEO. "Fledgling Anti-Semite Forcibly Sees the Light."
    Chicago Sun Book Week (November 11), p. 28.
        Review of Focus. The novel is a "tract for literates on
    the anatomy of native Fascism, an indictment of bigotry and
    social irresponsibility in a consummately skillful literary
    form." It may be to the "virus of American anti-Semitism
    what Uncle Tom's Cabin was to the institution of slavery."

9   NATHAN, G. J. "The Man Who Had All the Luck," in his Theatre
    Book of the Year, 1944-1945. New York: Alfred A. Knopf,
    1945, pp. 171-73.
        Though the theme of Miller's first play is venerable and
    obvious, its treatment is diffuse, disorderly and opaque.
    At times the play seems to be an unintentional burlesque of
    its theme.

10 ROSS, JEAN L. "Focus." Kirkus, 13 (August 15), 345-46.
        Despite its turning upon a mechanical device, Miller's
    "telling" first novel is "interesting and has a certain
    challenge."

11 _____. "Focus." Library Journal, 70 (October 15), 979.
        Brief notice of Focus. Advises caution before ordering,
    since the "Christian Front is attacked."

12 SMITH, HARRISON. "The Shape of a Human Face." Saturday Review
    of Literature, 28 (November 17), 11.
        Sincere and eloquently dramatic, Focus nevertheless deals
    with thoughts, motives and fears rather than with action.
    It is significant because Miller has taken a bogeyman fear,
    familiar since Hitler's day, and made it into a real and
    comprehensible theme for his readers.

1946

1   ANON. "Words Like Tracer Bullets." New York Post Week-End
    Magazine (April 27), p. 2.

Biographical sketch of Miller accompanying digest version
of Focus. "People often find themselves confused as to his
nationality--a fact which has an important bearing on the
theme of Focus." Miller calls himself an "inadvertent
chameleon."

2   BELLOW, SAUL. "Brothers' Keepers." New Republic, 114
     (January 7), 29.
          Review of Focus. Newman's transformation from Jew-hater
     to a man who accepts society's identification of him as
     Jewish is implausible. Miller has failed in his attempt to
     rescue this representative democratic man from misunder-
     standing.

3   WEILER, A. H. "By Way of Report." New York Times (July 21),
     sec. II, pp. 3, 6.
          The King Brothers purchase film rights to Focus. Jerome
     Chadarov is to write the scenario.

1947

1   ANON. "New Play in Manhattan." Time, 49 (February 10), 68,
     70.
          Review of New York premiere of All My Sons. A compelling
     rather than an entirely convincing play, All My Sons is
     social criticism presented in terms of the individual's
     moral responsibilities. Miller combines "purposefulness
     with power" and is the "most interesting of Broadway's new
     serious playwrights."

2   ANON. "Son and Father." Newsweek, 29 (February 10), 85.
          All My Sons is an honest, forceful study of postwar
     adjustment that "bogs down only because Miller burdens it
     with more plot and circumstance than the theme requires."
     Elia Kazan's direction is sympathetic.

3   ANON. "All My Sons." Life, 22 (March 10), 71-72.
          Brief notice of New York opening of All My Sons.

4   ANON. "All My Sons." Booklist, 43 (March 15), 220.
          Brief plot summary of a "serious but moving play about
     ordinary people and their family loyalty."

5   ANON. "Critics' Award Pleases Author of All My Sons." New
     Herald Tribune (April 23), p. 27.
          Interview and brief biography of Miller on the occasion
     of his New York Drama Critics' Circle award for All My Sons

1947

as best play of 1946–47 season. Miller was gratified because the award proved that "you could say what you wanted on Broadway without having to sugar-coat it or slick it up."

6   ANON. "To Sell All My Sons Script." New York Times (May 14), p. 31.
        The manuscript of All My Sons will be auctioned by the Progressive Citizens of America.

7   ANON. "Miller, Playwright, Buys Brooklyn Home." New York Times (June 1), sec. VIII, p. 1.
        Miller buys two-family house in Brooklyn Heights, intending to remodel part of the home into a studio.

8   ANON. "Miller Fails in Plea." New York Times (June 11), p. 33.
        U.S. State Department refuses to sponsor a production of All My Sons at World Youth Festival in Prague. In a resolution wired to the Department, Miller and others assert that the "participants have no special political affiliations."

9   ANON. "Death Merchants Again." New York Times (June 12), p. 24.
        Editorialist agrees with those who feel that All My Sons is "not the best possible representation for this country" to compete at World Youth Festival in Prague.

10   ANON. "Arthur Miller." Current Biography, 8 (October), 39–40.
        Review of Miller's life and career with quotations from Miller interviews. Reprinted: 1948.1.

11   ANON. "All My Sons a Hit in Holland." New York Times (October 21), p. 26.
        The Dutch version of All My Sons premieres to a capacity audience in Rotterdam.

12   ATKINSON, BROOKS. "All My Sons," in his Broadway Scrapbook. New York: Theatre Arts, pp. 277–79.
        Reprint of 1947.15.

13   _____. "Mare's Nest Inquiries." New York Times (September 7), sec. II, p. 1.
        Defends All My Sons against those who charge it smears the American business community. Such critics are encouraging censorship and their criticisms "suggest that American tolerance and flexibility, over which we have been thumping our chests internationally for some time, are getting a little thin."

14   ____. "The Play in Review." New York Times (January 30),
        p. 21.
            Helped by Elia Kazan's fine direction, All My Sons is
        "fresh and exciting drama." It is a "pitiless analysis of
        character that gathers momentum all evening and concludes
        with both logic and dramatic impact." Reprinted: 1947.22;
        1973.2.

15   ____. "Welcome Stranger." New York Times (February 9),
        sec. II, p. 1.
            All My Sons is the "most talented work by a new author
        in some time." Miller's talent for creating characters who
        are people rather than points of view, his compact and
        sinewy prose, his tight weaving of the plot are inspired.
        Like the play, the performance overflows with passion and
        life. Reprinted: 1947.12.

16   BARNES, HOWARD. "Too Many Duds." New York Herald Tribune
        (January 30), p. 15.
            Review. Though Miller has an "acute sense of theater
        and a certain sense of form," the skeins of tragedy in All
        My Sons become hopelessly snarled by the end. Perhaps this
        is because he tries to impose classical tragic form on sub-
        ject matter which is, at best, confused. Reprinted:
        1947.22.

17   BERNSTEIN, LESTER. "Miller Rejects Hollywood's Bid." New York
        Times (July 17), p. 15.
            Miller turns down a Hollywood script-writing offer for a
        film to be directed by Alfred Hitchcock.

18   BEYER, WILLIAM H. "The State of the Theatre: Midseason High-
        lights." School and Society, 65 (April 5), 250-51.
            All My Sons is the "most moving and provocative new play
        of the season," and Miller is a "playwright to be watched
        and keenly anticipated."

19   BROWN, JOHN MASON. "New Talents and Arthur Miller." Saturday
        Review of Literature, 30 (March 1), 22-24.
            Despite its "somewhat false and unresolved central
        theme," "overdressed dialogue," and debts to Chekhov and
        Ibsen, All My Sons makes a virtue of its "blazing emotional-
        ism" and the fervor of its convictions. Elia Kazan's
        staging is excellent.

20   CALTA, LOUIS. "All My Sons Wins Critics' Laurels." New York
        Times (April 22), p. 33.

1947

    All My Sons is selected as "best American play of the
season" by the New York Drama Critics' Circle. O'Neill's
The Iceman Cometh is runner up. All My Sons is cited for
its "frank and uncompromising presentations of a timely
theme, honesty of writing and accumulative power of the
scenes."

21   CHAPMAN, JOHN. "A Lot Goes on But Little Happens in Backyard
        Drama, All My Sons." New York Daily News (January 30).
           Review. Like The Man Who Had All the Luck, All My Sons
      is not "cohesive, progressive drama but has considerable
      quality in the writing." The play contains much "high
      temperature drama" played very coolly by the company, a
      kind of understatement that is theatrically effective.
      Reprinted: 1947.22.

22   COFFIN, RACHEL W., ed. "All My Sons." New York Theatre
        Critics' Reviews, 8 (February 3), 475-78.
           Reprints of New York critics' reviews: Atkinson
      (1947.14); Barnes (1947.16); Chapman (1947.21); Coleman
      (1947.23); Garland (1947.26); Hawkins (1947.30);
      Kronenberger (1947.32); Morehouse (1947.36); Watts (1947.42).

23   COLEMAN, ROBERT. "All My Sons Not Very Convincing." New York
        Daily Mirror (January 30).
           Review. All My Sons is a "grim indictment of war profit-
      eers and selfish mothers," but it is underwritten. The
      characters are too ordinary and seldom come to life. Elia
      Kazan's direction is pedestrian and placid. Reprinted:
      1947.22.

24   EATON, WALTER P. "In Too Many Directions." New York Herald
        Tribune Weekly Book Review (March 9), p. 19.
           The confusions in the writing of All My Sons, noted by
      some reviewers of the stage production, are not dispelled
      by publication of the text. It lacks the clarity and unity
      of effect of a fine play.

25   FREEDLEY, GEORGE. "All My Sons." Library Journal, 72 (March
        15), 466.
           Brief mention of publication of All My Sons by "Broadway's
      newest playwright of importance."

26   GARLAND, ROBERT. "All My Sons Bows at Coronet Theatre." New
        York Journal American (January 30).
           Review. All My Sons is an important play about an impor-
      tant subject. It is written with "controlled emotion and
      impressive skill." Reprinted: 1947.22.

27   GASSNER, JOHN. "The Theatre Arts." Forum, 107 (March),
      271-75.
          In All My Sons Miller's skillful dramatic narrative and
      his "knack for embodying his matter in frail and anguished
      flesh" qualify him for acclaim as the postwar theatre's
      first playwright of magnitude. A real drame bourgeois, All
      My Sons is nevertheless antibourgeois and a product of the
      so-called "left" theatre.

28   GILDER, ROSAMOND. "Broadway in Review." Theatre Arts, 31
      (April), 19.
          Review of New York opening of All My Sons. The play has
      "an urgency, an originality that argues well for Miller's
      future," while it "demonstrates his capacity to build char-
      acter and to plot compelling action."

29   GREEN, E. M. "All My Sons." Theatre World, 43 (April), 32.
          Brief review of London production of All My Sons.
      Packed with "drama, excellent dialogue, taut situations
      and very human characters," the play is "one of the most
      gripping and powerful dramas the theatre has told in many
      years." Reports that five London reviewers "showered the
      play with praise," while four "tagged it for oblivion."

30   HAWKINS, WILLIAM. "All My Sons a Tense Drama." New York
      World Telegram (January 30).
          Review. A forceful, tense drama written in simple,
      clear human speech, All My Sons is a play that offers no
      one "immunity from its comment." Elia Kazan's excellent
      production gives this play about "usual people with usual
      ambitions an intense reality." Reprinted: 1947.22.

31   HUTCHENS, JOHN K. "Mr. Miller Has a Change of Luck." New
      York Times (February 23), sec. II, pp. 1, 3.
          Interview with Miller concerning past and future plans
      for writing. The reaction of veterans to All My Sons was
      gratifying. Sidney Howard's The Silver Cord and Eugene
      O'Neill's Anna Christie "will give you an idea of the kind
      of theater I'm interested in."

32   KRONENBERGER, LOUIS. "A Serious Theme Makes for Compelling
      Theatre." New York PM Exclusive (January 31).
          Review of All My Sons. Miller's superiority to other
      contemporary American playwrights lies in the "personal
      intensity that charges what goes on with noticeable power"
      and his "social and moral perceptions that permit his story
      to vibrate and expand." The play has defects, but they are

1947

the defects of its virtues: its complexity sometimes seems congested; its characters unconvincing because they are not cut from whole cloth. Reprinted: 1947.22.

33   KRUTCH, JOSEPH WOOD. "Drama." Nation, 164 (February 15), 191, 193.
    Despite an overly neat plot, and overly warm respect for all the leftist pieties, All My Sons wrings "real dramatic force" from unpromising material. Miller has two important playwright's talents: an eye for character and real skill in the telling of a story.

34   LARDNER, JOHN. "The Theater: B for Effort." New Yorker, 22 (February 8), 50.
    All My Sons is a phony play by a worthy author. To a serviceman, the play must seem unrecognizable as a symbol of the problem of war profits, war complacency, and mis-understanding between home and war fronts.

35   MACKEY, JOSEPH. "Theater's Man of the Moment." New York Sun (February 4), p. 9.
    Biographical sketch and interview with Miller.

36   MOREHOUSE, WARD. "All My Sons, Intelligent and Thoughtful Drama." New York Sun (January 30).
    Review. Miller, a "new playwright of enormous promise," has written a play of great poignancy and power. In the Kazan-Clurman production the overall effect is one of "almost unendurable force." Though All My Sons fails when striving for comedy and does not bring its minor characters to life, the vibrancy of the principal roles and the excel-lent cast more than compensate. Reprinted: 1947.22.

37   NATHAN, GEORGE JEAN. "All My Sons," in his Theatre Book of the Year, 1946-1947. New York: Alfred A. Knopf, pp. 290-93.
    Though All My Sons is honest and sincere, it "says what we already know all too well in a manner we already know as well, and in terms and language that are undistinguished." Notes similarities to Ibsen's Pillars of Society.

38   PHELAN, KAPPO. "The Stage and Screen: All My Sons." Common-weal, 45 (February 14), 445-46.
    Though the language is "literary-sentimental," the climax ill-written and overdirected and the motivation occasionally unclear, All My Sons is a "grave, wholly absorbing, inevitable play." If it asks more questions

than it answers, it is because these are "the big inescap-
able questions and their statement and reiteration in terms
of theater is the current point." Abridged: 1960.23;
1969.11.

39   S., P. "All My Sons." San Francisco Chronicle, This World
      Magazine (May 18), p. 20.
          Brief review of published version of All My Sons. The
      play is a "bitter, brooding" and "incisive study of what
      war can do to the moral fiber of men who grow fat on its
      waste and extravagance."

40   STEVENS, VIRGINIA. "Seven Young Broadway Artists." Theatre
      Arts, 31 (June), 55-56.
          Interview. Miller discusses his career, All My Sons,
      his objectives in playwriting, and the economics of Broadway.

41   TERRY, C. V. "Broadway Bookrack." New York Times Book Review
      (April 6), p. 12.
          Despite his tendency to "speak in short parts," All My
      Sons has more than youth on its side. It is too soon to
      say this young dramatist has arrived, but he is definitely
      "a man to watch."

42   WATTS, RICHARD. "A Striking But Uneven Drama." New York Post
      (January 30).
          Review of All My Sons. Had the play been more skill-
      fully planned and written, it would be less overwrought and
      overburdened with plot. The force of its climaxes, its
      earnestness and its ability to be disturbing cannot be
      denied, however. Reprinted: 1947.22.

43   WYATT, EUPHEMIA VAN RENSSELAER. "The Drama: All My Sons."
      Catholic World, 164 (March), 552-53.
          Review of Broadway premier. The taut construction is
      strengthened further by Elia Kazan's sensitive direction,
      giving the actors a "sympathy for their parts that insures
      full freedom of expression."

44   YOUNG, STARK. "Theatre: Good Occasion." New Republic, 116
      (February 10), 42.
          All My Sons "brings a good new note into the season."
      The story is genuine, the theme has a good moral basis, the
      characters are varied and well drawn. Elia Kazan's direc-
      tion "does wonders for the thematic and human values of the
      play." Abridged: 1960.23; 1969.11.

1948

1948

1   ANON. "Arthur Miller," in Current Biography Yearbook. Edited
by Anna Rothe. New York: H. W. Wilson, pp. 438-40.
Reprint of 1947.10. Enlarged with bibliography: 1947.1.

2   ANON. "Book Ban Protested." New York Times (February 16),
p. 23.
Teachers at De Witt Clinton High School in the Bronx
protest the banning of Focus from the school library on
grounds that it "offends the Roman Catholic Church."

3   ANON. "Father and Sons." Newsweek, 31 (April 12), 89.
The film of All My Sons loses something of Miller's
bitter comment on the greed and irresponsibility of war
profiteers, but it "brings the personal narrative into
closer focus."

4   ANON. "The New Pictures." Time, 51 (April 12), 100, 103.
Review of film of All My Sons. Miller's "mannered,
deeply native style of dialogue" is better suited to stage
than screen; the play is "tainted with self-righteousness"
and not very bold or original in its indictment of business
ethics. Yet it is earnest, told with compassion as well as
passion, and not without "genuine dramatic vitality."

5   ANON. "All My Sons a Hit." New York Times (May 12), p. 33.
Brief quotations from generally favorable reviews of
London production.

6   CROWTHER, BOSLEY. "The Screen in Review." New York Times
(March 29), p. 17.
Review of film of All My Sons. Hollywood's timidity
caused the play's indictment of the capitalist system to be
confined to one man's greed and narrow-mindedness. Through
Edward G. Robinson's portrayal of Joe Keller, though, the
"film still lands a staggering right hook on the jaw of the
genius profiteer."

7   FLEMING, PETER. "The Theatre." Spectator, 180 (May 21), 612.
In its London Production All My Sons is "sincere, deft,
at times distinguished," with good dialogue, confident
characterization and strong situations. Its only fault was
the "not uncommon American tendency to moralize a shade too
explicitly."

8   HATCH, ROBERT. "A Matter of Ethics." New Republic, 118
(March 22), 33-34.

12

Review of film of All My Sons. Though the dénouement is awkwardly contrived, the film is characterized by serious thinking and honest acting. The gulf between business ethics and Christian morality is not new to ethics but has a look of brave innovation on the screen.

9 HOPE-WALLACE, PHILIP. "Plays in Performance." Drama, 10 (Autumn), 11.
   All My Sons has a strong moral argument, technical assurance and the popular appeal of a dramatized "living issue," but Joe Keller's fate matters less than it should. Such themes demand a poet like Eliot or Ibsen. Miller's play is merely an exciting "inquest revelation."

10 MCCALMON, GEORGE. "All My Sons." Players Magazine, 25 (November), 47-48.
    Though Miller's controversial views of war profiteering may give sense to directors contemplating a production of All My Sons, it is a play of "unrelenting and awesome power" and vibrantly human and individual characters. Its assets are large enough to dwarf its "contrived dramaturgy and strained coincidence."

11 MCCARTEN, JOHN. "The Current Cinema: The Disinherited." New Yorker, 24 (April 3), 58-59.
    Brief review of film of All My Sons, an "effective melo-drama" that is never dull despite the "incredible mélange of circumstances" underlying the plot.

12 WHITEBAIT, WILLIAM. "The Movies: All My Sons." New States-man and Nation, 36 (September 4), 193.
    Short review of an "eminently respectable" film, based on a "well-made play" that is effective though not very moving.

13 WORSLEY, T. C. "The Theatre." New Statesman and Nation, 35 (May 22), 412.
    Brief review of London production of All My Sons. Ibsen's technical influence is visible in every scene. A strong central situation results in a successful piece of "theatre" which effectively covers up the phoney, slick magazine quality of the characters and ideas.

1949

1 ANON. "Death of a Salesman." Life, 26 (February 21), 115, 117-18, 121.

13

1949

   Brief review of Broadway premier. Notes that the public
paid $250,000 for tickets in advance for a "play which pur-
sues its cause with firm purpose and a minimum of sex."

2 ANON. "Magnificent Death." Newsweek, 33 (February 21), 78.
   Review of New York opening of Death of a Salesman, "a
vivid, emotion-shattering, and deeply moving play that ranks
with the best in contemporary American drama." Praises
acting, direction, and the set.

3 ANON. "New Plays in Manhattan." Time, 53 (February 21),
  74-76.
   Review of New York premier of Death of a Salesman. In
revealing the "tragedy of a typical American who loses out
by trying too hard to win out," Miller has done something
so simple and terrible that most playwrights would not dare
attempt it. The idea of the play is "more moving than the
play itself, but it is written in solid, sometimes stolid
prose. No fake poetry, but no real poetry either." Brief
biography of Miller.

4 ANON. "Higher Call." New Yorker, 25 (March 26), 21.
   Interview with Lee J. Cobb on career and role as Willy
Loman. Willy has a "great potential in love and warmth.
He's an anonymous entity. We're crowded with men like
that.... The amazing thing is the identification the play
gives to so many slices of society."

5 ANON. "Page 1 Awards Made By Newspaper Guild." New York
  Times (March 29), p. 21.
   Mention of drama award of New York Newspaper Guild to
production of Salesman.

6 ANON. "Miller's Play Wins Stage Prize." New York Times
  (April 4), p. 26.
   Award of Theatre Club's prize medal to Miller for Death
of a Salesman, as the "outstanding play of the season."

7 ANON. "Miller Receives Award." New York Times (April 17),
  p. 63.
   Miller accepts New York Drama Critics' Circle award for
Salesman from John Mason Brown. He gives large measure of
credit for play's success to the "excellent cast."

8 ANON. "Salesman, Kate Win Perry Awards." New York Times
  (April 25), p. 19.

Salesman wins Antoinette Perry prize as an "outstanding contribution to the theatre." Elia Kazan was awarded a prize for directing Salesman. Arthur Kennedy was awarded a prize for acting in the New York production.

9 ANON. "Noted in Passing." House and Garden, 95 (May), 218.
   Brief review of Salesman.

10 ANON. "Death of a Salesman." Booklist, 45 (May 1), 289.
   Brief review of reading version of play.

11 ANON. "The Pulitzer Prizes." New York Times (May 3), p. 24.
   Editorial briefly compliments Miller on his Pulitzer prize for Salesman.

12 ANON. "Sketches of Pulitzer Prize Winners." New York Times
   (May 3), p. 22.
   Biographical sketch of Miller on occasion of Pulitzer Prize for Salesman.

13 ANON. "Pulitzer Prizes Announced by Columbia University."
   Publishers Weekly, 155 (May 7), 1877.
   Miller's Death of a Salesman is awarded the 1949 Pulitzer Prize for "the original American play, which shall represent in marked fashion the educational value and power of the stage."

14 ANON. "Death of a Salesman." New Yorker, 25 (May 21), 117.
   While Miller's tendency to overwrite is more evident in book form, Salesman in print is "still a deeply affecting tragedy."

15 ANON. "Named 'Father of the Year.'" New York Times (May 26),
   p. 5.
   Miller is one of ten outstanding fathers of the year chosen by the National Father's Day Committee.

16 ANON. "Miller Gets Writers Award." New York Times (June 1),
   p. 43.
   Miller receives Writer's Award from American Committee of Jewish Writers, Artists and Scientists, Inc. for Salesman, a "permanent contribution to contemporary literature."

17 ANON. "May Offer Salesman in Berlin." New York Times (June
   9), p. 35.
   Fritz Kortner announces plans to stage Salesman in Berlin.

1949

18   ANON. "Death of a Salesman." Times (London) (July 29), p. 9.
         Review of London production of Death of a Salesman. The
      play has two themes: the "straits in which an unnatural
      civilization puts natural man" and the "way in which the
      submerged ideal revenges itself upon the materialist by
      questioning the value of his achievements." The struggle
      of Biff to tear away the protective illusion by which his
      father has lived makes up the second and better half of the
      play.

19   ANON. "Death of Salesman Moves Londoners." New York Times
      (July 29), p. 12.
         Account of Salesman's reception on London stage with
      brief quotations from representative reviews.

20   ANON. "The Return of Paul Muni." Sphere, 198 (August 13),
      247.
         Brief notice, with photograph of set and actors, of
      London production of Salesman. Paul Muni makes a "pathetic
      figure of the salesman."

21   ANON. "Death of a Salesman at the Phoenix." Theatre World
      (October), pp. 11-18.
         Pictures and commentary on the London production of
      Salesman. It is "impossible not to be moved by Miller's
      dramatic play." The partnership of Elia Kazan (director)
      and Jo Mielziner (sets, lighting) is inspired.

22   ANON. "Moscow Acclaims a Hellman Play." New York Times
      (October 18), p. 34.
         Article discussing Moscow production of Lillian Hellman's
      Another Part of the Forest reports that a previous produc-
      tion of All My Sons there was "sharply criticized on the
      grounds that it presented an unsound philosophy."

23   ANON. "Death of a Salesman at the Phoenix." Theatre World,
      45 (December) 11-18.
         Photographs, with commentary, of London production of
      Salesman.

24   ANON. "Muni to Quit Salesman." New York Times (December 11),
      p. 84.
         Because of ill health, Paul Muni will withdraw from role
      of Willy Loman in London production of Salesman. The play
      "has played to packed houses in London."

25   ATKINSON, BROOKS. "At the Theatre." New York Times (February
      11), p. 27.

Enthusiastic review of New York premiere of <u>Salesman</u>, a
"rich and memorable drama that becomes poetry in spite of
itself." Simple in style, inevitable in theme, it has the
flow and spontaneity of a suburban epic. Elia Kazan has
pulled together the somewhat diffuse text into a "deeply
moving performance." Reprinted: 1949.42; 1962.5; 1973.2.

26 _____. "<u>Death of a Salesman</u>." <u>New York Times</u> (February 20)
sec. II, p. 1.
<u>Salesman</u> has stature and insight, awareness of life,
respect for people and knowledge of American manners and
modern folkways. Technically, it is a fresh creation in a
style of its own. The platonic pride audiences take in the
play stems from a recognition of the poignant truthfulness
of this simple story about an ordinary American family.
Reprinted: 1961.30.

27 _____. "Much Prized Play." <u>New York Times</u> (May 15), sec. II,
p. 1.
Compliments theatregoing public for its instinctive
recognition of <u>Salesman</u>'s integrity. In this "unearthly
requiem on the footloose life of an obscure commercial
traveller," the moral theme is the illusion of success,
that style is more important than substance. Miller's
"whirling tragedy" ranks with the finest works in our
theatre.

28 BARNES, HOWARD. "A Great Play is Born." <u>New York Herald
Tribune</u> (February 11), p. 14.
Review of <u>Death of a Salesman</u>. The play has "majesty,
sweep, and shattering dramatic impact." Its lucidity,
eloquence, and deep feeling make it far more than a good
job of craftsmanship. It is a "play to make history."
Reprinted: 1949.42.

29 BEAUFORT, JOHN. "Miller, Odets and Man's Dilemma." <u>Christian
Science Monitor</u> (March 5), p. 12.
Review of New York production of Clifford Odets' <u>The
Big Knife</u>. Compares Willy Loman with Charlie Castle. Both
men commit suicide to be free of the compromises that
vitiate personal integrity in modern society.

30 BENTLEY, ERIC. "Back to Broadway." <u>Theatre Arts</u>, 33
(November), 12-14.
Review of <u>Salesman</u>. Despite the "completeness of
<u>Salesman</u>'s Americanism," the "'tragedy' destroys the social
drama"; the "social drama keeps the 'tragedy' from having a

1949

fully tragic stature." The social theme of the little man
as victim arouses pity but no terror, and thus is not
tragic. Reprinted: 1953.11; 1961.30.

31   BEYER, WILLIAM H. "The State of the Theatre: The Season
Opens." School and Society, 70 (December 3), 363-64.
Salesman is Linda's tragedy, not Willy's. He is too
"unimportant, immature and commonplace to arouse more than
pity," but what Linda "stands for is important and when she
goes down the descent is tragic." Reprinted: 1967.48.

32   BREIT, HARVEY. "A Brief Visit and Some Talk with Thomas Mann."
New York Times Book Review (May 29), p. 12.
Mann says Salesman is an excellent play in all respects
but its style, which sometimes mixes realism and symbolism
in confusing fashion.

33   BROWN, IVOR. "As London Sees Willy Loman." New York Times
Magazine (August 28), pp. 11, 59.
Britons were impressed but not as overwhelmed by Willy
Loman's tragedy as New Yorkers. Perhaps the reason is
Willy's occupation of salesman and preoccupation with being
well-liked are seen as New York American rather than British
or universal. Reprinted: 1962.5; 1967.48.

34   _____. "Loman Over Jordan." Observer (London) (July 31),
p. 6.
Review of London production of Death of a Salesman.
Though it has "considerable merits as a piece of theatre,"
Salesman does not live up to expectations. New York audiences' applause for Willy is probably a "form of penitence,
since most of them would kick him out as a pestilent nui-
sance if he came badgering them for help." Britons can be
reassured that their "creed of the suburban villa" is less
childish and vulgar than Willy's belief in material goods
and popularity as measures of success.

35   BROWN, JOHN MASON. "Seeing Things: Even as You and I."
Saturday Review of Literature, 32 (February 26), 30-32.
Review of New York opening of Death of a Salesman, "not
only the best play to have been written by an American this
season, but a play which provides one of the modern theatre's
most overpowering evenings." In Salesman life is so mixed
with theatre that the two are indistinguishable. It is the
"most poignant statement of man as he must face himself to
have come out of our theatre," and Elia Kazan's production
is "as sensitive, powerful and human as the writing."
Reprinted: 1950.8; 1951.9; 1962.5; 1967.48.

36 CALTA, LOUIS. "Salesman Tops Theatrical Poll." New York Times
    (July 12), p. 31.
        Salesman wins Donaldson award as best play of 1948-49
    season. Lee J. Cobb is voted best actor of season. Arthur
    Kennedy and Mildred Dunnock are voted best supporting per-
    formers. Elia Kazan wins award for best direction, Jo
    Mielziner for "best background."

37 CASSIDY, CLAUDIA. "Death of Salesman." Chicago Daily Tribune
    (October 21), n.p.
        Though the requiem is anticlimactic, Salesman is "somber,
    compassionate, penetrating and powerful." Harold Clurman's
    staging of the Chicago production is excellent. Reprinted:
    1958.11.

38 CHAPMAN, JOHN. "Death of a Salesman a Fine Play." New York
    Daily News (February 11).
        Review. To see Death of a Salesman is to "have one of
    those unforgettable times in which all is right and nothing
    is wrong." It is an advance over Miller's previous plays
    in that he is preoccupied with people rather than ideas.
    The writing is not only "natural" but "terse, always in
    character and aimed at the furtherance of his drama."
    Reprinted: 1949.42.

39 CLARK, ELEANOR. "Old Glamour, New Gloom." Partisan Review,
    16 (June), 631-36.
        Death of a Salesman is unoriginal, pompous, flat and
    specious. Its lack of candor and intellectual muddle are
    "the main earmarks of contemporary fellow travelling."
    Reprinted: 1961.30; 1962.5; 1967.48.

40 CLURMAN, HAROLD. "The Success Dream on the American Stage."
    Tomorrow, 8 (May), 48-51.
        Review of Broadway opening of Salesman. The audience
    weeps not so much over Willy's fate but over the "millions
    of such men who are our brothers, uncles, cousins, neigh-
    bors." Willy's death symbolizes the breakdown of the whole
    concept of salesmanship on which our economic system is
    based. The value of Salesman lies in a "clean, moralistic
    rationalism that becomes a poetic attribute" and the "pene-
    trating clarity with which its theme is stated."
    Reprinted: 1958.12; 1961.30; 1967.48.

41 _____. "Theatre: Attention!" New Republic, 120 (February
    28), 26-28.
        Review of premier of Death of a Salesman. The play
    makes its audience recognize itself. Willy's wrong dream

1949

is one most of us still cherish. As a moralist, Miller has
a talent for a kind of humanistic jurisprudence that mar-
shalls evidence ineluctably and dispenses judgment that
"permits no soft evasion." Elia Kazan's production conveys
these qualities with a "swift and masterful thrust--like a
perfect blow." Reprinted: 1958.12. Abridged: 1960.23;
1969.11; 1972.47.

42   COFFIN, RACHEL W., ed. "Death of a Salesman." New York
      Theatre Critics' Reviews, 10 (February 14), 358-61.
            Reprints of New York critics' reviews: Atkinson
      (1949.25); Barnes (1949.28); Chapman (1949.38); Coleman
      (1949.43); Garland (1949.52); Hawkins (1949.58); Morehouse
      (1949.65); Watts (1949.79).

43   COLEMAN, ROBERT. "Death of a Salesman is Emotional Dynamite."
      Daily Mirror (February 11).
            Review. Salesman is an "exciting, devastating theatrical
      blast" which has many elements of Greek tragedy. The cast
      and production as a whole are magnificent. Reprinted:
      1949.42.

44   DARLINGTON, W. A. "London Sees Miller's Death of a Salesman."
      New York Times (August 7), sec. II, p. 1.
            Willy is a universal figure despite his American occupa-
      tion of traveling salesman. Salesman is a valid indictment
      of modern materialism everywhere.

45   DEDMON, EMMETT. "Drama of Salesman's Failure Is a Great
      American Tragedy." Chicago Sun (May 22), p. 8.
            Review of Viking edition of Death of a Salesman. The
      Lomans are as "recognizable as the family next door or down
      the street." Miller's evocation of pity for Willy "makes
      us realize that the tragedies of ordinary men may be as
      moving as the tribulations of rulers."

46   DOWNER, ALAN S. "Mr. Williams and Mr. Miller." Furioso, 4
      (Summer), 66-70.
            Though completely dissimilar as men and as playwrights,
      Miller and Tennessee Williams are alike in that they have
      given the American drama its first hopeful turn since the
      1930's. In Salesman, Miller's originality lies in the skill
      with which he makes his audience feel as well as intellect-
      ually recognize the situation. Willy is human and pathetic;
      had he been a king he would have fallen short of the tragic.

47   EATON, WALTER P. "The Salesman in Cold Type." New York Herald
      Tribune Weekly Book Review (May 22), p. 6.

Though the flatly realistic dialogue has no literary merit and the expressionism of the play's structure militates against a rewarding emotional experience in the reading, the text of Death of a Salesman has overtones of pathos, if not tragedy, that raise it above its limitations.

48 FLEMING, PETER. "The Theatre." Spectator, 183 (August 5), 173.
    Review of London production of Salesman. Elia Kazan's direction is very clever but somewhat portentous, and Miller would have been wiser to use "satire rather than sentiment in his approach to a way of life whose standards and atmosphere are really a matter for laughter rather than for tears."

49 FREEDLEY, GEORGE. "The Theatre." Library Journal, 74 (June 15), 960.
    Brief mention of Death of a Salesman as first play to be chosen by the Book-of-the-Month Club.

50 FULLER, A. HOWARD. "A Salesman is Everybody." Fortune, 39 (May) 79-80.
    Sees the salesman as the real hero of American society, the cutting edge of a competitive economy who exposes himself to slings and arrows of fortune to present new ideas and innumerable products of industry. Willy's enthusiasm, a necessary quality in a salesman, is unintelligent, self-deluded, and is thus responsible for his attempt to make Biff over into his own image. His failure to do so precipitates his suicide. Reprinted: 1967.48.

51 GABRIEL, GILBERT W. "Death of a Salesman." Theatre Arts, 33 (April), 15-16.
    Review of New York Production of Salesman. The play is a "fine thing, finely done and vastly well delivered." It contains "all the muck and melancholy joke of our petty-class life taken, shaken, rearranged, revitalized and somehow rehallowed into the stuff of a compelling, surging quasi-poetry, of a widespread pity, of a great-hearted dream." Abridged: 1960.23; 1969.11.

52 GARLAND, ROBERT. "Lee Cobb Is Excellent in 49's Prize Play." New York Journal-American (February 11), p. 16.
    Review of New York opening of Death of a Salesman. The emotional impact of the play is indicated by the audience's remaining seated well beyond the final curtain call, then breaking into "tumultuous appreciation that shattered the

1949

hushed expectancy." If Willy Loman is Everyman, his wife
is the "play's most poignant figure." Both Cobb and Dunnock
are superb in the main roles. Reprinted: 1949.42; 1967.48.

53 GASSNER, JOHN. "Aspects of the Broadway Theatre." Quarterly
    Journal of Speech, 35 (February), 289-94.
        Salesman is often moving, gripping and penetrative in
    characterization and social implication. Miller's judgments
    stem from close identification with his characters rather
    than from some intellectual eminence to raise the drama
    above the humdrum. Miller intensifies Willy's character
    through his consuming passion for the love of a favorite
    son and through the overall dramatized method of vertical
    rather than horizontal play building. The question "What
    is really the matter and why?" rather than "What will happen
    next?" points to basic realities. Reprinted: 1954.6;
    1959.10; 1967.48.

54 _____. "The Theatre Arts." Forum, 111 (April), 219-221.
        Review of Death of a Salesman. Miller succeeds where
    social playwrights of the 1930's failed; i.e., he bridges
    the gulf between social situation and human drama and makes
    them one. A "King Lear in mufti, Willy Loman is heroic
    because he can feel greatly, even if his thinking could be
    bounded in a nutshell." Though Salesman is tremendously
    moving to its audience, however, it lacks "the poetry, the
    nuances, the wonder, and insight" of the best plays of
    Williams and O'Neill. It is still "drame bourgeoise rather
    than high tragedy." Abridged: 1960.23; 1964.28; 1969.11.
    Reprinted: 1954.6; 1972.47.

55 GIBBS, WOLCOTT. "The Theatre: Well Worth Waiting For." New
    Yorker, 24 (February 19), 54, 56.
        Review of New York premiere of Death of a Salesman. The
    best serious play on Broadway in the 1949 season, Salesman
    combines "compassion, imagination and technical competence
    not often found in the theatre today." It is an unerring
    portrait of a failure, written with an accurate feeling for
    speech and behavior that few current playwrights can equal.

56 GIRSON, ROCHELLE. "Death of a Salesman." Saturday Review of
    Literature, 32 (August 13), 31.
        In the printed version of Death of a Salesman the tragedy
    comes off better in some respects than on stage. Charley's
    graveside lines do not sound as false, and it is easier to
    dovetail Willy's wandering mind with reality.

57   GRUTZNER, CHARLES. "Salesman is Pulitzer Play; Sherwood,
     Cozzens Cited." New York Times (May 3), pp. 1, 22.
          The Pulitzer award gives Salesman a "clean sweep" of the
     three major drama prizes: Pulitzer, New York Drama Critics
     Circle award, and the Antoinette Perry award.

58   HAWKINS, WILLIAM. "Death of a Salesman: Powerful Tragedy."
     New York-World Telegram (February 11), p. 16.
          Review of Broadway opening of Salesman. Compares play
     to a classical tragedy in that it shows the destruction of
     a man through flaws within himself. The failure of Willy's
     great potential is "moving and universally understandable
     because his happiness could have so easily been attained as
     an artisan glorying in manual effort." Reprinted: 1949.42;
     1967.48.

59   HOBSON, HAROLD. "From America." Sunday Times (London) (July
     31), p. 2.
          Review of London production of Death of a Salesman. A
     play of "enormous distinction," Salesman is the same pro-
     duction in London as New York except for the different
     acting styles of Paul Muni and Lee J. Cobb. Cobb's inter-
     nal "dynamo of energy" gives the New York production a
     "speed and certainty that are missing in London."

60   HOPE-WALLACE, PHILIP. "Death of a Salesman." The Guardian
     (Manchester) (July 30), p. 5.
          Review of London production of Salesman, which is less
     impressive than the New York production, despite Elia
     Kazan's excellent direction, because the "manner of expres-
     sion of the dramatic situation seems alien." In New York
     it was "comparable to an American King Lear."

61   KEOWN, ERIC. "At the Play." Punch, 217 (August 10), 163.
          Review of London production of Death of a Salesman. A
     "play of outstanding quality on a theme vital to the times,"
     Salesman is a "deeply understanding study, and extremely
     interesting in construction." Miller's "sleight-of-hand in
     the juggling of time is always strictly relevant."

62   KRUTCH, JOSEPH WOOD. "Drama." Nation, 163 (March 5), 283-84.
          Death of a Salesman is good in its own way, but rela-
     tively old-fashioned and limited in its naturalistic use of
     material, its failure to go beyond literal meaning, and its
     undistinguished dialogue. Unlike Tennessee Williams, Miller
     does not have a unique sensibility, new insight, fresh
     imagination or a gift for language.

1949

63   LERNER, MAX. "Sons and Brothers," in his Actions and Passions.
     New York: Simon & Schuster, pp. 22-24.
         All My Sons takes for granted the traditional virtues of
     courage, loyalty, patriotism and fortitude and celebrates
     the Judeo-Christian "sense of kinship that crosses all
     tribal boundaries." This ancient theme suddenly seems new
     and daring.

64   MOREHOUSE, WARD. "Arthur Miller," in his Matinee Tomorrow.
     New York: Whittlesey House, pp. 290-91.
         Brief biography of Miller. All My Sons has "a sharp
     sense of dramatic situation, a feeling for character, and
     a talent for trenchant dialogue."

65   _____. "Triumph at the Morosco." New York Sun (February 11).
         Review of Death of a Salesman. A "soaring triumph" of
     the living theater, Salesman is a poignant, shattering and
     devastating drama that has pathos, pitilessness, violence,
     tenderness, humor and vehemence. A play of "prodigious
     impact," it ends on a note of hope, not futility. It is
     the most powerful and exciting play of the season to date.
     Reprinted: 1949.42.

66   MORGAN, FREDERICK. "Notes on The Theatre." Hudson Review, 2
     (Summer), 272-73.
         Salesman is Broadway in a self-pitying mood and this
     accounts for its success with reviewers and audiences. The
     "language is undistinguished," the plot proceeds with "un-
     relieved vulgarity from cliché to stereotype," the tone is
     a "sustained snivel." Reprinted: 1962.5.

67   NATHAN, GEORGE JEAN. "Death of a Salesman," in his Theatre
     Book of the Year, 1948-1949. New York: Alfred A. Knopf,
     pp. 279-85.
         Salesman transcends the inferior melodramatics of All My
     Sons, despite director Kazan's "occasional melodramatic
     emphasis on the box-office's behalf." Among the play's
     many merits are the "uncompromising honesty of its emotion,"
     the "intermittent excellent flashes of imagery," and its
     evocation of the "commonplace details of everyday life with
     a sense of deep and pitiful recognition." Reprinted:
     1960.22; 1961.30.

68   _____. "Tragedy." American Mercury, 68 (June), 679-80.
         Argues that Death of a Salesman is ineffective as a
     "tragedy of the little man," since Willy Loman is not a
     "mind in strong conflict with the stronger fates" but a

"mindless man already beaten by them." Further, the language is too commonplace for first-rate drama, though it may make for first-rate theatre.

69   PHELAN, KAPPO. "Death of a Salesman." Commonweal, 49 (March 4), 520-21.
        Death of a Salesman, in the writing and the performances of Lee Cobb, Mildred Dunnock and Arthur Kennedy, is the most important drama in the U.S. since the earlier O'Neill. Miller's handling of technical problems--for example, the presentation of memory on stage--is especially praiseworthy.

70   S., F. "Death of a Salesman." Theatre World (September), pp. 9, 29.
        Attributes the mixed reviews of the London production of Death of a Salesman to the enthusiastic reception in New York. Critics "like to think they have discovered the great work themselves." Salesman, though, is a big London success and is relevant to English society as well.

71   SCHNEIDER, DANIEL E. "Play of Dreams." Theatre Arts, 33 (October), 18-21.
        All My Sons and Death of a Salesman exemplify Oedipal conflicts. If the theme of the former is that a "society that destroys fatherhood makes primitives (criminals) of its sons," the theme of the latter is that "he who pretends to godhead over me must fulfill his godhead or be revealed as a madman." Salesman could have been called All Our Fathers. Abridged: 1960.23; 1969.11. Reprinted: 1950.16; 1967.48.

72   SCHUMACH, MURRAY. "Arthur Miller Grew in Brooklyn." New York Times (February 6), sec. II, pp. 1, 3.
        Miller's dramas concentrate on the "significant commonplaces"--the relationship between father and son and between the individual and society. Miller explains flashback techniques in Salesman to maneuver themes into collision as an attempt to escape naturalistic plots. Schumach describes Miller's work habits, background, parallels with Salesman.

73   SHEA, ALBERT A. "Death of a Salesman." Canadian Forum, 29 (July), 86-87.
        Both a probing social study and a moral plea, Death of a Salesman is as great a drama as any seen on Broadway in the previous decade. Willy Loman is the epitome of a way of life involving us all. Through him Miller attacks the immorality of our commercial civilization with its salesman mentality and upholds the individual and his right to his own soul. Abridged: 1960.23; 1969.11.

1949

74   SLADEN-SMITH, F. "Theatre Bookshelf." Drama, No. 15 (Winter),
      p. 30.
          Brief review of English edition of Death of a Salesman.
      The play has "unforgettable qualities," and Willy's failure
      a "disturbingly personal flavour."

75   SYLVESTER, ROBERT. "Brooklyn Boy Makes Good." Saturday
      Evening Post, 222 (July 16), 26-27, 97-98, 100.
          Interview. Miller talks about his life, career, and the
      composition and staging of Death of a Salesman.

76   TAUBMAN, HOWARD. "Plays With Music Between the Lines." New
      York Times (March 27), sec. II, pp. 1, 3.
          Alex North's musical score for Salesman is brilliant,
      imaginative and a powerful aid to Miller in projecting the
      drama.

77   TREWIN, J. C. "Plays in Performance." Drama, No. 15 (Winter),
      p. 8.
          Brief review of London production of Death of a Salesman.
      The "vigour and humanity" of Paul Muni in the principal role
      "helps relieve an evening that is otherwise tangled, preten-
      tious and dull." The play is, however, a commercial success.

78   _____. "The World of the Theatre." Illustrated London News,
      125 (August 27), 320.
          Brief review of London production of Death of a Salesman.
      The play is an "over-coloured anecdote and needlessly por-
      tentous," and though Miller "has handled cunningly his
      play's old construction," it has nothing "very exciting to
      say." Nor are the characters "realised with imagination."

79   WATTS, RICHARD. "Death of a Salesman a Powerful Drama." New
      York Post (February 11).
          Review. Miller has replaced his "labored obeisance to
      Ibsen" with his own quality of "cold intellectual clarity
      mixed with simple and unashamed emotional force." Salesman
      is the "best and most important new American play of 1949."
      Without propagandizing, it goes "deeply enough into contem-
      porary values to be valid and frightening social criticism."
      The production is excellent. Reprinted: 1949.42.

80   WERTHAM, FREDERIC. "Let the Salesman Beware." New York Times
      Book Review (May 15), pp. 4, 12.
          Interview. Miller believes audiences respond to the
      attempt of Death of a Salesman to deal with the insecurities
      they must ultimately face, that the source of Willy's false
      notion of himself is the male need for an "efficient, suc-
      cessful, praiseworthy personality," that the "social

significance of <u>Salesman</u> is that man is happiest when he is
a giver," yet his "need to give and create is often contra-
dicted by his way of life." He accepts the label of
"romantic of realism," since "great art has always dealt
really with the commonplace."

81   WHITE, WARREN R. "Arthur Miller Writes of Death and the
     Drama." <u>San Francisco Chronicle, This World Magazine</u> (May
     22), pp. 19, 21.
     Review of Viking edition of <u>Death of a Salesman</u>. Com-
     pares play to characters in Josephine Lawrence's <u>If I Had
     Four Apples</u>, who are also victims of materialism. The
     message is not profound but served up with compassion,
     imagination and technical competence. "Had Willy been
     smarter his tragedy might have been more disturbing."

82   WORSLEY, T. C. "Poetry without Words." <u>New Statesman and
     Nation</u>, 38 (August 6), 146-47.
     Review of London premiere of <u>Salesman</u>. In an attempt to
     escape a naturalistic dramatic form while retaining a real-
     ist, contemporary subject Miller, like Saroyan, Wilder and
     Williams, uses a poetic approach without using poetry or
     even heightened speech. The words are not there. In
     addition, despite a certain power in <u>Salesman</u>, it is
     slighter than author or producer believes because there are
     only one and a half characters to carry it, and its episodic
     time and place switching are disjointed. Reprinted:
     1967.48.

83   WYATT, EUPHEMIA VAN RENSSELAER. "The Drama." <u>Catholic World</u>.
     169 (April), 62-63.
     Review of Broadway premiere of <u>Death of a Salesman</u>.
     Though it may not have been Miller's conscious idea, the
     play is a "picture of life without God," a drama of "dis-
     illusion without the catharsis of faith." Abridged:
     1960.23; 1969.11.

84   ZOLOTOW, SAM. "Miller Play Wins Critics' Plaudits." <u>New York
     Times</u> (April 13), p. 40.
     <u>Salesman</u> receives New York Drama Critics' Circle Award
     as one of three outstanding Broadway shows of 1948-49 sea-
     son. Brief summary of Miller's life and career to date.

1950

1   ANON. "<u>Death of a Salesman</u> Acclaimed in Vienna." <u>New York
     Times</u> (March 4), p. 10.
     Brief quotations from reviews of German production of
     <u>Salesman</u>. That the reviews were laudatory and understanding

1950

is surprising since salesmanship in the American sense is
unknown in Austria.

2   ANON. "Salesman in Denmark." New York Times (March 16), p. 41.
Hardly since the day of Ibsen and Strindberg had a play
been so eagerly awaited in Copenhagen as Salesman. Accord-
ing to critics it was one of the greatest theatrical
successes in several years.

3   ANON. "Salesman Opens in Two German Cities." New York Times
(April 28), p. 25.
The chief impact of the German production of Salesman on
reviewers in Düsseldorf and Munich was one of surprise that
capitalistic America could produce a story in which the
hero "goes to the dogs."

4   ATKINSON, BROOKS. "At the Theatre." New York Times (September
21), p. 20.
The new cast of Salesman, led by Thomas Mitchell, is
inferior to the original cast. The tone of the play is
lightened (Willy's problem becomes a mental one) and the
conclusion pathetic rather than tragic. The play is barely
retrieved by Peggy Allenby, as Linda, from a series of
"bouncing and inconsequential trivialities."

5   _____. "First Night at the Theatre." New York Times
(December 29), p. 14.
Favorable review of New York production of Miller's
adaptation of Ibsen's An Enemy of the People. The language
is a "vast improvement over the lugubrious Archer translation" in that it "releases the anger and scorn of the
father of realism." Reprinted: 1950.10.

6   _____. "Portrait of Willy." New York Times (March 12),
sec. II, p. 1.
After thirteen months of uninterrupted performances of
Salesman, Lee J. Cobb yields to Gene Lockhart in role of
Willy Loman. The play makes exceptional demands on the
imagination of its audience but appeals because of its
universality. The special circumstances of Willy's life
hardly matter. By some instinct Miller has caught a common
theme and written about it with the insight of a poet.

7   BARNES, HOWARD. "Ibsen Plus Miller." New York Herald Tribune
(December 29), p. 12.
Review of Miller's adaptation of Ibsen's An Enemy of the
People. Miller's broadening of Ibsen's drama to take in
present day events makes the play ungainly, rather like a
"nineteenth century canvas given a Picasso treatment." If

28

the characters speak with more color and authority than
they have had before in English, the appending of Miller's
notions to Ibsen's results in confusion and even hysteria.
Reprinted: 1950.10.

8   BROWN, JOHN MASON. "Even as You and I," in his <u>Still Seeing
     Things</u>. New York: McGraw-Hill, pp. 194-95, 197-204.
          Reprint of 1949.35.

9   CHAPMAN, JOHN. "Arthur Miller and Frederic March Put New
     Anger in Ibsen's <u>Enemy</u>." <u>New York Daily News</u> (December 29).
          Review of Miller's adaptation of Ibsen's <u>An Enemy of
     the People</u>. Miller has updated the play "without tampering
     with the content or intent of the original." It is once
     more a relevant political or sociological tract, and Miller's
     "skill at making characters talk like people has not re-
     cently been surpassed." Reprinted: 1950.10.

10   COFFIN, RACHEL W., ed. "<u>An Enemy of the People</u>." <u>New York
     Theatre Critics' Reviews</u>, 11 (December 29), pp. 154-56.
          Reprints: Atkinson (1950.5); Barnes (1950.7); Chapman
     (1950.9); Coleman (1950.11); Hawkins (1950.13); McClain
     (1950.15); Watts (1950.17).

11   COLEMAN, ROBERT. "<u>Enemy of People</u> Muddled in Version by
     Miller." <u>New York Daily Mirror</u> (December 29).
          Review of Miller's adaptation of Ibsen's <u>An Enemy of the
     People</u>. Miller's attempt to "state a drama of protest in
     the jargon of a modern underworld thriller" robs the orig-
     inal of stature and dignity. A "stilted problem play"
     becomes a "rip-roaring, muddle-mooded melodrama." Reprinted:
     1950.10.

12   DEKKER, ALBERT. "<u>Salesman</u>'s Travelling Understudy." <u>New York
     Times</u> (April 30), sec. II, p. 2.
          The trials of an understudy who must be ready to travel
     anywhere that a replacement for Willy is needed in a <u>Sales-
     man</u> production. Willy is "ninety-six sides long and the
     continuity of thought is held by a thread."

13   HAWKINS, WILLIAM. "Ibsen Play Turns Stage into Soapbox." <u>New
     York World Telegram and Sun</u> (December 29).
          Review of Miller's adaptation of Ibsen's <u>An Enemy of
     the People</u>. While Miller's workable vernacular frees the
     play from literal translations without marring its original
     form, the propaganda rules out emotional involvement on the
     audience's part, and the shift in emphasis from the mental
     rigidity to the lush living of the principal antagonist
     would surely not have met with Ibsen's approval. Reprinted:
     1950.10.

29

1950

14   KENNEDY, SIGHLE. "Who Killed the Salesman?" <u>Catholic World</u>,
         171 (May), 110-16.
              Miller does not blame economics or American values for
         Willy's failure. There are too many problems facing Willy
         for any one of them to be stressed. The defect of <u>Death</u>
         <u>of a Salesman</u> is really that Miller has no moral precepts,
         only pity to offer. What Willy might have been or what
         Biff Loman might become are unanswered questions. Neverthe-
         less, Miller's "far-reaching, sympathetic and insistent
         formulation of Willy's question has made millions of Willys
         in his audience care deeply about the answer."

15   MCCLAIN, JOHN. "Everything is Fine But Ibsen's Idea." <u>New</u>
         <u>York Journal American</u> (December 29).
              Review of Miller's adaptation of Ibsen's <u>An Enemy of the</u>
         <u>People</u>. The premise of Ibsen's play is wrong and the moral
         unacceptable, though Miller's adaptation and modernizing of
         the play is excellent. A "show should not slyly make a bum
         of our accepted way of life, especially at a time like
         this." Reprinted: 1950.10.

16   SCHNEIDER, DANIEL E. "A Modern Playwright," in <u>The Psycho-</u>
         <u>analyst and the Artist</u>. New York: International Univer-
         sities Press, pp. 241-55.
              Reprint of 1949.71.

17   WATTS, RICHARD. "Henrik Ibsen and Arthur Miller." <u>New York</u>
         <u>Post</u> (December 29).
              Review of Miller's adaptation of Ibsen's <u>An Enemy of the</u>
         <u>People</u>. An "earnest and impassioned tract for our time,"
         Miller's version nevertheless stays close to the original
         play. Some colloquialisms, however, add little to its
         timeliness, and on the whole it would be preferable to see
         Miller writing his own plays. Reprinted: 1950.10.

<u>1951</u>

1   ALPERT, HOLLIS. "Mr. Miller's Indignant Theme." <u>Saturday</u>
         <u>Review of Literature</u>, 34 (December 22), 34.
              The film version of <u>Salesman</u> has an "undeniable power to
         move" and is an "honest and dignified attempt" on the part
         of Stanley Kramer (producer) and Laslo Benedek (director)
         to portray the kind of subject matter that should be seen
         in films. The static quality is a result of the decision
         to do little more than photograph the play, and Fredric
         March is miscast as Willy.

2   ANON. "<u>An Enemy of the People</u>." <u>Time</u>, 57 (January 8), 31.
       Miller's adaptation of Ibsen's play is livelier theatre
  but seems even more contrived than the original. More
  topical melodrama than bitter satire, Miller's version,
  though it "replaces the old flaccid translator's English
  with new blood," has a "more agitated but less striking
  face."

3   ANON. "Theater: <u>An Enemy of the People</u>." <u>Newsweek</u>, 37
       (January 8), 67.
       Miller's adaptation "invigorates" the lines of Ibsen's
  play in the "language of today," and once again Ibsen is a
  "pamphleteer who uses the stage with electrifying dramatic
  effect."

4   ANON. "<u>An Enemy of the People</u>." <u>Theatre Arts</u>, 35 (March), 15.
       Review of Miller's adaptation of Ibsen's play. The plot,
  but not the mood, of the original has been retained, with
  the American version gaining in melodramatic excitement
  what it loses in subtlety. Carefully avoiding political
  implications, Miller "espouses only the cause of personal
  integrity in a fear-ridden society."

5   ANON. "<u>Death of a Salesman</u>." <u>Newsweek</u>, 38 (December 31),
       56-57.
       An "admirable screen adaptation of one of the finest
  plays in the contemporary American theater."

6   ANON. "The New Pictures." <u>Time</u>, 58 (December 31), 60.
       <u>Death of a Salesman</u> is a "bravely uncommon movie" that
  adheres too closely to Miller's original play. Verisimil-
  itude is lost when no one suggests Willy's rantings make
  him a candidate for a mental asylum, and the flashbacks
  clash with the everyday realism of the movie's settings.
  The cast is good with the exception of Fredric March, who
  "seems to be trying to play a drunk."

7   ATKINSON, BROOKS. "Ibsen in a Rage." <u>New York Times</u> (January
       7), sec. II, p. 1.
       Describes background against which Ibsen wrote <u>An Enemy
  of the People</u>. Ibsen's political aloofness is frustrating
  to contemporary savants, especially his lack of belief in
  democracy. Though Miller has tampered with the original
  in various ways, he does not misrepresent Ibsen's thesis.

8   BEYER, WILLIAM H. "The State of the Theatre: Revivals 'Front
       and Center.'" <u>School and Society</u>, 73 (February 17), 105.

1951

        Review of Miller's adaptation of Ibsen's <u>An Enemy of the</u>
<u>People</u>. The play has relevance still because human psychol-
ogy has changed little.

9   BROWN, JOHN MASON. "<u>Death of a Salesman</u>," in his <u>Dramatis</u>
      <u>Personae: A Retrospective Show</u>. New York: Viking, pp. 16,
      29-30, 94-100.
         Reprint of 1949.35.

10   CLURMAN, HAROLD. "Theatre: Lear and Stockmann." <u>New Republic</u>,
      124 (January 22), 21-22.
         Review of production of Miller's adaptation of Ibsen's
      <u>An Enemy of the People</u>. The youthful posturing and scream-
      ing, if out of keeping with Ibsen's play, are in order in a
      world where youthful indignation is more tonic than suave
      resignation. The issue in Miller's version is our own right
      to hold and express "unpopular" opinions. Miller's trans-
      formation of Ibsen's values produces some artistic and
      philosophic confusion, but this is "inevitable when art is
      caught in the tempest of social turmoil."

11   CROWTHER, BOSLEY. "<u>Death of a Salesman</u>." <u>New York Times</u>
      (December 21), p. 21.
         The film of <u>Salesman</u> enhances the episodic structure,
      makes the shifts in time and location seem more natural
      than on stage, and provides a broader frame of reference
      which "suggests it could happen in any American city to
      anyone who lives by false ideals."

12   DOWNER, ALAN S. <u>Fifty Years of American Drama</u>. Chicago:
      Henry Regnery, pp. 52-53, 73-75, 141-43.
         Discusses dramatic modes of Miller's plays. <u>All My Sons</u>
      is a "classic example of the well-made realistic play with
      a thesis." <u>Salesman</u> supplements its "selective realism"
      with symbolism while Miller's adaptation of Ibsen's <u>An</u>
      <u>Enemy of the People</u> approaches "highly literate and serious
      melodrama."

13   GIBBS, WOLCOTT. "The Theatre." <u>New Yorker</u>, 26 (January 13),
      44.
         Miller's adaptation of Ibsen's <u>An Enemy of the People</u>,
      which he has "modernized by inserting a few astonishing
      anachronisms," is naive and archaic. One can no longer
      believe that the dilemma of the idealist can be presented
      in terms as simple as Ibsen's.

14   HARTUNG, PHILIP T. "It Comes with the Territory." <u>Commonweal</u>,
      55 (December 28), 300.

1951

Review of film adaptation of <u>Death of a Salesman</u>. The theme of the play is already legend, though it is only two years old. Argues that Willy was not a failure, as he believed, because he was a "hard worker misled by his own empty dreams." Regrets absence of any "softening humor to relieve the play's lengthy tension."

15 HATCH, ROBERT. "Movies." <u>New Republic</u>, 125 (December 31), 22.
Review of film version of <u>Salesman</u>. The play succeeded because it permitted living salesmen, including most of us, to shiver pleasantly at their narrow escapes. However, Linda is the true focus of the play and film. Fredric March, "wings flapping and feathers awry...melodramatizes the emptiness of the role and will probably win an Oscar."

16 HUGHES, GLENN. <u>A History of the American Theatre 1700-1950</u>. New York: Samuel French, pp. 461-79, passim.
Discusses New York reception of Miller's plays through <u>Salesman</u>.

17 KERR, WALTER. "<u>An Enemy of the People</u>." <u>Commonweal</u>, 53 (January 19), 374.
Review of Miller's adaptation of Ibsen's play, starring Fredric March and Morris Carnovsky. Miller has done nothing to remove the ambiguity of the play, though he has put it into contemporary, acceptable English.

18 KRUTCH, JOSEPH WOOD. "Arthur Miller Bowdlerizes Ibsen." <u>Nation</u>, 172 (May 5), 423-24.
Criticizes Miller's substitution, in his version of Ibsen's <u>An Enemy of the People</u>, of "correct liberal platitudes" for Dr. Stockmann's fulminations against the weakness and stupidity of the masses. Recommends that Miller "cultivate a certain tough-mindedness in the face of the heresies of which he does not approve."

19 MCCARTEN, JOHN. "The Current Cinema." <u>New Yorker</u>, 27 (December 22), 70.
If the soul searchings of the Loman family had a touch of logorrhea about them, they nevertheless seemed significant on stage. On celluloid they seem ridiculous. The film gives only an occasional glimpse of the play's main thesis--that the Golden Calf and the Bitch-Goddess Success are a hell of a pair of icons to have around the house.

20 MARSHALL, MARGARET. "Drama." <u>Nation</u>, 172 (January 6), 18.
Brief notice of performance of Miller's adaptation of Ibsen's <u>An Enemy of the People</u>. "The weaknesses of the original are played up in this confused version."

33

1951

21   NATHAN, GEORGE JEAN. "Enemy of the People," in his Theatre
      Book of the Year, 1950-1951. New York: Alfred A. Knopf,
      pp. 167-70.
         Miller's adaptation of Ibsen's An Enemy of the People
      has a "superficial theatrical life but scarcely any inner
      dramatic vitality." It becomes an "over-accentuated melo-
      drama" written in the language of the gangster movie.
      Miller adds material that attempts to draw a parallel be-
      tween Stockman and contemporary liberals, but he leaves
      Ibsen even further in the past instead of bringing him up
      to date.

22   ROSS, GEORGE. "Death of a Salesman in the Original."
      Commentary, 11 (February), 184-86.
         Review of Toyt Fun a Salesman, a Yiddish production of
      Death of a Salesman. In "translating" from his American-
      Jewish experience, Miller censored out the Jewish part,
      making the Loman family anonymous. The Yiddish version
      catches Miller "in the act of changing his name, and has
      turned up the original for us." Discovers Jewish character
      and situation in the play. Reprinted: 1967.48.

23   THOMPSON, ALAN. "Professor's Debauch." Theatre Arts, 35
      (March), 27.
         Discusses Miller's changes in his adaptation of Ibsen's
      An Enemy of the People. Stockman emerges as a "Hollywood-
      ish--heroical Champion of Democracy." The whole play is
      molded to "appeal to contemporary fears of tyranny and
      sentiment for individual freedom." The applause Miller's
      adaptation wins from its audience is for the "agitational
      propaganda, not for Ibsen."

24   WILLIAMSON, AUDREY. "From Across the Atlantic," in her
      Theatre of Two Decades. London: Rackliff, pp. 181-82.
         Death of a Salesman "crystallizes something of the
      frustration of the New World concentration on material
      success." Miller's experimenting with chronology is effec-
      tive and offers sudden revelations. Willy's character is
      skillfully drawn and the play has vitality, though it "lacks
      the highest distinction of writing."

25   WYATT, EUPHEMIA VAN RENSSELAER. "Theatre." Catholic World,
      172 (February), 387.
         Review of New York production of Miller's adaptation of
      Henrik Ibsen's An Enemy of the People. Objects to instances
      where Miller expands on original, and finds the applause
      that welcomes Dr. Stockman's denunciations of the majority
      that opposes him a "dubious attitude toward our treasured
      concept of democracy."

1952

1   ANON. "Death of a Salesman." Life, 32 (January 14), 63-64,
         66.
              Brief review of film version. Stanley Kramer has made
         "an impressive movie adaptation which follows the play
         almost too literally."

2   ANON. "Current Feature Films." Christian Century, 69
         (February 20), 231.
              Favorable review of screen version of Death of a Salesman,
         though the occasional tendency to picture the hero as merely
         mentally unbalanced weakens the moral argument.

*3   FISHER, WILLIAM J. "Trends in Post-Depression American Drama:
         A Study of the Works of William Saroyan, Tennessee Williams,
         Irwin Shaw and Arthur Miller." Ph.D. dissertation, New
         York University, [No Dissertation Abstracts entry].

4   HINE, AL. "Death of a Salesman." Holiday, 11 (March), 14,
         16, 18.
              Salesman succeeds as a film because it was a play packed
         with the easily transferable emotion of the soap opera, and
         because Hanley Roberts' screenplay is sharper and more mov-
         ing than the stage version.

5   KASS, ROBERT. "Film and TV." Catholic World, 174 (February),
         386.
              The film of Death of a Salesman is monotonously pessi-
         mistic and overemphasizes Willy's mental deterioration.
         The tragedy of Biff is "more touching since his defeat is
         less self-impelled."

6   KECK, MARILYN. "Symposium: Death of a Salesman." Folio
         (Indiana University), 17 (March), 22-26.
              The significance of Willy Loman is not that his American
         dream is false, but that he aspires to emulate people like
         his father and brother, who engage "not only in a struggle
         for brute power, but in civilizing the jungle, in bringing
         human fruit from unplowed land, and in shaping their own
         nature in the face of an undetermined future and, ultimately,
         death." These desires are an American version of the Jason
         myth, and to "deny them in Willy's dream is to deny him his
         birthright as a man."

7   MCDONALD, GERALD D. "Death of a Salesman." Library Journal,
         77 (January 15), 140.
              Brief, favorable review of film of Death of a Salesman.

1952

8   MALOFF, SAUL. "Symposium: <u>Death of a Salesman</u>." <u>Folio</u>
    (Indiana University), 17 (March), 9-18.
        <u>Salesman</u> advances beyond the "manipulations and masonry
    of the <u>pièce bien faite</u>" in <u>All My Sons</u> to an approximation
    of tragedy and a "free functional use of presentational
    and expressionist forms," which extend, through the use of
    symbols, the "possibilities of realism." The central
    themes are that failure to achieve self-knowledge is dis-
    aster, and that doing violence to one's identity is self-
    betrayal and inevitably betrayal of others, one's sons.

9   SEIGER, MARVIN L. "Symposium: <u>Death of a Salesman</u>." <u>Folio</u>
    (Indiana University), 17 (March), 19-22.
        Out of his dissatisfaction with the limitations of
    theatrical realism and traditional methods of staging,
    Miller in <u>Salesman</u> (perhaps in collaboration with Elia Kazan
    and Joe Mielziner) has "produced an original synthesis, a
    contribution to American staging."

10 STALLKNECHT, NEWTON P. "Symposium: <u>Death of a Salesman</u>."
    <u>Folio</u> (Indiana University), 17 (March), 3-9.
        Americans do not regard <u>Salesman</u> as a condemnation of
    American society because its argument is too intimate and
    personal. We tend more to criticize our own motives and
    decisions. <u>Salesman</u>'s moral is a Socratic one: Know
    Thyself. If the purpose of drama since Sophocles has been
    to help audiences "attain the insight that only the truth
    can set us free, then <u>Salesman</u> deserves consideration in
    this context."

11 WARSHOW, ROBERT. "The Movie Camera and the American."
    <u>Commentary</u>, 13 (March), 275-81.
        Review of screen version of <u>Death of a Salesman</u> and
    analysis of the "aura that undeniably surrounds a drama
    that does not come to life on its own terms." The movie
    is inferior to the Broadway stage presentation, yet it has
    a power which the play lacked. The play is superficial in
    that Willy is a man possessed by a "humor" rather than a
    valid creation and Miller offers us not the fact but the
    atmosphere of thought. Pessimism is the basic appeal of
    the play to those weary of the cheap optimism of "official"
    American culture, but pessimism is not a measure of
    seriousness.

1953

1   ANON. "Witchcraft and Stagecraft." New York Post (February
    1), p. 9 M.
        Criticizes Miller for implying in The Crucible that the
    "Soviet challenge is an elaborate hallucination of Western
    man, as fanciful as the madness that bedeviled Salem."
    Reprinted: 1971.43.

2   ANON. "The Crucible." Newsweek, 41 (February 2), 68.
        Γ   Review of New York premiere. Without insisting on the
    modern parallel to the 1692 witch trials in Salem, Miller
    has dramatized a grim chapter in American history with
    "eloquence, force and a sense of theater given to few
    practicing playwrights." If the play lacks Salesman's
    emotional intensity, it is because the characters follow a
    predestined pattern that shrouds emotion in a cool, imper-
    sonal light.

3   ANON. "The Theater." Time, 61 (February 2), 48.
        At its best The Crucible is "hard-hitting sociological
    melodrama" with "many scenes of real theatrical power,"
    but it blurs the real point of Salem by slighting the
    "psychological tragedy of fierce Calvinist repression" that
    erupted in hysteria in children and their parents. It is
    more interested in manifestations than motives.

4   ANON. "Satan Came to Salem." Life, 34 (February 9), 87-88,
    90.
        Brief, favorable notice of Broadway premier of The
    Crucible.

5   ANON. "The Crucible." Theatre Arts, 37 (April), 65.
        Perhaps the first successful play on an important social
    theme since Death of a Salesman, The Crucible is a "dramatic
    statement of a contemporary issue that besets our times."
    Miller's theme reminds one that the theatre has not remained
    free of fear and that "such fear has handed over much of
    the theatre to the trivial and the innocuous."

6   ANON. "The Crucible." Booklist, 49 (May 15), 299.
        The analogy between the Salem of 1692 and the U.S. of
    1953 is not always clear, but Miller "intensifies the
    dramatic values of the play without any sacrifice of
    historical accuracy."

7   ATKINSON, BROOKS. "At the Theatre." New York Times (January
    23), p. 15.

1953

> While lacking the universality, power and simple elo-
quence of the theme of Salesman, The Crucible shows a sure
instinct for dramatic form and makes a genuine contribution
to the season. Reprinted: 1953.16; 1971.43; 1973.2.

8 _____. "At the Theatre." New York Times (July 2), p. 20.
> The revised version of The Crucible freshens the most
genuine parts of the original production. The excitement
is less metallic; the emotion is more profound. However,
the prologue is still too crowded with information and the
last scene still vacillates between points of view.
Reprinted: 1971.43.

9 _____. "The Crucible." New York Times (February 1), sec. II,
p. 1.
> Despite overwrought direction by Jed Harris, The Crucible
is the most notable play of the season and professional
theatre on a much higher plane than most of the work done
on Broadway. More interested in his theme than his people,
however, Miller has difficulty finding room for his chief
characters. The contemporary parallels are incidental to
the play as a whole.

10 _____. "Return of a Classic." New York Times (March 15),
sec. II, p. 1.
> Disapproves request of American Bar Association that
Miller alter dialogue in The Crucible that allegedly dis-
parages the legal profession.

11 BENTLEY, ERIC. In Search of Theatre. New York: Knopf,
411 pp., passim.
> Reprint of 1949.30 on pp. 84-87.

12 _____. "Miller's Innocence." New Republic, 128 (February
16), 22-23.
> Review of New York premiere of The Crucible. Miller's
unreconstructed liberalism argues falsely for a parallel
between Salem witch hunts and the "red-baiting" of the
McCarthy era. The play is a melodrama of indignation not
because it paints its villains too black, but because it
paints its heroes too white. Enlarged and Reprinted:
1954.5; 1968.11; 1971.43.

13 BEYER, WILLIAM H. "The State of the Theatre: The Devil at
Large." School and Society, 77 (March 21), 185-86.
> The overcrowded, frenetic scenes of The Crucible resolve
it into a melodrama that beats the audience into insensi-
bility eventually. Dramatizing history robs the play of

the suspense inherent in an original work; and Miller fails
to "digest history to the point that the social and aesthetic
values flow into a dramatic life-blood giving us pure tragedy
which beats with the pulse of conviction."

14 BROWN, JOHN MASON. "Seeing Things: Witch-Hunting." Saturday
Review of Literature, 36 (February 14), 41-42.
    Lacking the "depth and fire" of Miller's earlier plays,
The Crucible is undramatic because the playwright is more
interested in his theme than the people it concerns, and
it is too crowded with incident for the characters to
establish themselves as individuals. Its "one indisputable
virtue is that it is about something that matters."

15 CHAPMAN, JOHN. "Miller's The Crucible Terrifying Tragedy
about Puritan Bigotry." Daily News (January 23).
    Review. The Crucible is a "stunning production, splen-
didly acted and strongly written." It is not a political
parable, like Miller's adaptation of Ibsen's An Enemy of
the People, but a tragedy about the Puritan purge of witchcraft. The big moment is the trial scene, a chilling,
blood-curdling, terrifying depiction of the course of
bigotry and deceit. Reprinted: 1953.16.

16 COFFIN, RACHEL W., ed. "The Crucible." New York Theatre
Critics' Reviews, 14 (January 23), 383-86.
    Reprints: New York critics' reviews: Atkinson (1953.7);
Chapman (1953.15); Coleman (1953.17); Hawkins (1953.23);
Kerr (1953.28); McClain (1953.32); Watts (1953.41).

17 COLEMAN, ROBERT. "The Crucible, a Stirring Well-Acted Melodrama." Daily Mirror (January 23).
    Review. The Crucible is staged in vigorous style, acted
in the grand manner, and has refreshing doses of sheer
vitality. It makes for a "harrowing, suspenseful, intensely
dramatic evening" of "real drama, conflict and impassioned
action." There appear to be no "deep implications" for the
modern playgoer. Reprinted: 1953.16.

18 FREEDLEY, GEORGE. "The Crucible." Kirkus, 21 (March 15), 207.
    Brief notice of Viking edition of The Crucible. Notes
Miller's additions to the acting text of the play.

19 _____. "The Crucible." Library Journal, 78 (May 15), 920.
    Brief mention of publication of The Crucible, "an excel-
lent play about witchcraft and bigotry in 17th century New
England."

1953

20   FUNKE, LEWIS. "Thoughts on a Train Bound for Wilmington."
     New York Times (January 18), sec. II, pp. 1, 3.
          Interview with Miller and Jed Harris, director of The
     Crucible. Harris believes that if the play has value, it
     is as a theatrical experience. He objects to seeing Miller
     as a "big social thinker, a sort of Brooklyn Ibsen."

21   GIBBS, WOLCOTT. "The Theatre: The Devil to Pay." New Yorker,
     28 (January 31), 39-40.
          Review of New York premiere of The Crucible, a "powerful
     play, handsomely executed and conceivably the most interest-
     ing one of the year." Miller writes with a compassion and
     felicity only slightly below the level achieved in Salesman.

22   GRIFFIN, JOHN and ALICE GRIFFIN. "The Crucible." Theatre
     Arts, 37 (October), 33-34.
          Interview. Miller had thought of dramatizing the Salem
     witch trials while in college. The Salem people appealed
     because they were articulate and, though defeated, "did not
     die helplessly." Unlike Willy, the characters had insight
     into their situations. Hence, it was easier to avoid
     pathos. "My weakness is that I can create pathos at will."

23   HAWKINS, WILLIAM. "Witchcraft Boiled in The Crucible." New
     York World Telegram and Sun (January 23).
          Review. A "big, bold, very theatrical" play, The
     Crucible gets its power from "unusual complexities" rather
     than "blatant modern comparisons." It states "timeless
     truths about guilt, conscience, hysteria and bandwagon
     instincts" and represents also an important advance in the
     poetic quality of Miller's writing. Reprinted: 1953.16.

24   HAYES, RICHARD. "The Stage: The Crucible." Commonweal, 57
     (February 20), 498.
          Review of New York opening of The Crucible. The play
     "enriches and again asserts the range, variety and continu-
     ing interest of the American polemic tradition," though the
     political complexities are handled with less vitality and
     appreciation of ambiguity than the moral complexities.
     Even if it is the "product of theatrical dexterity and moral
     passion rather than fruitful, reverberating imagination,"
     it has an "urgent boldness" that does not "shrink from the
     implications of a large and formidable design." Abridged:
     1960.23; 1969.11; 1972.19.

25   HEWES, HENRY. "Arthur Miller and How He Went to the Devil."
     Saturday Review of Literature, 36 (January 31), 24-26.

Interview. Miller discusses the Puritan background,
themes, characters, historical and political parallels, and
the director, Jed Harris, at a rehearsal for the New York
opening of The Crucible. Abridged: 1960.23. Reprinted:
1971.43.

26 HOBSON, HAROLD. "The Involved Theatre," in The Theatre Now.
London: Longmans Green, pp. 121-25.
Discusses differences between London and New York productions of Death of a Salesman, Elia Kazan's direction,
the opinions of George Jean Nathan and George Freedley,
and differences between English and American methods of
directing drama.

27 HOGAN, WILLIAM. "Plays for Those Who Like Their 'Two on the
Aisle' at Home." San Francisco Chronicle, This World Magazine (October 4), p. 22.
Brief notice of Viking edition of The Crucible. The
play has "depth and intelligence," and the "parallel between unintelligent men in Old Salem and unintelligent men
in contemporary America who hurl accusations of 'witchcraft'
indiscriminately, is unmistakable."

28 KERR, WALTER. "The Crucible." New York Herald Tribune,
(January 23), p. 12.
Review of New York opening of The Crucible. The play is
a "step backward into mechanical parable" and "lives not in
the warmth of humbly observed human souls, but in the ideological heat of polemic." Reprinted: 1953.16; 1971.43.
Abridged: 1972.19.

29 ____. "The Crucible Retells Salem's Violent Story." New
York Herald Tribune (February 1), sec. IV, p. 1.
The Crucible is a half-realized work of art in that its
characters remain abstractions, and its effect is more that
of social investigation than drama. Miller's portrayal of
the small minds that go to make up a mob is excellent,
though, and his points--with their contemporary relevance--
are often "strikingly apt and stingingly phrased."

30 KIRCHWEY, FREDA. "The Crucible." Nation, 176 (February 7),
131-32.
Brief review of The Crucible. Though the play is not
contained by time and place, the reviewer "cannot shed the
sense of having experienced simultaneously the anguish and
heroism of Salem's witch hunt and of today's." Abridged:
1960.23; 1969.11.

1953

31 KRUTCH, JOSEPH WOOD. "American Drama," in his "Modernism"
    in Modern Drama. Ithaca, N.Y.: Cornell University Press,
    pp. 102, 106, 123-26.
        Though Salesman can be dismissed as brutal naturalism,
    it is also a "study of the effects of moral weakness and
    irresponsibility." Miller's tragic guilt is thus "a very
    old fashioned one--he was not true to himself." Expanded:
    1957.33. Reprinted: 1961.30.

32 MCCLAIN, JOHN. "Play of Enormous Strength and Depth." New
    York Journal American (January 23).
        Review. The Crucible has enormous strength, depth and
    intelligence but lacks plausibility of plot and character.
    Reprinted: 1953.16.

33 MORRIS, LLOYD. "Toward Tomorrow," in his Curtain Time: The
    Story of the American Theater. New York: Random House,
    p. 362.
        In Salesman Miller invents a "dramatic form for the ex-
    pression of a tragedy wholly subjective."

34 NATHAN, G. J. "American Playwrights, Old and New: Arthur
    Miller," in his The Theatre in the Fifties. New York:
    Alfred A. Knopf, pp. 105-109.
        The Crucible's internal power does not communicate it-
    self to the audience because the characters lack humanity.
    The overly intense opening weakens the tension that should
    come later, and the contemporary parallels are propa-
    gandistic.

35 _____. "Henrik Miller." Theatre Arts, 37 (April), 24-26.
        Review of New York opening of The Crucible. Though the
    play has power and intellectual purpose, "the power is that
    of an impersonal machine, and the intellectual purpose that
    of a historical analyst." The play is "all theme and no
    character." Thus it is repetitious and lacks warmth. Its
    author appears indifferent to his audience.

36 RASKIN, A. H. "Maids and Lawyers Assail Stage 'Slurs.'"
    New York Times (March 9), pp. 1, 23.
        The American Bar Association demands removal of lines
    disparaging lawyers in The Crucible. Miller refuses to
    make any changes.

37 RAYMOND, HARRY. "The Crucible, Arthur Miller's Best Play."
    Daily Worker (January 28), p. 7.
        Review. Notes parallel between Salem witchcraft and
    "current persecution of Communists and other progressives."

The Salem persecutions were an "attempt by a ruling class to suppress a new class of society which is challenging the old rulers' right to rule." Miller hints at the alliance between clergy and ruling class but fails to elaborate. Objects to the "Aunt Jemima black stereotype" in Tituba.

38 ROTHMAN, STANLEY, BERNARD MARCUS and ROBERT WARSHOW. "The Crucible." Commentary, 16 (July), 83-84.
    An exchange of letters concerning Warshow's previous analysis of The Crucible as "confused and unsubstantial liberalism."

39 SHIPLEY, JOSEPH T. "Arthur Miller's New Melodrama Is Not What It Seems to Be." New Leader, 36 (February 9), 25-26.
    There is great power in the "big scene" of The Crucible, but it is the "calculating craftsman, not the deeply moved creator at work." The Soviet Union today provides a better parallel to the Salem witch trials than contemporary America. Reprinted: 1971.43.

40 WARSHOW, ROBERT. "The Liberal Conscience in The Crucible." Commentary, 15 (March), 265-71.
    The Crucible, when it does not ignore the facts of the Salem trials, alters them to fit its author's "constricted field of vision" and the "assured simplicity of his view of human behavior." It says nothing about the Salem trials, merely suggests that a great deal might be said about the "present atmosphere," and offers its audience little more than a "sense of their close community of right-mindedness in the orthodoxy of 'dissent.'" Reprinted: 1955.38; 1962.35; 1969.10; 1971.43. Abridged: 1973.23.

41 WATTS, RICHARD. "Mr. Miller Looks at Witch Hunting." New York Post (January 23).
    Review. Emotionally successful, The Crucible lacks the intellectual insight of Death of a Salesman. Miller is more concerned with what happened than why and this results in superficiality. Compared with the Inquisitor in Shaw's Saint Joan, Danforth is a cardboard villain. Still, the play is hard-hitting, effective and does not insist on contemporary parallels. Reprinted: 1953.16.

42 WHITLEY, ALVIN. "Arthur Miller: An Attempt at Modern Tragedy." Transactions of the Wisconsin Academy of Sciences, Arts and Letters, 42: 257-62.
    All My Sons and Death of a Salesman are inconsistent with Miller's own theory of tragedy. The fallacy of Miller's theory is that a search for dignity is not as powerful as

1953

"dignity already achieved and playing a great part in a significant universe." Willy Loman ends where Hamlet begins.

43   WOLFERT, IRA. "Arthur Miller, Playwright In Search of His Identity." New York Herald Tribune (January 25), sec. IV, p. 3.
     Biographical sketch and interview with Miller on his career and background of The Crucible.

44   WYATT, EUPHEMIA VAN RENSSELAER. "Theatre." Catholic World, 176 (March), 465-66.
     Review of New York opening of The Crucible. Under the direction of Jed Harris, the play is "forthright and un-relenting," though Leftists applauding it must realize that its theme "is in direct opposition to the principle behind the purge trials of the Soviet." Perhaps someone should also write the story of Mrs. Hale "with its more hopefully American climax."

1954

1   ANON. "Playwright Arthur Miller Refused Visa to Visit Brussels to See His Play." New York Times (March 31), p. 16.
     U.S. State Department denies Miller a passport under "regulations denying passports to persons believed to be supporting the Communist movement." Miller denies "sup-porting any Communist movement," says he withdrew his pass-port application shortly after making it since the passport would not have come in time for him to attend The Crucible's opening in Brussels anyway.

2   ANON. "Play Group Ignores Salesman Protest." New York Times (November 12), p. 23.
     Thomas E. Parradine, a vice-president of the Coca Cola Company and former national vice-commander of the American Legion, withdraws from role of Willy Loman in Long Island production of Salesman because of Miller's alleged "left wing affiliations."

3   ANON. "Protested Play Given." New York Times (December 10), p. 42.
     Long Island production of Salesman opens with a replace-ment in the role of Willy. In rehearsals the actor origi-nally chosen for the part quit because of Miller's "alleged association with un-American activities."

1954

4   AYMÉ, MARCEL. "I Want to Be Hanged Like a Witch." Translated
      by Gerald Weales. Arts (December 15-21), pp. 1, 3.
           In his French translation of The Crucible, Aymé was
      forced to blacken the character of Abigail far beyond her
      culpability in the original, because the sympathy of French
      audiences would otherwise have gone to her rather than
      Proctor. Reprinted: 1971.43.

5   BENTLEY, ERIC. "The Innocence of Arthur Miller," in his The
      Dramatic Event: An American Chronicle. New York: Horizon
      Press, pp. 90-94.
           Reprint of 1953.12.

6   GASSNER, JOHN. "Death of a Salesman: First Impressions,
      1949," in his Theatre in Our Times. New York: Crown,
      pp. 364-373.
           Reprints 1949.53, 54.

7   HOBSON, HAROLD. "Fair Play." Sunday Times (London) (November
      14), p. 11.
           Review of London production of The Crucible. Holds that
      Miller, by implication, gives a better case to Senator
      McCarthy than might have been expected, refusing to "let
      personal convictions interfere with the dramatist's respon-
      sibility to present every character with understanding and
      sympathy." Not only does Miller admit there is a basis for
      the investigation, but shows it proceeding legally under a
      judge who is "genuinely concerned to see justice done."
      Reprinted: 1971.43.

8   HOPE-WALLACE, PHILIP. "Theatre." Time and Tide, 35:   1544.
           Review of Bristol Old Vic production of The Crucible.
      The play has less impact than it should in England because
      "all witch hunt plays are the same in the long run; unless
      they are written by someone like Shaw." Miller's trial
      scene is filled with anger and self-pity, whereas Shaw's
      (in St. Joan) is so "human, wise and balanced that it
      cleaves the heart."

9   SAMACHSON, DOROTHY and JOSEPH. Let's Meet the Theatre. New
      York: Abelard-Schuman, pp. 15-20.
           Interview. Miller discusses critics, community theatre,
      the set of Death of a Salesman, the best plays for non-
      commercial production, and the best training for aspiring
      playwrights.

10 SMALL, CHRISTOPHER. "Theatre." Spectator, 193 (November 19),
      608.

1954

> Review of Bristol Old Vic production of The Crucible.
> Rather than illuminating current or past affairs, the play
> "does not much more than provide its author with a whipping
> boy on whom to work off honest indignation." Miller leaves
> the historical parallels unfinished. The play is "good,
> strong, rugged stuff," though, with "a lot more kick in it
> than Death of a Salesman."

11 TREWIN, J. C. "Blanket of the Dark." The Illustrated London
      News, 225 (November 27), 964.
>   Review of Bristol Old Vic production of The Crucible.
> Compares Miller's play to Longfellow's Giles Corey of Salem
> Farms. As a historical melodrama, The Crucible is "pro-
> foundly affecting" and a play in which "suspense can choke."
> The "fantastic bigotry" of the judges is hard to believe,
> though.

12 TYNAN, KENNETH. "American Blues: The Plays of Arthur Miller
      and Tennessee Williams." Encounter, 2 (May), 13-19.
>   Biographical and critical summaries of Miller's and
> Williams' careers to date. Like their American predeces-
> sors, both playwrights deal with the martyrdom of modern
> man. Trapped in the present, Miller's preoccupation is
> with action and incident; Williams' is with nostalgia and
> hope, the past and the future. Reprinted: 1961.30;
> 1961.46; 1967.42.

13 WORSLEY, T. C. "A Play of Our Time." New Statesman and Nation,
      48 (November 20), 642.
>   Review of Bristol Old Vic production of The Crucible.
> The development of a language that is not awkwardly archaic
> or falsely poetic and careful organization of complicated
> dramatic material successfully solve the two main problems
> of Miller's subject. The play is forceful, compelling and
> the atmosphere of panic brilliantly evoked. The trouble
> is that the parallel between witch hunting and Communist
> hunting is forced and the characterization is simplistic.

1955

1 ANON. "Crucible Hailed in Argentina." New York Times (July
      29), p. 8.
>   Brief mention of Buenos Aires production of The Crucible.

2 ANON. "Miller Work Hailed." New York Times (August 31),
      p. 16.

Report of Falmouth Playhouse production of A Memory of
Two Mondays and A View from the Bridge. The audience gave
the pre-Broadway production a standing ovation.

3   ANON. "A View from the Bridge." Time, 66 (October 10), 53.
Review of New York opening of A Memory of Two Mondays
and A View from the Bridge. The former is a "pat, shapeless
picture," but the latter is "better than good theatre at
its best," though "not quite good drama as a whole." In
evoking the Greek origins of drama, Miller actually emphasizes how little his characters have in common with Greek
tragedy.

4   ANON. "Nostalgia and Passion by the River." Life, 39
(October 17), 166-67.
Brief mention with pictures of New York premiere of A
View from the Bridge.

5   ANON. "A View from the Bridge." Theatre Arts, 39 (December)
18-19.
Review of New York production of A View from the Bridge.
The play is portentous, though the excellent acting gives
the characters "greater stature than Miller might reasonably
have expected." The play is written as a "lean, taut narrative that certainly fulfills the second half of Aristotle's
pity-and-terror formula." A Memory of Two Mondays is an
"evocative, evanescent wordy piece" which is a good deal
more than a curtain-raiser, even if not in the main event
class.

6   ANON. "Youth Board Set to Approve Film." New York Times
(December 5), p. 33.
The New York City Youth Board will ratify a film contract signed in July 1955 for production of Miller's film
script on street gangs. The script was originally com-
missioned by the Board.

7   ANON. "City Drops Plans for a Youth Film." New York Times
(December 8), p. 47.
New York City Youth Board votes not to film Miller's
script dealing with street gangs. Board officials said an
investigation of Miller showed he had "been associated with
some subversive groups at one time."

8   ANON. "Miller Hits Back at Youth Agency." New York Times
(December 9), p. 29.
Miller criticizes Youth Board for overriding its sub-
committee's recommendation that his script on street gangs

1955

be filmed. "Let us see whether fanaticism...can perform a
creative act. Let it take its club in hand and write what
it has just destroyed."

9 ATKINSON, BROOKS. "Foreword," in <u>New Voices in the American
Theatre</u>. Edited by Brooks Atkinson. New York: Modern
Library, pp. vii-ix.
    Two brief paragraphs on Miller and <u>Salesman</u> in foreword
to this anthology.

10   . "Theatre: <u>A View from the Bridge</u>." <u>New York Times</u>
(September 30), p. 21.
    Though <u>A View from the Bridge</u> contains material for a
forceful drama of simple people caught in a terrible crisis,
Miller's blunt, spare characterizations are not big enough
for his tragedy. The play is self-conscious in writing and
acting, as though author and actors were trying for something more exalted than the narrative can yield. Reprinted:
1955.15.

11   . "<u>A View from the Bridge</u>." <u>New York Times</u> (October 9),
sec. II, p. 1.
    Review of New York opening of <u>Bridge</u> and <u>A Memory of Two
Mondays</u>, an "exercise in theatrical photography that is
flat and diffuse." <u>Bridge</u> is ambitious, however, and
achieves most of what it attempts. But because Miller has
not told us enough about Eddie Carbone, he remains mean and
vicious to the end, unable to enlist the sympathy necessary
for a tragic hero.

12 BENNETT, CHARLES G. "City Hall Dodges Youth Film Issue."
<u>New York Times</u> (November 30), p. 38.
    New York's Board of Estimates defers to New York City
Youth Board concerning action on a production contract for
Miller's film script on the Youth Board's work with street
gangs. The contract had been held up pending results of an
investigation of Miller's left-wing activity. The investigation found no evidence of present left-wing associations
of Miller.

13 BENTLEY, ERIC. "Theatre." <u>New Republic</u>, 133 (December 19),
21-22.
    Review of <u>A View from the Bridge</u> and <u>A Memory of Two
Mondays</u>. Whereas Elia Kazan's <u>On the Waterfront</u> makes a
virtue of informing, <u>View</u> condemns it--a significant difference in view of the relationship between Miller and
Kazan and their appearances before congressional investi-
gators. Nevertheless, <u>View</u> is "isolated from the great

debates of our time," though it was well received on the
road. With tightening, <u>Memory</u> could have been an unforced
and touching drama, rather than an unsuccessful evocation
of Odets and Saroyan.

14   CHAPMAN, JOHN. "Miller's <u>View from the Bridge</u> Is Splendid,
     Stunning Theatre." <u>New York Daily News</u> (September 30).
          Review. <u>A View from the Bridge</u> marks a further develop-
     ment in Miller's "human insight, theatrical skill and
     quality as a poet." A classical tragedy, it is also a
     modern classic that "wastes no time, has no false moves,
     and has the beauty that comes from directness and simplic-
     ity." Reprinted: 1955.15.

15   COFFIN, RACHEL W., ed. "<u>A View from the Bridge</u>." <u>New York</u>
     <u>Theatre Critics' Reviews</u>, 16 (September 30), 272-75.
          Reprints New York critics' reviews: Atkinson (1955.10);
     Chapman (1955.14); Coleman (1955.16); Hawkins (1955.24);
     Kerr (1955.30); McClain (1955.33); Watts (1955.39).

16   COLEMAN, ROBERT. "Twin Bill at Coronet Fine for Box Office."
     <u>New York Daily Mirror</u> (September 30).
          Review. While <u>A Memory of Two Mondays</u> is Chekhovian,
     with a lot of salty talk but little action, <u>A View from the</u>
     <u>Bridge</u> is a violent, sensational, realistic "slice of life."
     Reprinted: 1955.15.

17   COUCHMAN, GORDON W. "Arthur Miller's Tragedy of Babbitt."
     <u>Educational Theatre Journal</u>, 7 (October), 206-11.
          Compares <u>Death of a Salesman</u> with Sinclair Lewis's
     <u>Babbitt</u>. Miller brings Lewis up to date and at its best
     his play shares with <u>Babbitt</u> "a rare gift for the poetic
     in the colloquial which redeems both works from being merely
     depressing." Reprinted: 1972.47.

18   FARRELL, ISOLDE. "From the Seine." <u>New York Times</u> (February
     27), sec. II, p. 3.
          Brief notice of <u>Les Sorcières de Salem</u>, the French stage
     version of <u>The Crucible</u> adapted by Marcel Aymé. The
     <u>Figaro</u> critic expressed the unanimous opinion of French
     critics in applauding this "original, vigorous and signif-
     icant play; one of the finest shows ever presented in
     Paris."

19   FAST, HOWARD. "I Propose Arthur Miller as the American
     Dramatist of the Day." <u>Daily Worker</u> (November 8), p. 6.
          Compares Miller favorably with the left-wing writers,
     Clifford Odets and Lillian Hellman. Sees <u>The Crucible</u> as

1955

a tribute to the courage of Ethel and Julius Rosenberg, and
notes that A View from the Bridge is also a drama of betrayal.
Miller's dependence on the "inner neurotic conflict" of
Eddie Carbone reflects the constraints under which the playwright must work on Broadway in the cold war. Congratulates
Miller for "fighting with all the wit and skill at his com-
mand for his survival as an artist."

20 GIBBS, WOLCOTT. "The Theatre." New Yorker, 31 (October 8),
    92, 94-95.
        Review of New York premiere of A View from the Bridge and
    A Memory of Two Mondays. A "shocking study of a sick mind,"
    Bridge shows Miller's skill in transforming illiterate
    speech into harsh and grotesquely eloquent dialogue, and a
    fine discipline in the treatment of dramatic incident. The
    lawyer, however, is a "distractingly literary touch." A
    Memory is an interesting collection of "eccentric character
    studies."

21 GOODMAN, WALTER. "How Not to Produce a Film." New Republic,
    133 (December 26), 12-13.
        An account of Miller's aborted efforts to make a film on
    juvenile delinquency for the New York City Youth Board.
    Because of his "questionable political background," the
    city fathers were pressured by the American Legion, the
    Catholic War Veterans and the New York Police Department
    into canceling the project.

22 GRUTZNER, CHARLES. "Mayor Halts City TV Plans." New York
    Times (October 26), pp. 1, 62.
        The New York Civil Liberties Union criticizes Mayor
    Wagner's investigation of Miller's political beliefs in
    connection with the film script he wrote on the work of
    the New York City Youth Board.

23 _____. "39 TV Films Based on City Planned." New York Times
    (October 25), pp. 1, 21.
        New York's Mayor Wagner is investigating charges that
    Miller, who had written a film script on New York for the
    New York City Youth Board, had "left-wing affiliations."
    Emphasizing that nothing derogatory had yet been found,
    Wagner said, "We are not having a witch hunt or anything;
    we are just trying to find out."

24 HAWKINS, WILLIAM. "2-in-1 Bill Staged at Coronet." New York
    World Telegram and Sun (September 30).
        Review. While A Memory of Two Mondays is a "plotless
    group of character studies," A View from the Bridge has

50

more bold plot than most opera. Miller's attempt to criticize the current attitude toward immigration sinks in bom-
bastic emotion, though the audience is breathless with
suspense until the violent finale. The tale is "absorbed
in a single emotion" and fails to "inspire sympathy for its
principal character." Reprinted: 1955.15.

25   HAYES, RICHARD. "The Stage: I Want My Catharsis." Commonweal, 62 (November 4), 117-18.
        Review of A Memory of Two Mondays and A View from the
Bridge. The latter play fails as tragedy since it lacks
the "finely structured articulation of pain" and a "suf-
ficiently flexible language to register the shocks of per-
sonality and fate." Miller is not interested in artistically
shaping the material of pain, but rather in a "willed melodrama of sensation."

26   HEWES, HENRY. "Death of a Longshoreman." Saturday Review, 38
(October 15), 25-26.
        A View from the Bridge must rise or fall on its dramatic
effectiveness as a study of Eddie Carbone. As such it is
"gripping, unflinchingly real as well as poetic." A Memory
of Two Mondays is a "real and important part of Arthur
Miller's exploration of modern man's struggle against
indignity." Abridged: 1960.23; 1969.11.

27   _____, ed. "American Playwrights Self-Appraised." Saturday
Review, 38 (September 3), 18-19.
        Miller's answers to a questionnaire. The only important
trend in theatre today "is represented by Bertolt Brecht";
the only materials for a possible new trend in the U.S. are
"new insights into social and psychological mechanisms."

28   KERNODLE, GEORGE R. "The Death of the Little Man." Tulane
Drama Review, 1 (1955-56), 47-60.
        In connection with Death of a Salesman, discusses the
figure of the Little Man in other plays and American popular culture. Compares film and stage versions of Salesman.

29   KERR, WALTER. How Not to Write a Play. New York: Simon and
Schuster, pp. 55-58.
        Discusses All My Sons and Salesman as thesis plays. The
thesis play that is clear in its argument (All My Sons) is
not memorable in its characterization; the one whose argument is clouded (Salesman) has an unforgettable character
in Willy Loman.

1955

30   ____. "A View from the Bridge." New York Herald Tribune
        (September 30), sec. III, p. 8.
           Review. A View from the Bridge has "taut lines," direct
        dialogue, and theatrical images that lend vividness and
        color to every crisis. The human majesty, warmth and pity
        suggested by the setting are missing from the play, however.
        In clinging to the facts, Miller omits the poetry the
        classical parallels hint at. A Memory of Two Mondays is an
        "interesting and affecting mood piece," though it could have
        been sacrificed in the interests of the larger work.
        Reprinted: 1955.15.

31   LEVIN, DAVID. "Salem Witchcraft in Recent Fiction and Drama."
        New England Quarterly, 28 (December), 537-42.
           Miller's faulty understanding of the period "damages The
        Crucible as 'essential' history, as moral instruction, and
        as art." Discusses historical errors, misleading impres-
        sions in the play that undermine its brilliant dramatization
        of the dilemma of an innocent man. Abridged: 1971.43.

32   LEWIS, THEOPHILUS. "A View from the Bridge." America, 94
        (November 19), 223-24.
           Brief review of Broadway debut of A Memory of Two Mondays
        and A View from the Bridge. Sees latter play as variation
        of Cenci story.

33   MCCLAIN, JOHN. "Hail Heflin in Two Plays." New York Journal
        American (September 30).
           Review. While A Memory of Two Mondays is not a very
        absorbing or conclusive play, and A View from the Bridge is
        pedestrian and lacking in verisimilitude, Miller has an
        "unqualified ear" and a "legitimate understanding of the
        people he writes about." The plays are not a fair indica-
        tion of Miller's talents or a fruitful excursion in the
        theatre. Reprinted: 1955.15.

34   SARTRE, JEAN-PAUL. "Jean-Paul Sartre nous parle de théâtre."
        Translated by Nora L. Magid. Théâtre Populaire, No. 15
        (September-October), p. 9.
           Sartre's comments on Marcel Aymé's stage adaptation of
        The Crucible. Objects to Aymé's universalizing of a
        "specifically American phenomenon," argues that the basis
        of the social conflict in the play is the battle between
        the old and new settlers for possession of the land, between
        the rich and the poor. Reprinted: 1971.43.

35   SELZ, JEAN. "Raymond Rouleau Among the Witches." Les Lettres
        Nouvelles, 3 (March), 422-26.

Review of French production of The Crucible. The performance was enhanced by Marcel Aymé's adaptation, Raymond
Rouleau's direction, and an excellent cast led by Simone
Signoret and Yves Montand. Reprinted in translation:
1971.43.

36 SIEVERS, W. DAVID. "Tennessee Williams and Arthur Miller,"
in his Freud on Broadway. New York: Hermitage, pp. 388-99.
Traces psychology of father-son, Oedipal relationships
in early plays, concentrating on Salesman, the twentieth
century American tragedy that best succeeds in "compressing
deeply understood psychological relationships into a form
that is vibrantly alive in the theatre." The Crucible
breaks new dramatic ground by "synthesizing historical and
psychoanalytic insight." Pages 376-80, 388, 391-96
reprinted: 1961.30.

37 TRAUBER, SHEPARD. "Theater." Nation, 181 (October 22),
348-49.
Brief favorable review of Broadway premiere of A View
from the Bridge and A Memory of Two Mondays. The plays,
though minor works, are always interesting, frequently
stirring and "steadily illuminated by the incandescence of
an author whose thinking about human beings is always
profound."

38 WARSHOW, ROBERT. "The Liberal Conscience in The Crucible,"
in The Scene Before You: a New Approach to American
Culture. Edited by Brossard Chandler. New York: Rinehart,
pp. 191-203.
Reprint of 1953.40.

39 WATTS, RICHARD. "Those New Plays by Arthur Miller." New York
Post (September 30).
Review. A Memory of Two Mondays has credible atmosphere,
a brooding sadness and believable characters, but its
"dramatic aimlessness keeps it from being more than mod-
erately interesting." A View from the Bridge, despite
excellent characterization, atmosphere and dialogue, is
"commonplace and lacking in freshness of viewpoint or insight." Tennessee Williams could probably have told the
same story more powerfully. Reprinted: 1955.15.

40 WYATT, EUPHEMIA VAN RENSSELAER. "Theatre." Catholic World,
182 (November), 144-45.
Review of Broadway premiere of A View from the Bridge and
A Memory of Two Mondays. The former play never approaches

1956

classic tragedy because its hero lacks nobility of motive
and horror is substituted for catharsis. The latter play
is a "vividly graphic sketch" spoiled by an offensively
lewd and blasphemous interlude.

1956

1   ANON. "Cultural Group Rebukes Miller." New York Times
        (February 14), p. 5.
            The American Committee for Cultural Freedom denies it
        invited Miller to write an appeal for cultural freedom in
        the U.S. and Russia. Miller is "almost certain" the Com-
        mittee asked for his statement. The Committee further
        objects to Miller's equation of the suppression of cultural
        freedom in the two countries.

2   ANON. "Soviet Challenged to Reveal Criticism." New York
        Times (February 15), p. 28.
            The American Committee for Cultural Freedom and Radio
        Liberation challenges the Soviet Union to publicize Miller's
        statement denouncing political interference with artistic
        freedom.

3   ANON. "London Critics Hail Miller's The Crucible." New York
        Times (April 11), p. 28.
            Summary of reviews of English Stage Company's production
        of The Crucible at Royal Court Theatre, London.

4   ANON. "Arthur Miller Gets Divorce." New York Times (June 12),
        p. 24.
            In Reno, Nevada, Miller wins uncontested divorce from
        his first wife, Mary Grace Slattery, charging her with
        "extreme cruelty, entirely mental in nature."

5   ANON. "Investigation of the Unauthorized Use of United States
        Passports - Part 4." Hearings Before the Committee on Un-
        American Activities, House of Representatives: 84th Con-
        gress, 2nd Session (June 14, 21). Washington, D. C.: U.S.
        Government Printing Office, pp. 4655-91.
            Record of Miller's appearance before HUAC in response to
        a subpoena charging misuse of his passport. The hearing
        degenerates into an inquisition into Miller's leftist
        sympathies and his belief in artistic freedom of expression.

6   ANON. "Michigan U. Honors Nine." New York Times (June 17),
        p. 8.
            Miller receives honorary degree from the University of
        Michigan.

7   ANON. "Miller Ordered to Reveal Names." <u>New York Times</u> (June 28), p. 10.
        The House Un-American Activities Committee votes to give Miller ten days to reveal the names of those he saw at Communist Party meetings in the 1940's. Miller's passport to visit Britain is being held up "until he furnishes a satisfactory affidavit regarding his past associations."

8   ANON. "Marilyn Monroe, Arthur Miller Married." <u>New York Times</u> (June 30), p. 19.
        Report of wedding in White Plains, New York.

9   ANON. "Engagement Party." <u>Newsweek</u>, 48 (July 2), 21-22.
        Announcement of wedding plans of Miller and Marilyn Monroe.

10   ANON. "Millers Remarried." <u>New York Times</u> (July 3), p. 16.
        Marilyn Monroe and Miller remarry in Jewish faith after an earlier civil ceremony.

11   ANON. "Miller Granted Europe Passport." <u>New York Times</u> (July 7), p. 15.
        After refusing for two years, the U.S. State Department grants Miller a six-month passport for a European honeymoon. Affidavits recently submitted by Miller apparently persuaded officials he was not now pro-Communist.

12   ANON. "Miller Declines to Identify Reds." <u>New York Times</u> (July 8), p. 25.
        In a letter to the House Un-American Activities Committee, Miller again refuses to name those he saw at Communist meetings in the 1940's and cites legal precedents against being penalized for contempt of Congress.

13   ANON. "People." <u>Time</u>, 68 (July 9), 36.
        Report of Miller's marriage to Marilyn Monroe and return to home in Connecticut.

14   ANON. "Reds Linked to Film." <u>New York Times</u> (July 9), p. 3.
        <u>Neues Deutschland</u>, an East German newspaper, reports that a French-East German team plans to film <u>The Crucible</u>, using a movie script by Jean-Paul Sartre. In the U.S. Miller says any East German connection with the production would seem to be a violation of his French contract.

15   ANON. "German Link to Movie Denied." <u>New York Times</u> (July 10), p. 26.

1956

> A French film company denies it plans to join an East
> German company in making a film of The Crucible.

16   ANON. "Arthur Millers Leave for London." New York Times
        (July 14), p. 33.
           In London, Miller will work on the British production of
        A View from the Bridge, while Miss Monroe makes a film, The
        Prince and the Show Girl, with Sir Laurence Olivier.

17   ANON. "Proceedings Against Arthur Miller, July 25, 1956,
        Report #2922." House Reports, 2800-2974. Vol. 5.
           Record of Miller's appearance before House Committee on
        Un-American Activities in its investigation of the unauthor-
        ized use of U.S. passports.

18   ANON. "Arthur Miller on Way Here." New York Times (August
        27), p. 15.
           Miller will interrupt his European visit to return to
        New York for a ten-day vacation with his children.

19   ANON. "Playwright Flies Here From London for Visit." New
        York Times (August 28), p. 13.
           While in the U.S. Miller will take a trip with his two
        children by a previous marriage, then return to London to
        supervise a production of A View from the Bridge.

20   ANON. "Drama by Miller Opens in London." New York Times
        (October 12), p. 35.
           Brief quotations from reviews, generally favorable, of
        London production of A View from the Bridge. The play was
        presented at a private club because of the Lord Chamberlain's
        ban on public presentation, a ban attributed to the homo-
        sexual references.

21   ANON. "Revised Bridge Given in Capital." New York Times
        (November 9), p. 34.
           The scenes added to A View from the Bridge clarify the
        story considerably in the Washington production, though the
        lawyer-commentator character is still troublesome.

22   ANON. "Marilyn Monroe Here." New York Times (November 22),
        p. 50.
           Miller accompanies wife home from London after her com-
        pletion of filming of The Prince and the Show Girl.

23   BENTLEY, ERIC. "Do We Believe in Discussion?" New Republic,
        135 (July 2), 22.

Discussion of several controversial plays. Notes that
The Crucible, one of the decade's most controversial plays,
aroused very little controversy in the New York press.

24   _____. "The Miller Case." New Republic, 135 (September 10),
        23.
        Rebuttal to Gerald W. Johnson's support in August 6
        issue of New Republic of Miller's refusal to name names
        before the House Un-American Activities Committee. Miller's
        connection with Communism was not limited to "half a dozen
        meetings." It is part of the "deep involvement of a large
        class of persons in a movement inadequately defined by words
        like giddy." Miller, Johnson, and other liberals are beg-
        ging the question, who has been betrayed by whom?

25   BREIT, HARVEY. "Dostoevsky." New York Times (February 26),
        sec. VII, p. 8.
        While it is absurd of Miller to equate American and
        Soviet injustice in his statement on the anniversary of
        Dostoevsky's death, it is to his credit that he refused the
        gambit of the Soviet Writer's Union, which had hoped to
        create a pro-Soviet cause célèbre by inviting him to Russia
        in the expectation that he would be denied a passport.

26   COOK, JIM. "Their Thirteenth Year Was the Most Significant."
        Washington Post & Times Herald (July 10), p. 24.
        Parallel biographical sketches of Miller and Marilyn
        Monroe. Interviews with Miller and his sister on his early
        years. Miller regards his thirteenth year as the most
        significant in his life, since the Depression hit his family
        in that year (1929).

27   DRURY, ALLEN. "Arthur Miller Admits Helping Communist Front
        Groups in '40's.'" New York Times (June 22), pp. 1, 9.
        Before House Un-American Activities Committee, Miller
        admits signing several appeals and protests issued by Red
        front groups in the last decade, and attending four or five
        Communist meetings. He denies membership in the Communist
        party or that he was ever "under Communist discipline" and
        refuses to name others at Communist meetings. Plans to wed
        Marilyn Monroe are announced.

28   _____. "House Votes 373-9 for Citing Miller." New York Times
        (July 26), p. 7.
        Because of his refusal to give the House Committee on
        Un-American Activities the names of persons with whom he
        attended Communist writers meetings in 1947, Miller is cited

1956

by the House of Representatives for contempt of Congress.
Miller had not resorted to the Fifth Amendment or other
Constitutional protections in testifying before the
committee.

29   FARRELL, JAMES T. "Curbs on Art Opposed." New York Times
     (February 21), p. 32.
          Farrell, Chairman of the American Committee for Cultural
     Freedom, denies Miller was invited to issue a statement on
     the anniversary of Dostoevski's death and denies the impli-
     cation in Miller's statement that the Committee was
     "attempting to draw the memory of Dostoevski onto a polit-
     ical platform."

30   FREEDLEY, GEORGE. "A View from the Bridge." Booklist, 52
     (January 15), 205-206.
          Brief descriptions of A View from the Bridge and A Memory
     of Two Mondays.

31   _____. "A View from the Bridge." Library Journal, 81
     (January 1), 101.
          Brief notice of publication of View and A Memory of Two
     Mondays.

32   GASSNER, JOHN. Form and Idea in Modern Theatre. New York:
     Dryden, pp. 13, 43, 66, 84-85.
          Discusses alternation between realistic and stylized
     staging of Salesman. The play's flow of action is deter-
     mined by an explicit issue or argument: what values shall
     a man live by?

33   GRIFFIN, ALICE. "The Crucible at York." Theatre Arts, 40
     (February), 80.
          Excerpts from reviews of York, Pennsylvania, production
     of The Crucible. Though it was uncertain, in view of the
     play's "serious and provocative theme," what the reaction
     would be, the production was an "overwhelming success."

34   HARTLEY, ANTHONY. "Good Melodrama." Spectator, 196 (April
     20), 547.
          Review of London production of The Crucible. The play
     has "more guts than we have seen in an English-language
     play for many a long day," and the writing is "fundamentally
     poetic without the self-conscious striving after artifici-
     ality which is the bore of the West End stage." The play's
     political parallels are questionable but can be "neglected
     without much loss."

35   _____. "Waterfront." Spectator, 197 (October 19), 538, 540.
        Review of Peter Brook's London production of A View from
    the Bridge. Though Elia Kazan and the Group Theatre, Wait-
    ing for Lefty, and Winterset are oppressive influences,
    this "powerful play has enough strength to overcome its
    defects." Despite momentary lapses of the rhetoric into
    bad prose poetry, the View has Miller's usual economy of
    language, "humanity in its approach to the characters,"
    and fast-paced action once it gets going.

36   HOPE-WALLACE, PHILIP. "Theatre: A View from the Bridge."
        Time and Tide, 37 (October 20), 1267.
        Review of London production of A View from the Bridge,
    a "fine piece that enriches London drama." Peter Brook's
    production "packs a tremendous punch," but the play is not
    tragedy since it lacks "fine feelings" and characters who
    understand and can express their motives.

37   JOHNSON, GERALD W. "Undermining Congress." New Republic, 135
        (August 6), 10.
        Supports Miller's refusal before the House Un-American
    Activities Committee to name others who were "half-inclined
    to swallow the Communist rumble-bumble" in the 1940's. The
    real issue is whether the desirability of blasting the
    reputation of Miller's friends "justifies the risk of
    blasting the reputation of Congress among honorable people."

38   LEWIS, ANTHONY. "House Unit Asks Miller Citation." New York
        Times (July 11), p. 10.
        The House Committee on Un-American Activities votes
    unanimously in closed session to recommend to the full
    House that Miller be cited for contempt of Congress for
    refusing to name those he saw at Communist meetings in the
    1940's.

39   LUMLEY, FREDERICK. Trends in 20th Century Drama: A Survey
        Since Ibsen and Shaw. Fair Lawn, N. J.: Essential Books,
        pp. 185-86, 191-93.
        Abridged version of 1972.40.

40   MCCARTHY, MARY. "Introduction," in her Sights and Spectacles
        1937-1956. New York: Farar, Straus and Cudahy,
        pp. xiv-xvi.
        Striving to be tragedy, Salesman instead becomes "con-
    fused and hortatory." Though Willy seems Jewish, he is not
    individualized enough to be recognizably anything; and the
    play as a whole is "conceptualized, like the ads to which
    it gives a bitter retort."

1956

41   MULLER, HERBERT J. "Tragedy in America: O'Neill," in his
      The Spirit of Tragedy. New York: Alfred A. Knopf,
      pp. 316-17.
         Salesman is a humane, honest work, despite the play's
      "supra-realistic effects which are too fancy for little
      Willy." The critics' divergent judgments of Willy stem
      from Miller's own uncertain understanding of him.

42   O'CONNOR, FRANK. "The Most American Playwright." Holiday, 19
      (February), 65, 68, 70.
         Discusses father-son relationships in Miller. Reviews
      View from the Bridge and A Memory of Two Mondays, preferring
      the latter (as does Miller) because it deals with differ-
      ences in opportunity between brothers and social classes.

43   PAYNE, DARWIN R. "Unit Scenery." Players Magazine, 33
      (December), 59, 62.
         Description of scenery for a production of The Crucible
      at Southern Illinois University. The aim was to "match
      visually the forceful simplicity of Miller's poetic drama,"
      as well as to present a "succession of historically accurate,
      architecturally feasible rooms and locales."

44   ROVERE, RICHARD H. "Monroe Doctrine." Spectator, 196 (June
      29), 877.
         Miller announces after HUAC hearing that he will wed
      Marilyn Monroe, a "supremely American activity." Chairman
      Walter's attempt to regain the limelight by announcing he
      will move to have Miller cited for contempt of Congress "is
      probably just talk."

45   SCHWARTZ, HARRY. "Red and Anti-Red Curbs on Art Denounced."
      New York Times (February 13), p. 9.
         In response to requests from two anti-Communist organi-
      zations, Miller appeals to Soviet Communists and American
      anti-Communists to recognize that true art is above politics.
      The occasion was the seventy-fifth anniversary of the death
      of Feodor Dostoevski.

46   SIEGEL, PAUL N. "Willy Loman and King Lear." College English,
      17 (March), 341-45.
         The cause of the catastrophe of the King of ancient
      Britain and the salesman of today is the same: neither
      knows himself nor the world he lives in. The grim, ironic
      humor of Willy's floundering self-contradictions is similar
      to the Fool's in Shakespeare's King Lear and serves to

heighten pathos in both plays. Willy has some of Lear's
greatness of spirit, and like Lear elicits not merely pity
but fear (that we are all Willy Lomans selling nothing but
ourselves).

47   TREWIN, J. C. "Quick Change." Illustrated London News, 229
        (October 27), 720.
             Review of Peter Brook's production of View from the
        Bridge, an "honest theatrical melodrama" that is "sternly
        inevitable," "economically wrought," and atmospherically
        intense.

48   WALKER, PHILIP. "Arthur Miller's The Crucible: Tragedy or
        Allegory?" Western Speech, 20 (Fall), 222-24.
             The Crucible suffers from Miller's uncertainty about
        whether it is a personal tragedy or a political allegory.
        Neither the allegorical or tragic element is sufficiently
        developed to be exclusive of the others. The confusion can
        only be resolved in performance by "establishing an empathic
        relationship between Proctor and the audience" of such
        strength and intensity that no parallel between Salem in
        1692 and Washington in 1954 will suggest itself.

49   WORSLEY, T. C. "The Arts and Entertainment: Realistic Melo-
        drama." New Statesman, 52 (October 20), 482.
             Review of Peter Brook's production of A View from the
        Bridge. A "tense, vivid, atmospheric" production despite
        the fact that Miller "leaves his melodrama unredeemed by
        language." To redeem it, he resorts to a "passionate
        intensity of truthfulness," which succeeds, and an attempt
        to "establish from the outside of the play some sort of
        universality," which fails.

50   _____. "Producers at Play." New Statesman and Nation, 51
        (April 14), 370-71.
             Brief notice of Royal Court production of The Crucible.
        Though Miller has solved the problems of language and
        organization inherent in his dramatic material, the climax
        "does more credit to his feelings for goodness than truth."
        The play "could have bitten much deeper."

                                    1957

1   ANON. "Moscow Backs Miller." New York Times (February 20),
        p. 2.
             Moscow radio perceives a parallel between Miller's in-
        dictment for contempt of Congress and The Crucible. "This

1957

very same situation occurs in <u>The Crucible</u>. In it the in-
quisitor is about to arrest a character for contempt of
court. Is this really a coincidence? No."

2   ANON. "Miller and Nathan Disavow Contempt." <u>New York Times</u>
     (March 2), p. 14.
          Miller pleads not guilty in Federal District Court to an
     indictment charging him with contempt of Congress for refus-
     ing to answer questions of the House Committee on Un-
     American Activities.

3   ANON. "Miller Must Stand Trial." <u>New York Times</u> (April 13)
     p. 9.
          Judge Charles F. McLaughlin of the Federal District
     Court in Washington, D. C. refuses to discuss an indictment
     charging Miller with contempt of Congress. Miller must
     stand trial on May 13, 1957.

4   ANON. "Miller Trial Delay Refused." <u>New York Times</u> (May 4),
     p. 26.
          Federal District Judge Bolitha J. Laws refuses to post-
     pone the contempt trial of Miller scheduled for May 13.

5   ANON. "Reds' 'Discipline' of Miller Argued." <u>New York Times</u>
     (May 17), p. 10.
          At Miller's trial for contempt of Congress, lawyers
     argue over the point at which a person comes under Communist
     discipline. Richard Arens, staff director of HUAC, testi-
     fies that it could be assumed that a person who attended
     meetings to which only known Communists were admitted was
     under party discipline.

6   ANON. "Judge Denies Point to Miller in Trial." <u>New York
     Times</u> (May 21), p. 30.
          In Miller's trial on contempt of Congress charges, Judge
     McLaughlin denies his lawyer's contention that government
     testimony asserting that Miller was a Communist in the
     1940's is inadmissible because it is based on hearsay.

7   ANON. "Judge Bars Data on Miller Romance." <u>New York Times</u>
     (May 22), p. 17.
          Judge McLaughlin rejects Joseph L. Rauh's trial dis-
     missal motion based on his argument that HUAC had called
     Miller as a witness to capitalize on publicity he was
     receiving as Miss Monroe's suitor.

8   ANON. "Miller Trial Ends." <u>New York Times</u> (May 24), p. 9.
        Miller's trial on charges of contempt of Congress con-
cludes with Harry P. Cain, a former Washington Republican
senator, testifying that he believes Miller's statement
that he has never been under Communist discipline. Cain
was a former member of the Subversive Activities Control
Board.

9   ANON. "Arthur Miller: Act II." <u>Economist</u>, 183 (June 1), 790.
        An account of Miller's trial for contempt of Congress.

10   ANON. "Playwright in Trouble." <u>New York Times</u> (June 1), p. 8.
        Biographical sketch of Miller through his trial for con-
tempt of Congress.

11   ANON. "When Silence is Contempt of Congress." <u>U. S. News
and World Report</u>, 42 (June 7), 14.
        Miller is found guilty of contempt of Congress by Judge
McLaughlin for refusing to answer questions of the House
Committee on Un-American Activities.

12   ANON. "Innocent and Guilty." <u>Newsweek</u>, 49 (June 10), 32.
        Miller is found guilty on two counts of contempt of
Congress. Sentencing is deferred.

13   ANON. "Morality and Law." <u>Commonweal</u>, 66 (June 14), 268-69.
        The Court's finding that Miller is guilty of contempt
of Congress for refusing to name people he saw at Communist
party meetings in 1947 is an attack on the right of the
individual to follow his own conscience, and lends support
to those "sincere Americans who fail to see that a defense
of the democratic rights of American Communists is a defense,
not of Communism, but of democracy."

14   ANON. "Collected Plays." <u>Booklist</u>, 53 (June 15), 523.
        Brief review. Plays are for readers who can "accept a
realistic, tough-minded approach to play-writing."

15   ANON. "Inquiry Reform Seen Inevitable." <u>New York Times</u> (June
19), p. 16.
        As a result of the Supreme Court's reversal of the con-
tempt of Congress conviction of John T. Watkins, Miller
asks a Federal Court to throw out his conviction for contempt of Congress. Watkins was convicted for refusing on
grounds of conscience to identify former Communist
associates.

1957

16   ANON. "Judge Reaffirms Guilt of Miller." <u>New York Times</u>
      (June 29), p. 4.
           Judge McLaughlin refuses to throw out Miller's convic-
      tion for contempt of Congress, despite the Supreme Court's
      reversal of the conviction of John T. Watkins on a similar
      charge. The Judge did reverse himself on the second of
      two counts on which he had found Miller guilty, explaining
      that HUAC had wrongly refused, when challenged, to state
      to the defendant the pertinency of the second of two ques-
      tions Miller had declined to answer.

17   ANON. "One Round for Congress." <u>U. S. News and World Report</u>,
      43 (July 5), 12.
           Judge McLaughlin refuses to set aside Miller's convic-
      tion for contempt of Congress.

18   ANON. "New Plea by Miller." <u>New York Times</u> (July 17), p. 3.
           Miller's attorneys ask Judge McLaughlin to reverse him-
      self and acquit Miller of the remaining count that he had
      unlawfully refused to name writers with whom he attended
      Communist meetings in 1947 in New York. The plea was based
      on the Federal Court of Appeals' setting aside of the simi-
      lar contempt of Congress conviction of Marcus Singer.

19   ANON. "Arthur Miller Fined; Plans an Appeal." <u>New York Times</u>
      (July 20), p. 4.
           Judge McLaughlin rejects Miller's motion to have his
      conviction set aside. Miller is fined $500 and given a
      suspended one-month jail sentence. In lieu of the jail
      sentence, Miller is placed on probation for three months.

20   ANON. "Miller Asks Reversal." <u>New York Times</u> (July 26),
      p. 8.
           Joseph L. Rauh, Miller's attorney, asks the U.S. Court
      of Appeals in Washington, D. C. to reverse Miller's con-
      tempt of Congress conviction. Rauh tells the court that
      Miller's case is in the same category as two similar cases
      recently reversed by the Supreme Court and the Appeals
      Court.

21   ANON. "Curtain." <u>Newsweek</u>, 50 (July 29), 26, 29.
           Brief account of Miller's sentencing to a $500 fine, a
      one-month suspended jail term, and three months probation
      after his conviction for contempt of Congress for refusing
      to tell the House Un-American Activities Committee the
      names of Communists he saw at a meeting in New York in 1947.

1957

ATKINSON, BROOKS. "Five by Miller." New York Times (June 9)
sec. II, p. 1.
Miller's Collected Plays reveal a fine mind, an austere
conscience and a creative pen. The record of achievement
here proves that the early masterpiece, Death of a Salesman,
was no accident. His refusal to "turn his private conscience over to administration by the State is the measure
of the man who has written these high-minded plays."

23 BREIT, HARVEY. "Politics II." New York Times (May 19), sec.
VII, p. 8.
Miller relates his experiences with HUAC, denies any
bitterness toward the Committee, and reasserts the freedom
necessary to the writer in any society.

24 COGLEY, JOHN. "The Witnesses' Dilemma." Commonweal, 65
(March 15), 612.
Discusses the dilemma posed by inquiries of the House
Un-American Activities Committee into the political views
of Miller, Lillian Hellman and Larry Parks. Few wish to
limit Congress's right to investigate subversion, but
"many Americans who want to protect that right are dis-
turbed by the problem Arthur Miller faces," that of naming
others to redeem himself or risking imprisonment.

25 DORN, NORMAN K. "Arthur Miller's Collected Plays." Kirkus,
25 (March 15), 256.
Brief notice of Collected Plays, summarizing Miller's
introduction. Expanded in 1957.26.

26 _____. "Arthur Miller's Collected Plays." San Francisco
Chronicle, This World Magazine (June 2), p. 24.
Expanded version of 1957.25.

27 FINDLATER, RICHARD. "No Time for Tragedy?" Twentieth
Century, 161 (January) 56-62.
Review of London production of A View from the Bridge.
The play is "most exciting, well-made and well-written,"
though Eddie Carbone is "too much of a clot to wear the
cothurnus" and the author is afflicted with an "idolatrous
faith in the forms of classic tragedy."

28 HUNTER, FREDERICK J. "The Value of Time in Modern Drama."
Journal of Aesthetics & Art Criticism, 16 (December),
199-200.
Analyzes the handling of time in Death of a Salesman.
The play's combination of the "intensity of compact time

as well as the extremity of the full, retrospective story"
provides a "probable and causal basis for the presentation
of the scenes and the actions as they appear in the play."

29 HUSTON, LUTHER A. "Miller's Past Tie With Reds Retold." New
York Times (May 16), p. 17.
At the second day of Miller's trial on contempt of Congress charges, prosecutor William Hitz asserts that as
early as 1922 Communists in the U.S. had obtained passports
by concealing their intentions to visit Iron Curtain
countries. Thus there is a connection between the questions Miller refused to answer and the misuse of passports.

30 ____. "Teacher Cleared in Contempt Case." New York Times
(July 10), p. 18.
The U.S. Court of Appeals in Washington, D. C. sets
aside the conviction of Marcus Singer on contempt of Congress charges resulting from his refusal before HUAC to
name other persons with whom he had been associated in
Communist activities. Joseph L. Rauh, Miller's attorney,
says he will make the court's decision the basis for a new
appeal to have Miller's conviction set aside.

31 ____. "Trial of Miller Attracts Crowds." New York Times
(May 15), p. 19.
Mistakenly expecting Miss Monroe to accompany him, crowds
of spectators, reporters, feature writers and sketch artists
appear at the opening of Miller's trial for contempt of
Congress in Washington Federal District Court. The issue
argued was the pertinency to legislative purpose of the two
questions Miller refused to answer out of 200 put to him by
the House Committee on Un-American Activities.

32 KALVEN, HARRY, JR. "A View from the Law." New Republic,
136 (May 27), 8-13.
Reviews history of First Amendment claims by persons
under investigation for suspected Communist activities in
connection with Miller's forthcoming trial for contempt of
Congress.

33 KRUTCH, JOSEPH WOOD. "Postwar," in his American Drama Since
1918. New York: Braziller, pp. 324-29, 332.
Revised version of 1953.31.

34 LEWIS, ANTHONY. "A Red-Party Form Linked to Miller." New
York Times (August 25), p. 20.
HUAC produces Miller's alleged application in 1943 for
Communist party membership. The card was unsigned, however,

and Miller claims it is "either a forgery or was done unknown to me." It is a "transparent attempt to influence
the course of my appeal."

35 LOFTUS, JOSEPH A. "Arthur Miller and Dr. Nathan Indicted on
Contempt Charges." New York Times (February 19), pp. 1,
14.
Miller is indicted by a Federal Grand Jury on charges
of contempt of Congress for refusing to name names before
the House Committee on Un-American Activities. Miller's
lawyers argue that the questions put to Miller were un-
related to the stated purpose of the hearing ("The Investigation of the Use of Unauthorized United States Passports")
and therefore not a valid basis for contempt action.

36 _____. "Miller Convicted in Contempt Case." New York Times
(June 1), pp. 1, 8.
Miller is convicted of contempt of Congress, Judge
McLaughlin ruling that the two questions Miller refused to
answer before HUAC were pertinent to the committee's
inquiry.

37 MCCARTHY, MARY T. "Naming Names: The Arthur Miller Case."
Encounter, 8 (May), 23-25.
Summarizes Miller's appearance before the House Un-
American Activities Committee at which he declined to name
persons he had seen at Communist-sponsored meetings.
Argues that since HUAC already had the names, its real
purpose was to force Miller to accept the "principle of
betrayal as a norm of good citizenship" and to "reduce the
private conscience to a niggling absurdity." Reprinted:
1961.38.

38 MCCOLLOM, WILLIAM G. "The World of Tragedy," in his Tragedy.
New York: MacMillan, pp. 16-17.
Salesman fails as tragedy because it is set against the
temporary social and political climate of American super-
ficiality, greed and commercialism.

39 QUIGLY, ISABEL. "Sabbath Witches." Spectator, 199
(September 6), 310.
Review of The Witches of Salem, a film adaptation of
The Crucible. The film is both grim and brilliant. The
direction of this "appalling politically pointed tale" is
intense without being oppressive and obscene without being
disgusting.

1957

40   ROVERE, RICHARD H. "Arthur Miller's Conscience." New
      Republic, 136 (June 17), 13-15.
         Traces Miller's thinking on the subject of informing
      and its relation to a sense of self in his plays. Argues
      that Miller's simplistic position is the product of polit-
      ical and moral confusion. The frivolous, mischievous
      attitude of HUAC does not give a witness the right to stand
      mute without being held in contempt. Abridged: 1960.23;
      1969.11. Reprinted: 1962.31; 1963.20; 1971.43.

41   STEINBECK, JOHN. "The Trial of Arthur Miller." Esquire, 47
      (June), 86.
         The Congressional investigation of Miller represents a
      "clear and present danger to our changing and evolving way
      of life." Should Steinbeck ever be in Miller's position,
      he hopes he "would be brave enough to fortify and defend
      my private morality as he has." Reprinted: 1963.22;
      1973.27.

42   WAIN, JOHN. "Arthur Miller." Observer (September 8), p. 5.
         Interview. Miller discusses the social mission of the
      writer, his criteria for good plays, his rejection of
      "social realism," and the theme of A View from the Bridge.

43   WEALES, GERALD. "Plays and Analysis: Arthur Miller's Col-
      lected Plays." Commonweal, 66 (July 12), 382-83.
         Miller's chief virtue as a playwright is his ability to
      uncover the emotions of human beings in their most per-
      sonal relationships, though he attempts to reach beyond
      domestic tragedy by placing personal conflict on a moral
      rather than a psychological level. Theme and character are
      sometimes in conflict, as in Willy Loman, and Miller's
      limited facility with language "often weakens what it
      should strengthen."

44   WEBSTER, MARGARET. "A Look at the London Season." Theatre
      Arts, 41 (May), 28-29.
         Review of London production of A View from the Bridge.
      Peter Brook has emphasized the play's melodramatic values,
      while losing the "sense of a people of ancient lineage,
      reborn on the Brooklyn waterfront, yet still the prey of
      those smoldering, buried passions which wrought the classic
      tragedies."

45   WHITEBAIT, WILLIAM. "Witch Doctors." New Statesman, 54
      (September 7), 276.

1958

Brief review of Jean-Paul Sartre's film The Witches of
Salem, based on The Crucible. If the film-makers wanted
Sartre on the Salem witches, why drag in Miller? Or why
drag in Sartre to add the party line to Miller? Two dis-
similar talents are wasted where one might have succeeded.

46 WIEGAND, WILLIAM. "Arthur Miller and the Man Who Knows."
    Western Review, 21 (Winter), 85-103.
       For ten years Miller has been writing "modern-dress ver-
    sions of classical martyrdoms." In each play a man who
    knows the "truth" that something is wrong with society but
    cannot communicate it is destroyed; yet arriving at this
    knowledge is his only chance of saving his soul. Reprinted:
    1967.48; 1971.43.

                          1958

1   ANON. "Ten Are Elected to Arts Institute." New York Times
    (February 11), p. 28.
       Miller is elected a member of the National Institute of
    Arts and Letters.

2   ANON. "Miller Files Appeal." New York Times (February 22),
    p. 6.
       Miller's attorneys ask the U.S. Court of Appeals in
    Washington to set aside his conviction for contempt of
    Congress on the grounds that HUAC used his romance with
    Marilyn Monroe to seek publicity for itself, rather than
    information for legislation.

3   ANON. "Arthur Miller's Appeal Slated." New York Times (May
    28), p. 21.
       The U.S. Court of Appeals in Washington will hear
    Miller's appeal of his contempt of Congress conviction in
    June.

4   ANON. "Miller in Court Appeal." New York Times (June 12),
    p. 26.
       Miller's attorneys argue before Federal Court of Appeals
    that it should throw out his contempt of Congress
    conviction.

5   ANON. "Arthur Miller Cleared of Contempt of Congress."
    Publisher's Weekly, 174 (August 18), 31-32.
       Miller's conviction for contempt of Congress is reversed
    (August 7) by U.S. Court of Appeals for the District of
    Columbia.

1958

6   ANON. "Our Colossal Dad." <u>Times Literary Supplement</u> (August
        29), p. 482.
            Review of <u>Collected Plays</u>. Traces father-son relation-
        ship in the plays, compares with Ibsen and O'Neill, and
        notes the use that British playwrights (Osborne, Bolt,
        Shaffer) are making of this theme. Reprinted: 1961.30.

7   ATKINSON, BROOKS. "<u>Crucible</u> Restaged." <u>New York Times</u>
        (June 1), sec. II, p. 1.
            Review of New York revival of <u>The Crucible</u>. To see the
        play again is to "admire again the scope and principle of
        Mr. Miller's accomplishment." The arena style of staging
        makes the play as exciting as it was originally.

8   ____. "Theatre: <u>The Crucible</u>." <u>New York Times</u> (March
        17), p. 21.
            Review of Hollywood production of <u>The Crucible</u>. More
        like a tract than a drama about people, the play needs all
        the warmth and color a cast can give it. Unfortunately,
        the actors are more interested in their private careers
        than in the play or audience. The production lacks flow,
        cohesion and spirit, though it is noisy enough.

9   BIERMAN, JUDAH, JAMES HART and STANLEY JOHNSON, eds. "Arthur
        Miller: <u>Death of a Salesman</u>," in <u>The Dramatic Experience</u>.
        New York: Prentice Hall, pp. 490-93.
            The terror of Miller's vision in <u>Salesman</u>, and the point
        where he joins Sophocles and Shakespeare, is that it forces
        us to ask: Have we created a society so inimical to man
        that in cutting him off from the sun and the earth, it
        threatens his very survival? "The tragic vision is not
        focussed on the station or status of man, but on the motives
        of his soul." Reprinted: 1967.48.

10 BRIEN, ALAN. "There was a Jolly Miller." <u>Spectator</u>, 201
        (August 8), 191-92.
            Review of <u>Collected Plays</u>. Though "painfully and often
        clumsily written," Miller's introduction is "one of the
        most important texts in the modern theatre." Discusses
        Miller's socialism and optimism.

11 CASSIDY, CLAUDIA. "Claudia Cassidy Reviews <u>Death of a
        Salesman</u>," in <u>The Passionate Playgoer</u>. Edited by George
        Oppenheimer. New York: Viking, pp. 600-601.
            Reprint of 1949.37.

12 CLURMAN, HAROLD. "Arthur Miller," in his <u>Lies Like Truth</u>.
        New York: Macmillan, pp. 64-72.

1958

> Refutes criticisms of All My Sons that Miller makes the
> "system" responsible for Keller's guilt, that the plot is
> too complicated, that war-profiteering is the meaning
> rather than the material of the play. Miller's is a
> "moral talent with a passionate persistence that resembles
> that of the New England Preacher who fashioned our first
> American rhetoric." Also reprints 1949.40, 41.

13   CROWTHER, BOSLEY. "Screen: French Crucible." New York Times
      (December 9), p. 54.
>   Jean-Paul Sartre's and Raymond Rouleau's French film
> version of The Crucible achieves a "deepening of emotional
> perception," and Miller's "cramped and parochial account"
> of what happened in Salem "comes forth as a sort of time-
> less drama of the unwholesome misplacement of zeal."

14   FUNKE, LEWIS. "Theatre: The Crucible." New York Times
      (March 12), p. 36.
>   Review of New York revival of The Crucible, which
> "remains a provocative, stimulating and inspiring creation."
> Though the faults found with the play originally still have
> validity, they are "minor compared with the scope and force
> of Miller's achievements."

15   GASSNER, JOHN. "Tragic Perspectives: A Sequence of Queries."
      Tulane Drama Review, 2 (May), 20-22.
>   Willy Loman qualifies as a classical tragic hero in
> all but one respect--he lacks an interesting mind. Death
> of a Salesman is low (or modern, democratic) tragedy, as
> distinguished from high (or earlier, aristocratic) tragedy.
> Reprinted: 1961.30.

16   GELB, PHILLIP. "Death of a Salesman: A Symposium." Tulane
      Drama Review, 2 (May) 63-69.
>   Gore Vidal, Richard Watts, Philip Gelb (moderator) and
> Miller discuss the tragic qualities present and absent in
> Willy Loman, his values or lack of them, the sentimentality
> of the play, and the "true-to-life portrayal of a certain
> type of American as old as Sam Slick and as current as the
> modern huckster." Reprinted: 1961.30.

17   _____. "Morality and Modern Drama: Arthur Miller as inter-
      viewed by Phillip Gelb." Educational Theatre Journal, 10
      (October), 190-202.
>   An interview ranging over a wide variety of literary and
> social topics: values and ideals in Willy Loman; realism
> in Shaw, Eliot and Williams; the nature of the artist's

71

1958

role and influence in society; Miller's attitudes toward
writing and production of his plays; the hostility of con-
servatives toward his liberal approach; the racial situation in the South and the obligations of the dissenting
conscience in the democratic process. Abridged: 1967.48.

18 KAUFFMANN, STANLEY. "Torture, New and Old." New Republic,
139 (December 22), 21.
Review of The Witches of Salem, a film adaptation of
The Crucible. Jean-Paul Sartre overemphasizes the love
triangle and converts Miller's play into a proletarian
allegory. A distorted film that strives but fails, Witches
of Salem confirms that there are such things as national
temperaments and they color art. No Frenchman can really
know Miller or Shakespeare; no American can really know
Molière.

19 KLAPP, ORIN E. "Tragedy and the American Climate of Opinion."
Centennial Review of Arts and Sciences, 2 (Fall), 408, 411.
To the superficial American view, Willy Loman is merely
a failure. At best there is an obscurely implied triumph
in his downfall. In Miller's view Willy's victimization
by society provides an opportunity for heroic determination,
the essence of tragedy. Willy's tragic stature lies in his
"willingness to throw all he has into the contest" to
maintain his "chosen image" of what and who he is in the
world. Reprinted: 1961.30.

20 KNOX, SANKA. "Prizes Are Given in Arts, Letters." New York
Times (May 22), p. 31.
Miller is inducted into the American Academy and
National Institute of Arts and Letters for "distinguished
achievement in literature and the arts."

21 LEWIS, ANTHONY. "Miller is Cleared of House Contempt." New
York Times (August 8), pp. 1, 7.
Citing a 1955 Supreme Court ruling that a contempt conviction could not stand unless the witness had been clearly
warned of the possible penalty for not answering a Congressional committee's questions, the U.S. Court of Appeals
for the District of Columbia reverses Miller's conviction
for contempt of Congress. Miller says the decision "made
the long struggle of the past few years fully worth it."

22 MCCARTEN, JOHN. "The Current Cinema." New Yorker, 34
(December 13), 209-10.
Review of Witches of Salem, Jean-Paul Sartre's film
based on The Crucible. Whereas Miller was content to show

72

the "awful evils of superstition running amuck in a theo-
cratic society" and the degeneration of law into demonology,
Sartre depicts the Salem peasants as politically agitated
in the manner of the sans-culottes of the French Revolu-
tion. If the film is accepted as fiction, though, it has
many strong moments.

23 MORTIMER, JOHN. "Arthur Miller's Collected Plays." Encounter,
      11 (October), 87.
          Brief review of Collected Plays. Just as Willy Loman
      represents no single dramatic theory or political view-
      point, "Miller belongs neither to America nor England. He
      is us because he contains us all."

24 NEWMAN, WILLIAM J. "The Plays of Arthur Miller." Twentieth
      Century, 164 (November), 491-96.
          Review of Collected Plays. Discusses father-family
      theme in Miller, the nature of the American family, and
      the freedom of choice of Miller's heroes. Reprinted:
      1961.30.

25 WORSLEY, T. C. "American Tragedy." New Statesman, 56
      (August 23), 220.
          Review of Collected Plays. Though Miller's preface makes
      clear that his intentions go beyond writing social drama,
      these do not appear in his plays. A successful way of
      writing the tragedy of the little man, for example, still
      eludes him; yet the fact that he continues to pursue this
      goal "gives his plays an intensity beyond their mere
      statement."

                              1959

1 ALLSOP, KENNETH. "A Conversation with Arthur Miller."
      Encounter, 13 (July), 58-60.
          Interview. Miller's views on American society and
      theater in the 1950's. The protest drama of the 1950's is
      decadent and limited in point of view. It fails to address
      the paradox of a collapsing respect for authority in our
      society at the same time that "authority takes on greater
      pretensions for itself." Also discusses his work in
      progress, The Misfits.

2 ANON. "Witches of Salem." Time, 73 (January 5), 84.
          Review of Jean-Paul Sartre's film version of The
      Crucible. Like Miller, Sartre misses the lesson of Salem.
      It may be, as both argue, that the Devil in Salem was not

1959

in the witches but those who burned them, but Sartre's case
is not helped when he "identifies the witch burners as
colonial capitalists and the hero as a son of the suffering
masses."

3   ANON. "Gold Medal Winners." New York Times (January 28),
      p. 21.
         The National Institute of Arts and Letters awards Miller
      its Gold Medal for Drama "for distinguished achievement
      characterizing the entire work of the recipient."

4   ANON. "Memo." New York Times (May 17), sec. II, p. 1.
         The Crucible's 500 performances to date have been
      exceeded only by the 565 of Eugene O'Neill's The Iceman
      Cometh.

5   ANON. "Arthur Miller to be Honored." New York Times
      (September 9), p. 50.
         Miller will be honored by the American Friends of
      Hebrew University of Philadelphia for "distinguished
      achievement in the dramatic arts."

6   ATKINSON, BROOKS. "Miller's Ibsen: An Enemy of the People."
      New York Times (February 5), p. 24.
         Review of New York revival of Miller's adaptation of
      Ibsen's An Enemy of the People. In one of the best off-
      Broadway productions of the year, an excellent cast gives
      a "rabble-rousing drama a rabble-rousing performance."

7   BRUSTEIN, ROBERT. "Why American Plays Are Not Literature."
      Harper's, 219 (October), 167-72.
         Discusses shortcomings of American plays, playwrights
      and theatre. Singles out Miller as the only American play-
      wright with the "ambition to write a mature drama which
      transcends the family crisis, the sexual conflict and the
      individual psychosis." Miller's defects might have been
      overcome if there had been more opportunity for debate,
      conversation and intercourse with his equals in other
      disciplines.

8   CALTA, LOUIS. "Phoenix Begins Subscriber Drive." New York
      Times (April 29), p. 28.
         To help launch a subscription drive for New York's
      Phoenix Theatre, Miller declares that the Phoenix is adding
      "a new element in this country, a theatre which we hope
      will ultimately be comparable to the Old Vic and the
      Comédie Française."

*9   DATTA, T. R. "Illusion and Reality in the Plays of Arthur
      Miller." Andhra University Magazine (Waltair, India), 20:
      30-34.

10   GASSNER, JOHN. "Home Grown Tragedy," in Theatre U. S. A.:
      1668 to 1957. Edited by Barnard Hewitt. New York:
      McGraw-Hill, pp. 444-48.
           Reprint of 1949.53 with some additional comments by
      Hewitt.

11   GEIER, WOODROW A. "Images of Man in Five American Dramatists:
      A Theological Critique." Ph.D. dissertation, Vanderbilt
      University. Dissertation Abstracts, 20 (October), 1463-64.
           Miller's plays signal the passing of Liberal Man and a
      rejection of the materialistic image of man. In its place
      is the prevailing image of Imperfect Man. The plays are a
      report of "modern man's yearnings and questions which are
      fulfilled in the Christian doctrine of Incarnation -
      Resurrection."

12   GROFF, EDWARD. "Point of View in Modern Drama." Modern Drama,
      2 (December), 268-82, passim.
           Compares Miller's use of flashbacks in Salesman with
      O'Neill's in The Emperor Jones. Both playwrights are seek-
      ing "not simply the memory of an earlier event but a new
      experience, a fusion of past and present." Both seek to
      go beyond objective reality to a subjective drama.

13   HARTUNG, PHILIP T. "The Screen: Many Things to Many People."
      Commonweal, 69 (January 2), 363-64.
           In Witches of Salem, based on The Crucible, Miller's
      theme concerning the dignity of man works out better as a
      movie than as a play, despite the fact that the great power
      of Sartre's script is lessened by overtelling the story.

14   HEWES, HENRY. "Conscience Makes Valiants of Us All."
      Saturday Review of Literature, 42 (February 21), 34.
           The off-Broadway production of An Enemy of the People,
      Miller's adaptation of Ibsen's play, is a "vigorous polemic
      exercise that makes its points by demonstrating rather than
      exploring the truth."

15   KAUFMANN, WALTER. "Dialogue with a Critic," in his From
      Shakespeare to Existentialism. Boston: Beacon, p. 27.
           A play about hollow values, Salesman shows that "what
      is tragic today is not what was tragic in former times."

1959

16   KRUTCH, JOSEPH WOOD. "Ten American Plays that Will Endure."
      New York Times Magazine (October 11), pp. 34, 39.
          Death of a Salesman will endure because it is less
      dependent than Miller's other plays on passing themes and
      attitudes.

17   MCDONALD, GERALD D. "Witches of Salem." Library Journal, 84
      (January 1), 70, 88.
          Brief review of Jean-Paul Sartre's film Witches of Salem,
      based on The Crucible. The film is "curious but compelling,"
      though Sartre is more interested in a Freudian and Marxian
      interpretation than the injustices of Salem and latter-day
      witch-hunting.

18   MALCOLM, DONALD. "The Theatre." New Yorker, 34 (February 14),
      68, 70.
          In Miller's adaptation of Ibsen's An Enemy of the People,
      he plays the reactionary for once, emphasizing scenes with
      the sharpest antiquarian flavor. He has brought the play
      up to date because he believes with Ibsen that men cannot
      live with the harshest truth, whereas today we live very
      comfortably with it. Miller's colloquial translation is
      scarcely more meaningful than the original Norse text to a
      reviewer unfamiliar with that language.

19   MILLSTEIN, GILBERT. "Ten Playwrights Tell How it All Starts."
      New York Times Magazine (December 6), pp. 63, 65.
          Miller reveals the sources of his inspiration for All
      My Sons, Death of a Salesman, and The Crucible.

20   SEAGER, ALLAN. "The Creative Agony of Arthur Miller."
      Esquire, 52 (October), 123-26.
          Describes Miller's methods and work habits in the pre-
      writing and writing of plays. Gives samples of notebook
      jottings. Miller "has made fewer concessions to box-
      office standards than any other living artist." He is
      ultimately preoccupied with "man's lack of any profound
      concern with his own true nature and his consequent failure
      to recognize the true nature of his inevitable bonds with
      others." Reprinted: 1967.48.

21   SHARPE, ROBERT BOIES. "Modern Trends in Tragedy," in his
      Irony in the Drama. Chapel Hill: University of North
      Carolina Press, pp. 194-203.
          Discusses Miller's use of irony in the plays. Miller
      has discovered, or rediscovered, the "value of building

tension just before a play's turning point" and invented a
"modified form of ironic self-expression" through a "memory
variant of the flashback" in the character of Willy Loman.

22   WALSH, MOIRA. "He Who Must Die and The Witches of Salem."
      America, 100 (January 17), 480-82.
          Brief review of Jean-Paul Sartre's film based on The
      Crucible. Sartre's version differs in omitting contem-
      porary parallels and stressing the value of the martyrs'
      sacrifice in restoring the community to its senses.

23   WATTS, RICHARD, JR. "Introduction," in The Crucible. New
      York: Bantam, pp. ix-xiv.
          Our "one important social dramatist," Miller in The
      Crucible makes an eloquent statement about man's universal
      need to struggle against mass pressures to conform to
      social or political dictates. It has transcended the night-
      mare era of its conception and grows in stature as a modern
      morality play as time passes.

24   WEALES, GERALD C. "American Drama Since the Second World
      War." Tamarack Review, 13 (Autumn), 91-93.
          Despite "infelicities of language and unnecessary
      tricks," Miller's plays grow with each rereading. His
      strength is in giving flesh to personal relationships so
      that they become societal, and thus the plays become more
      than mere self-revelations.

25   WEBER, EUGEN. "The Crucible." Film Quarterly, 12 (Summer),
      44-45.
          Review of Jean-Paul Sartre's French film version of The
      Crucible. In Sartre's script, social commitment replaces
      individual conscience, an "interpretation that serves
      neither historical likelihood nor the original purpose of
      the play." In addition, "symbolism grows solicitous with
      elephantine explicitness," so that the original material
      is "stretched beyond its endurance." The unrelieved grim-
      ness of the setting is in the spirit of the original, but
      a film should range more widely and do so without mislead-
      ing the audience.

26   WILLIAMS, RAYMOND. "The Realism of Arthur Miller." Critical
      Quarterly, 1 (Summer), 140-49.
          Miller has revived the drama of social questions. The
      key to his social realism lies in a particular conception
      of the relationship of the individual to society "in which
      neither is the individual seen as a unit nor the society
      as an aggregate, but both are seen as belonging to a

1959

continuous and inseparable process." In reaching for this new social consciousness, Miller is a "central figure in the drama and consciousness of our time." Reprinted: 1959.27; 1967.48; 1969.10.

27   ____. "The Realism of Arthur Miller." Universities and Left Review, 7 (Autumn), 34–37.
          Reprint of 1959.26.

28   YORKS, SAMUEL A. "Joe Keller and His Sons." Western Human-ities Review, 13 (Autumn), 401–407.
          Argues that the theme of All My Sons is that local and personal loyalties should not be sacrificed to abstract and universal loyalties.

1960

1   ADLER, HENRY. "To Hell with Society." Tulane Drama Review, 4 (May), 53–76.
          A wide-ranging criticism of the "sociological approach to drama" which limits its vitality and the "playwright's freedom as observer and witness." Caught in this trap, Miller's plays fail as tragedy because of their "rational-ism and democratic social consciousness," the qualities he seems to think make him superior to Ibsen. Reprinted: 1963.2.

2   ANON. "Soviet to Print Arthur Miller." New York Times (August 11), p. 6.
          A Moscow publisher will publish a collection of Miller's plays (All My Sons, Death of a Salesman, The Crucible, A View from the Bridge).

3   ANON. "Out of the Fish Bowl." Newsweek, 56 (November 21), 37.
          Brief account of divorce plans of Miller and Marilyn Monroe.

4   ANON. "Popsie and Poopsie." Time, 76 (November 21), 61.
          Announcement of divorce plans of Miller and Marilyn Monroe.

5   ATKINSON, BROOKS. "Art Takes Second Place." New York Times (November 11), p. 28.
          Comments and elaborates on Miller's interview with Henry Brandon ["The State of the Theatre." Harper's, 221 (November), 63–69]. See 1960.7.

6   BRANDON, HENRY ARTHUR. "A Conversation with Arthur Miller and
     Marilyn Monroe." Sunday Times (London) (March 20),
     pp. 14-15.
         Interview. Miller's opinions on American drama as an
     authentic expression of American life and American anti-
     intellectualism; Britain's Angry Young Men and the legacy
     of McCarthyism. Calls for plays that will "heighten our
     awareness of what living in our time involves," rather than
     a theatre of "sexual sensationalism, self-pity and senti-
     mentality." The 1950's is an "era of gauze" in the drama,
     attributable mainly to Tennessee Williams' "translation of
     current life into the man within the self." Reprinted:
     1960.7. Expanded: 1961.14. Abridged: 1962.7.

7   _____. "The State of the Theatre: A Conversation with Arthur
     Miller." Harper's, 221 (November), 63-69.
         Reprint of 1960.6.

8   BRUSTEIN, ROBERT. "The Memory of Heroism." Drama Review, 4
     (March), 5-7.
         In Miller's attempt to make "tragedy conform to American
     liberal dogma," the pessimistic basis of tragedy is lost.
     It is something to be illustrated in order to be corrected.
     Social and political reform are valid functions of Miller's
     drama but not of tragedy. Reprinted: 1969.9. Abridged:
     1976.19.

9   CALTA, LOUIS. "Marilyn Monroe to Divorce Miller." New York
     Times (November 12), pp. 1, 14.
         Divorce plans of Miller and Miss Monroe are announced.
     Miller's career since the marriage is reviewed.

10   CASSELL, RICHARD A. "Arthur Miller's 'Rage of Conscience.'"
     Ball State University Forum, 1 (Winter), 31-36.
         The focus of Miller's plays is his image of conscience
     in which the sense of wonder of his naive characters con-
     fronts the moral emptiness and confusion in American life.
     Miller's shift in his later plays from conscience in con-
     flict with the protagonist-father or state to the skepti-
     cism of the narrator figure is an "admission that he is
     addicted to putting himself and his conscience on stage"
     and does not trust "himself or his audience to let the play
     be the thing."

11   DE SCHWEINITZ, GEORGE. "Death of a Salesman: A Note on Epic
     and Tragedy." Western Humanities Review (Winter),
     pp. 91-96.

1960

Salesman has a traditional epic and tragic structure in that its "poles of value" are clearly distinguishable and objectified; and they effectively precipitate a tragic situation that gives a sense of a "universe in the throes of unresolved conflict and agony." Reprinted: 1967.48; 1972.47.

12 DILLINGHAM, WILLIAM B. "Arthur Miller and the Loss of Con-
    science." Emory University Quarterly, 16 (Spring), 40-50.
        Miller's plays are discussed from the standpoint of
    their central theme: the obligation to assume one's
    "rightful place in a world unified by love and a sense of
    responsibility." Failure to recognize one's place in
    society or surrendering it because of false values leads to
    tragedy. Although the settings and social order in Miller's
    tragedies are modern, he is concerned with the traditional
    problem of moral decision and represents an unusual modern
    synthesis of the artist concerned with both the polis and
    the integrity of the individual. Reprinted: 1967.48.

13 DRIVER, TOM F. "Strength and Weakness in Arthur Miller."
    Tulane Drama Review, 4 (May), 45-52.
        Miller's strengths are an awareness of the public nature
    of the theatre, an ability to report life realistically,
    and a desire to write plays of heightened consciousness.
    His weaknesses are a narrow view of man in society, and a
    basic contradictoriness in wanting a "universal moral
    sanction" while arguing that "man's potentialities and
    limitations lie entirely within himself." Reprinted:
    1969.10. Abridged: 1973.23.

14 DUSENBURY, WINIFRED L. "Personal Failure," in her The Theme
    of Loneliness in Modern American Drama. Gainesville:
    University of Florida Press, pp. 16-26.
        An other-directed individual, Willy Loman in Salesman
    is lonely because he fails to understand the moral prin-
    ciples that underlie society. His separateness results
    from his seeking only the kind of success that will gain
    him social approbation.

15 GASSNER, JOHN. "Affirmations?," in his Theatre at the Cross-
    roads. New York: Holt, Rinehart & Winston, pp. 63-64,
    274-78.
        Argues Death of a Salesman is "low tragedy" because
    Willy lacks an interesting mind to go with his capacity for
    suffering, his dignity, and his unwillingness to surrender
    to failure or the "heat of days." Miller was one of the

very few writers of the McCarthy period to speak out for
reason and justice, and The Crucible will live long after
the criticisms of its political implications have been for-
gotten. Its durability is attributable to the "excitement
of the action, the author's underlying passion and the
character drama and tragic pattern." Reprinted (Crucible
section): 1972.19.

16 HULSOPPLE, BILL G. "Theatre in Southeast Missouri." Players
    Magazine, 36 (February), 106-107.
        In an attempt to "win acceptance of theatre in complacent
    communities," Southeast Missouri State College successfully
    staged The Crucible, among other plays. The production was
    followed by invitations to return to both towns where it
    played.

17 HUNT, ARTHUR. "Realism and Intelligence: Some Notes on Arthur
    Miller." Encore (London), 7 (May-June), 12-17, 41.
        The Crucible is an important example of realist art
    because of Miller's intense, lucid and objective concen-
    tration on the past. Miller offers us the "spectacle of a
    powerful mind struggling to come to artistic terms with the
    complex reality of modern society." Reprinted: 1971.43.

18 KAZAN, ELIA. "Excerpts from Elia Kazan's Notebooks for Death
    of a Salesman," quoted in A Theatre in Your Head. By
    Kenneth Thorpe Rowe. New York: Funk & Wagnalls, pp. 44-59.
        Director's notes on various elements in Salesman, plus
    annotated pages for opening of Act II.

19 KITCHIN, LAURENCE. "The Potent Intruder," in his Mid-Century
    Drama. London: Faber and Faber, pp. 57-64.
        Miller and Tennessee Williams forced the lifting of
    political and sexual taboos in English theaters and the
    "new English drama shows many traces of Miller's influence."
    Williams fails to achieve Miller's "combination of social
    perceptiveness and organically rich dramatic construction."

20 LAWSON, JOHN HOWARD. "The Dilemma of Arthur Miller," in his
    Theory and Technique of Playwriting. New York: Hill and
    Wang, pp. xxvi-xxxii.
        Brief survey of themes of Miller's plays through A View
    from the Bridge. Miller's dilemma is that "pathos comes
    easily to him but he wants to achieve the greatness of
    tragedy." Though there is pathos in the plight of people
    driven by fate, there is no tragedy in people who have lost
    their will.

1960

21 NANNES, CASPAR H. Politics in the American Drama. Washington,
      D. C.: Catholic University of America, pp. 184-85.
        Plot summary of The Crucible showing parallels between
    McCarthyism and the Salem witch hunts of 1692.

22 NATHAN, GEORGE JEAN. "Arthur Miller," in his The Magic Mirror.
      New York: Alfred A. Knopf, 1960, pp. 243-50.
        Reprint of 1949.67.

23 NYREN, DOROTHY, ed. Modern American Literature. Library of
      Literary Criticism. New York: Ungar, pp. 337-41.
        Abridged reprints of 1947.38; 1947.44; 1949.41; 1949.51;
    1949.54; 1949.71; 1949.73; 1949.83; 1953.24; 1953.30;
    1955.26; 1957.40. All the preceding reprinted: 1969.11.

24 POPKIN, HENRY. "Arthur Miller: The Strange Encounter."
      Sewanee Review, 68 (Winter), 34-60.
        In Miller's plays up to A View from the Bridge there is
    a confrontation between banality and guilt. From this
    "strange encounter" Miller draws a "liberal parable of
    hidden evil and social responsibility." The plays have
    moved inward, making the large issues increasingly dim.
    The "studied ambiguity" of Miller's method in his response
    to the political climate. Reprinted: 1965.48. Abridged:
    1969.11.

25 RAPHAEL, D. D. "The Dramatist as Philosopher," in his The
      Paradox of Tragedy. Bloomington: Indiana University
      Press, pp. 103-105.
        In The Crucible the "genius of the dramatist swamps the
    motives of the propagandist." The play concretely exempli-
    fies moral philosophy and explores the "complex relations
    between moral good and moral evil." It is by far the best
    of Miller's plays.

26 ROWE, KENNETH THORPE. A Theater in Your Head. Funk &
      Wagnalls, pp. 67-69, 149, 239-40, 253.
        Discusses Jo Mielziner's staging of Salesman, and the
    tragic elements and theatrical effectiveness of The Crucible.

27 SAISSELIN, RÉMY G. "Is Tragic Drama Possible in the Twentieth
      Century?" Theatre Annual, 17: 20-21.
        Whereas the absurdist plays of Anouilh, Sartre, and
    Camus are "tragedy on the edge of society," Death of a
    Salesman's hero is pathetic. The values of Willy's society
    are those of the eighteenth century Enlightenment, which,
    the philosophy of the absurd points out, were always false.
    Willy never learns this and thus lacks universal interest
    and nobility. Reprinted: 1972.47.

28 STEINBERG, M. W. "Arthur Miller and the Ideas of Modern
    Tragedy." Dalhousie Review, 40 (Autumn), 329-40.
        Examining Miller's plays and essays on tragedy reveals
    the terms of his definition and the relation between mod-
    ern tragedy and that of earlier periods. Miller's tragedies
    fluctuate uneasily between Greek and Christian drama,
    though he seeks an explanation of the human situation in
    rationalistic or humanistic rather than transcendental
    terms. Miller's later plays focus more on the individual,
    subordinating the social issue to the inner crisis. His
    protagonists are now worthier opposites of the forces op-
    posing them. Reprinted: 1969.10. Abridged: 1972.19;
    1973.23.

29 WEATHERBY, W. J. Making "The Misfits." Manchester Guardian
    (November 3), p. 8.
        Interviews with Miller, John Huston (director), and
    Marilyn Monroe (star). Miller announces that his aim is to
    move people--on all levels. "I haven't done it yet but
    that's my aim." On the more optimistic ending of The
    Misfits, Miller admits it has taken a long time for him to
    create characters who rise above the tragedy of existence
    to die with dignity.

30 WHITCOMB, J. "Marilyn Monroe: The Sex Symbol versus the Good
    Wife." Cosmopolitan, 149 (December), 53-57.
        Interview with Miller and Marilyn Monroe during filming
    of The Misfits. Miller wrote The Misfits for his wife, to
    alleviate her depression at losing a baby. Miller discusses
    his contributions to the filming, and his marriage to a
    Hollywood celebrity.

1961

1   ALPERT, HOLLIS. "Arthur Miller: Screenwriter." Saturday
    Review, 44 (February 4), 27, 47.
        The Misfits "presents the American West and the cowboy
    figure in a totally new and comprehensible light." A study
    of the book and movie shows that the book was followed
    faithfully. The form of Miller's screenplay opens up a
    "new vista for writers interested in saying something
    directly for the screen."

2   ANGELL, ROGER. "The Current Cinema: Misfire." New Yorker,
    36 (February 4), 86, 88.
        Review of film The Misfits. Though the casting is
    impeccable, the screenplay is so "obtrusively symbolic and

1961

sentimental as to be unintelligent." To pose valid dramatic
questions about the survival of personal goodness in a
cynical society through a fallen child and three true-blue
buckaroos is to guarantee false, uninteresting answers.

3   ANON. "Miss Monroe Divorced." New York Times (January 25),
    p. 35.
        Miller signs waiver on right to court appearance and
    reaches property agreement with Marilyn Monroe.

4   ANON. "The Misfits." Time, 77 (February 3), 68.
        Though the "image of innocence hunted down and converted
    to dog meat makes a shattering comment on an aspect of
    modern life," The Misfits is rambling, banal, and "loaded
    with logy profundities." Yet the main themes of the film,
    "mercifully disburdened of Miller's words," do make for
    fluent and exciting dramatic action.

5   ANON. "Arthur Miller's Mother Dies." New York Times (March
    7), p. 35.
        Miller's mother dies. She is survived by Miller and
    two other children: Kermit, and Joan Miller Kupchik.

6   ANON. "Rome Sees Opera of Miller Play." New York Times (March
    13), p. 36.
        Summary of mixed reviews of Rome production of Uno
    Sguardo del Ponte, an opera based on A View from the Bridge.
    The opera is a condensed version of Girardo Guerriri's
    Italian translation of the play, composed by Renzo
    Rossellini and produced by Roberto Rossellini.

7   ANON. "Movies." McCalls, 88 (April), 6, 21.
        Brief review of The Misfits. The film says something
    important about American life (that "contemporary society
    has killed individual endeavor and freedom") through
    interesting characters and events. It contains good acting,
    direction, and writing.

8   ANON. "The Misfits." Booklist, 57 (April 15), 519.
        The importance of the book lies in the author's name and
    the interest in the motion picture.

9   ANON. "The Written Film." Times Literary Supplement (May 12),
    p. 296.
        Review of book of The Misfits. The ideas in this example
    of the new literary cinema emerge with greater clarity and
    force in print than on screen. Despite the protestations

that Roslyn is the life-force incarnate, she is treated
almost with contempt; because, though she cares for everything, she understands nothing.

10   ANON. "Church Upheld on Play." New York Times (November 10),
      p. 11.
         A Circuit Court in Milford, Connecticut, rules that
      Sunday performances of All My Sons do not violate State
      statutes. The Citizens' Anti-Communist Committee, citing
      Miller's appearance before HUAC, had filed a complaint
      against the play's "objectionable content," and its alleged
      violation of laws barring Sunday performances.

11   ARCHER, EUGENE. "Pirated U. S. Play Filmed in Soviet." New
      York Times (March 10), p. 24.
         Lenfilm Productions has made and exhibited in Russia a
      film version of Death of a Salesman, entitled The Bridge
      Cannot Be Crossed. Miller and Columbia Pictures, which
      made the U.S. film of Salesman, express concern about copy-
      right infringement.

12   BECKLEY, PAUL V. "Graphic Reality in Miller's Film." New
      York Herald Tribune Lively Arts and Book Review (February
      5), p. 10.
         Favorable review of film of The Misfits. A film of
      "rich vitality," it is a "paean to freedom but with an
      accurate account of its costs."

13   BOGGS, W. ARTHUR. "Oedipus and All My Sons." Personalist,
      42 (Autumn), 555-60.
         Despite superficial similarities between Oedipus and
      All My Sons, the latter is not a true tragedy of recognition
      like the former and thus is not a "superior, modern trag-
      edy." The social message of the play (one's responsibility
      to one's fellow men) emphasizes man in the mass rather than
      the outstanding individual who goes wrong, and this decreases
      the tragic effect.

14   BRANDON, HENRY. "Sex, Theater and the Intellectual: A Con-
      versation with Arthur Miller and Marilyn Monroe," in his
      As We Are. New York: Doubleday, pp. 102-31.
         Expands 1960.6 to include comments on Chekhov and Beckett.

15   CROWTHER, BOSLEY. "The Misfits." New York Times (February 2),
      p. 24.
         Despite "dynamic, inventive and colorful" direction by
      John Huston, and a lot of absorbing details, the characters
      and theme of The Misfits "do not congeal."

1961

16   DENT, ALAN. "Alien Values." <u>Illustrated London News</u>, 238
         (June 10), 992.
             Brief negative review of film of <u>Misfits</u>.

17   DOWNER, ALAN. <u>Recent American Drama</u>. Minnesota Pamphlets on
         American Writers, No. 7. Minneapolis: University of
         Minnesota Press, pp. 33-39.
             Brief critical survey of Miller's plays. Taken as a
         whole they have had "a high purpose, a sweep and excite-
         ment, a willingness to deal rigorously with the most impor-
         tant of unanswerable questions." If he has returned to the
         exemplary drama, the oldest of American theatrical tradi-
         tions, he nevertheless refuses to repeat himself, as so
         many of his contemporaries do.

*18   _____. "The Two Worlds of Arthur Miller and Tennessee
         Williams." <u>Princeton Alumni Weekly</u>, 72 (October 20), 8-11,
         17, 20.

19   DUDEK, LOUIS. "Arthur Miller and <u>The Misfits</u>." <u>Delta</u>, 15
         (August), 26-27.
             Review of film of <u>The Misfits</u>. Miller's old but still
         incomprehensible theme is that "men are alone, homeless
         and miserable because they are incapable of compassion."
         The realities of life have taught them brutality, but the
         opportunities for "heroic hardness," as Hemingway knew, no
         longer exist. Man will be a misfit in the universe, since
         his heroic cruelty is inimical to all forms of life, until
         he learns not to lie or kill.

20   DUPREY, RICHARD A. "<u>The Crucible</u>." <u>Catholic World</u>, 193
         (September), 394-95.
             Review of Philadelphia production directed by Nina Vance.
         Inspired direction brings Miller's long-winded polemics
         down to the level of the human heart. <u>The Crucible</u> remains
         an arresting, if dramatically clumsy play, in a day when
         its "universality can burn through the unfortunate circum-
         stances of its birth."

21   EDWARDS, JOHN. "Arthur Miller: An Appraisal." <u>Time and Tide</u>,
         42 (May 4), 740-41.
             Though his social preoccupation provides "much of the
         motive power" in his plays, Miller has always sought a
         "tragic formula to accommodate the experience of ordinary
         man." Because of the "weak realisation of the social frame-
         work" surrounding Eddie Carbone, however, <u>A View from the
         Bridge</u>, Miller's most explicit attempt to write a tragedy,

falls short. If Miller "over-fashions his formula and undernourishes his materials," his aims are nevertheless laudable; and his plays stand out from those of his contemporaries for their "craftsmanship, seriousness and daring."

22 FARNSWORTH, T. A. "Arthur Miller: Moralist and Crusader." Contrast (Capetown, South Africa), I (Winter), 84-87.
    Contrasts Miller and Terence Rattigan; briefly comments on All My Sons, The Crucible, and Death of a Salesman. For Miller the theater is an "instrument of passion," and "no other living playwright can match his power and intensity."

23 FOSTER, RICHARD J. "Confusion and Tragedy: The Failure of Miller's Salesman," in Two Modern American Tragedies. Edited by John D. Hurrell. New York: Scribner's, pp. 82-88.
    Death of a Salesman fails as classical or modern tragedy because of the "failure of its intellectual content and order." It is sentimental in that Miller does not rely on ideas but on "a frequently self-contradictory and often quite arbitrary mélange of social and moral clichés and the stock emotional responses attached to them."

24 FREEDLEY, GEORGE. "The Misfits." Library Journal, 86 (March 15), 1155.
    Brief mention of novel version of The Misfits--a picaresque novel with an inner meaning that Miller's social conscience senses and portrays.

25 GRAUMAN, LAWRENCE, JR. "The Misfits." Film Quarterly, 14 (Spring), 51-53.
    An attempt at treating most of the social and psychological conflicts of American literature for the past hundred years, the film sinks under its own weight; though the last third (director John Huston's rather than Miller's) partially succeeds in fulfilling the ambitiousness of the story.

26 HAMILTON, WILLIAM. "Of God and Woman." Christian Century, 78 (April 5), 424-25.
    The Misfits is an attempt to use the western movie for a serious purpose, that of examining competitive myths of freedom and conformity, the cowboy and the commuter, in the modern American imagination.

27 HARTUNG, PHILIP T. "The Screen: Woe, Woe, Whoa." Commonweal, 73 (February 17), 532-33.

1961

The Misfits is a "fascinating study of maladjusted people
who deserve understanding," a western version of The Sun
Also Rises, despite its "sentimental ideas on life and
death, occasional lapses in taste and a tacked-on, corny
ending."

28 HATCH, ROBERT. "Films." Nation, 192 (February 18), 154-55.
        Short negative review of film of The Misfits. Shallow
    characterization, and director John Huston's "bashful solem-
    nity" in the face of an original script by the author of
    Death of a Salesman, combine to give the picture a hollow
    sound.

29 HURRELL, JOHN D. Introduction, in Two Modern American
    Tragedies: Reviews and Criticism of "Death of a Salesman"
    and "Streetcar Named Desire." Scribner Research Anthology.
    Edited by John D. Hurrell. New York: Scribner, pp. 1-3.
        Brief discussion of the significance of Miller and
    Williams in American drama and the differences between them
    as revealed in the plays included here. Miller's plays
    "reach out from the individual to society as a whole, while
    Williams' move in from society to the individual." Miller's
    tragedy is closer to the Greeks and Ibsen, while Williams'
    is closer to Chekhov and Strindberg.

30 _____, ed. Two Modern American Tragedies: Reviews and
    Criticism of "Death of a Salesman" and "Streetcar Named
    Desire." Scribner Research Anthology. New York: Scribner,
    153 pp.
        Reprints: Atkinson (1949.26); Bentley (1949.30); Clark
    (1949.39); Clurman (1949.40); Nathan (1949.67); Krutch
    (1953.31); Tynan (1954.12); Sievers (1955.36); Anon.
    (1958.6); Gassner (1958.15); Gelb (1958.16); Klapp (1958.19);
    Newman (1958.24).

31 HUTCHENS, JOHN K. "The Misfits." New York Herald Tribune
    Lively Arts and Book Review (February 5), p. 27.
        The printed version of The Misfits, despite Miller's
    insistence that it is "neither novel, play, nor screenplay,"
    is in fact a novel that emphasizes manner and form rather
    than the story. Though the idea of the book is vibrant, it
    remains a placid story on the page.

32 JOHNSON, WILLIAM. "Movie Viewer." Modern Photography, 25
    (May), 24-25.
        Short favorable review of film of The Misfits. The cor-
    respondence between "inner and outer action creates a strong
    sense of space and movement."

33 KAUFFMANN, STANLEY. "Across the Great Divide." New Republic, 144 (February 20), 26, 28.
      The screenplay of The Misfits is "several universes above most American films in idea and in much of its execution," but the film fails because of implausible character development, bathetic dialogue, and Miller's infatuation with, rather than perceptiveness about, Roslyn. Basically, Miller is a theater-writer with an orthodox and socially utilitarian view of art for which dialectical dialogue is the life blood. Unfortunately, this results in a "talked-out" film.

34 LEONARD, JOHN. "Who's a Misfit?" National Review, 10 (May 20), 321-22.
      Reviews film of The Misfits. The film fails because the story is too static for film adaptation, and because Miller is thinking out loud about his wife, Marilyn Monroe, as part of his continuing private, personal search to figure her out.

35 LEONARD, WILLIAM. "Letter to Mrs. Miller Well Worth Reading." Chicago Sunday Tribune (February 12), sec. IV, p. 6.
      Brief review of movie script of The Misfits. It has the qualities that have made Miller one of America's most important writers--power, compassion, melancholy, sincerity.

36 MCCARTHY, MARY. "Americans, Realists, Playwrights." Encounter, 17 (July), 24-31.
      Discusses Miller's search for a dimension beyond realism, his "thirst for universality" that regards the specific as trivial. Compares Miller with other American realists: Williams, Inge, Chayevsky, Rice. Reprinted: 1961.37.

37 _____. "Americans, Realists, Playwrights." Harper's, 223 (July), 45-52.
      Reprint of 1961.36.

38 _____. "Naming Names: the Arthur Miller Case," in her On the Contrary. New York: Farrar, Straus and Cudahy, pp. 147-54.
      Reprint of 1957.37.

39 MCLAUGHLIN, RICHARD. "The Misfits by Arthur Miller." Springfield Republican (March 12), p. 5.
      Miller's "pretentious, symbol-laden screen script" has been made into a film, The Misfits, a "rather lugubrious attempt on the part of Miller to psychoanalyze his own misfitted marriage to Marilyn Monroe."

1961

40   MAYNE, RICHARD. "Shoot the Moralist." <u>New Statesman</u>, 61
         (April 28), 678.
             Brief review of film of <u>The Misfits</u>. It lacks the
         "knotted quality of truth that would make it more than a
         good film," though the milieu is excellently done and the
         technique of the book--in the form of a literary film
         script--is quite hypnotic. Perhaps "dissatisfaction with
         subtopia makes a feeble springboard for art."

41   MILLER, JORDAN Y. "Arthur Miller," in his <u>American Dramatic</u>
         <u>Literature: Ten Modern Plays in Historical Perspective</u>.
         Edited by Jordan Y. Miller. New York: McGraw-Hill,
         pp. 558-59.
             Biographical sketch.

42   MITGANG, HERBERT. "Books of the Times." <u>New York Times</u>
         (February 8), p. 29.
             Because of the economy of language characteristic of the
         drama and screenplays, <u>The Misfits</u> lacks the description of
         incident and character necessary in fiction. However,
         Miller's artistry is everywhere present and there are
         explorations of the heart as good as any he has written.

43   POPKIN, HENRY. "Arthur Miller Out West." <u>Commentary</u>, 31
         (May), 433-36.
             Review of screen version of <u>The Misfits</u>. The theme is
         communication but the characters are inarticulate, and
         effective language is absent. The story is haphazard,
         unified only by Roslyn's inspiring presence, and the action
         is without motivation. The sequence on the trapping of the
         mustangs has a simple eloquence precisely because it is
         unembarrassed by speech.

44   QUIGLY, ISABEL. "The Light that Never Was." <u>Spectator</u>, 206
         (June 9), 840.
             The film of <u>The Misfits</u> never rises above the "preten-
         tious triviality" of John Huston's direction. The main,
         if morbid, interest is personal and lies in the real-life
         facts; and "in spite of a sentimental story and much weird,
         battered symbolism about masculinity and mustangs, it all
         sounds only too true to life."

45   ROLO, CHARLES. "Reader's Choice." <u>Atlantic Monthly</u>, 207
         (March), 115-16.
             Discusses <u>The Misfits</u> as a "cinema-novel," a new fic-
         tional form which is far less effective than the conven-
         tional novel, even in its ability to make things visual.

46 TYNAN, KENNETH. "The American Theatre," in his Curtains.
    New York: Atheneum, pp. 123-24, 253-54, 257-62.
      Review of British Old Vic's production of The Crucible
    in 1954. The play is weakened by the strength of Miller's
    convictions. He presents Danforth as a "motiveless mon-
    ster," prejudges those he accuses of prejudice, and the
    last scene "plays like old melodrama." In comparing
    Miller with Tennessee Williams, Tynan finds them "comple-
    mentary yet irreconcilable" and equal in virtuosity. To-
    gether they have "produced the most powerful body of dramatic
    prose in modern English." Also reprints 1954.12.

47 WALSH, MOIRA. "The Misfits." America, 104 (February 18),
    676, 678.
      The film sinks under the weight of "accidental overtones
    of tragedy" (the death of Clark Gable just before its
    release) and "clinical psychology" (Miller's intimate per-
    sonal knowledge of the leading female character, played by
    Marilyn Monroe). Sporadically, however, it is a "desperate
    cry from human beings seeking to live without hurting or
    being hurt."

48 WEALES, GERALD. "The Tame and Wooly West." Reporter, 24
    (March 2), 46-47.
      The Misfits is a dull film because of poor acting and
    direction and Miller's abandonment of tragedy to go the
    way of Broadway and Hollywood. Whereas the trouble with
    the film is its theme, the book fails because its hybrid
    form restricts Miller's genius for dialogue.

49 WEATHERBY, W. J. "The Misfits: Epic or Requiem?" Saturday
    Review of Literature, 44 (February 4), 26-27.
      An eye-witness account of the filming of The Misfits.
    In "eloquently and honestly assessing Western life in the
    America of today, Miller does for the modern cowboy what
    Hemingway once did for the bullfighter."

50 WELLAND, DENNIS. Arthur Miller. New York: Grove;
    Edinburgh, Scotland: Oliver and Boyd, 124 pp.
      A critical survey of Miller's output through The Misfits.
    Miller's plays, like the writings of Nathaniel Hawthorne
    and Henry James, are "original and thoughtful enquiries
    into the complex fate of being an American." The strongest
    impulses in Miller's work are his "sense of wonder at the
    multiplicity of experience" and his concern with the pro-
    cesses of living. A "salutary restlessness of spirit and
    zest for experience" characterize all his plays, while his
    "powers of construction and command of language" increase
    with every play. Excerpted: 1972.19.

1961

51   ZOLOTOW, MAURICE. <u>Marilyn Monroe</u>. New York: Bantam,
     pp. 83-84, 260-70.
         Chronicles the Miller-Monroe romance, beginning in 1949.
     He was early attracted to Monroe's "incandescence and vital-
     ity," and <u>The Crucible</u> and <u>A View from the Bridge</u> are
     "triangle plays" in which Miller, still married to Mary
     Slattery, subconsciously attempts to rationalize guilt
     feelings caused by his attraction to Monroe. In the 1957
     revision of <u>View</u> for the London production, Miller iden-
     tifies with Eddie Carbone and writes a dramatic <u>apologia</u>
     <u>pro amore sua</u>.

1962

1   ANON. "Oedipus in Flatbush." <u>Time</u>, 79 (January 19), 55.
        Miller's screenplay of <u>A View from the Bridge</u> is written
    with clear intelligence and rude male force. Sidney Lumet's
    direction often achieves a "noble seriousness that makes
    the drama seem almost a rite," and the acting is excellent.
    But Miller misuses Greek tragedy. In Eddie Carbone, as
    distinct from the Greek hero, there is nothing specifically
    human. Thus, he is not tragic but pathetic: "Oedipus in
    a gorilla suit."

2   ANON. "What's Eating Eddie?" <u>Newsweek</u>, 59 (January 22),
    80-81.
        Review of film of <u>A View from the Bridge</u>. Miller and
    screenwriter Norman Rosten "invoke the subconscious as a
    cover for implausibility." Even Eddie Carbone is per-
    plexed at his own behavior, and the audience has few clues
    to the mystery.

3   ANON. "Arthur Miller Reweds." <u>New York Times</u> (February 22),
    p. 19.
        Miller's marriage to Inge Morath is announced.

4   ANON. "Arthur Millers Have Child." <u>New York Times</u> (September
    29), p. 15.
        A daughter, Rebecca Augusta, is born to Miller and Inge
    Morath.

5   BENTLEY, ERIC, ed. <u>The Play: A Critical Anthology</u>. Engle-
    wood Cliffs, N. J.: Prentice-Hall, pp. 729-47.
        Reprints <u>Salesman</u> and five articles and reviews of the
    play: 1949.25; 1949.33; 1949.35; 1949.39; 1949.66.

92

6   BETTINA, SISTER M. "Willy Loman's Brother Ben: Tragic Insight
    in Death of a Salesman." Modern Drama, 4 (February),
    409-12.
        Ben's function is to provide tragic insight into Willy
    Loman by personifying in Willy's consciousness the dream of
    material success. Ben's character, conveyed through expres-
    sionism, is a projection of Willy's personality, just as
    expressionism fuses with realism in the play as a whole.
    Reprinted: 1972.47.

7   BRANDON, HENRY. "A Conversation with Arthur Miller." World
    Theatre, 11 (Autumn), 229-40.
        Abridged version of 1960.6.

8   CALTA, LOUIS. "Miller Donates Papers." New York Times
    (February 13), p. 38.
        Miller donates his manuscript collection to the Univer-
    sity of Texas Humanities Research Center. The collection
    includes original drafts and revised and final versions of
    his plays from They Too Arise (1935), his first play,
    through Death of a Salesman and The Crucible.

9   CROWTHER, BOSLEY. "Questions of Choice." New York Times
    (January 28), sec. II, p. 1.
        Free of the "Hollywood mentality," A View from the Bridge
    is a film of consummate sincerity in the neo-realist style,
    but the focal character is a stubborn boor rather than a
    tragic figure.

10 _____. "A View from the Bridge." New York Times (January 23),
    p. 36.
        The film of A View from the Bridge has excellent acting
    and authentic atmosphere, but its boorish hero merits no
    sympathy. Unlike his salesman, Miller's longshoreman is
    better off dead.

11 EISENSTATT, MARTHA T. "Arthur Miller: A Bibliography."
    Modern Drama, 5 (May), 93-106.
        A reasonably complete checklist of secondary sources
    through A View from the Bridge.

12 ESTEROW, MILTON. "Miller Is Writing Play for Center." New
    York Times (October 26), p. 5.
        A new Miller play, to be directed by Elia Kazan, will be
    the first production of the Lincoln Center repertory com-
    pany. Miller refuses to give details other than to say it
    is a "contemporary play that will run 3 1/2 hours, is set
    in New York, and has 14 characters."

1962

13   FRUCHTER, NORM. "On the Frontier: The Development of Arthur
       Miller." Encore, 9 (January-February), 17-27.
           Reviews Dennis Welland's Arthur Miller (1961.50).
       Welland's view that the idea of the polis is the aim of
       Miller's drama is rejected, as is the view that Miller's
       work has increased in power with each play. In fact, after
       The Crucible Miller returned to the naturalist convention
       that marred his early work, and narrowed his dramatic con-
       cern from the "relationship between a man and his society to
       the possible relationship between two emotional cripples"
       (The Misfits). Miller's development and failure reflects an
       American society become too absurd to serve as meaningful
       context for drama or cinema.

14   GASCOIGNE, BAMBER. "Arthur Miller," in his Twentieth-Century
       Drama. London: Hutchinson, pp. 49-50, 72-73, 174-83.
           Contrasts Miller with Tennessee Williams. Though Miller's
       output has been small, it is of a high standard. Miller
       needs outside stimuli, such as the McCarthy episode, and
       these seem few and far between.

15   GILL, BRENDAN. "The Current Cinema." New Yorker, 37 (January
       27), 82-83.
           A View from the Bridge is a highly effective film.
       Sidney Lumet's direction is brilliant. Miller, taking a
       "consciously simple-minded view of his craft," builds plays
       of "good, sound ibsenwood." When they are dealt with
       kindly, "they give an impression of moral grandeur much
       greater than they actually possess."

16   HAGOPIAN, JOHN V. "Death of a Salesman." Insight (Frankfurt,
       Germany), I: 174-86.
           An analysis of Salesman, accompanied by discussion ques-
       tions and answers. Argues that Biff is the central charac-
       ter, but that critics believe Willy is because "his mind is
       the frame, the controlling intelligence, the stream of con-
       sciousness within which is enacted the drama of Biff." The
       outer drama (Willy's) of social criticism is "daringly
       experimental in form and technique." The inner drama
       (Biff's) is classical in form and technique and a "uniquely
       American manifestation of the eternal humanizing struggle
       of a man to discover his own identity." Reprinted (without
       discussion questions): 1963.12.

17   HARTUNG, PHILIP T. "The Screen: Mother Wins, Uncle Loses."
       Commonweal, 75 (February 9), 518.

Despite an admirable script by Norman Rosten, superb
direction by Sidney Lumet, and acting "worthy of an Oedipus
or Othello theme," the film of A View from the Bridge
"strains too hard to be great tragedy."

18   HATCH, ROBERT. "Films." Nation, 194 (February 10), 125.
Although psychologically convincing, the film of View
from the Bridge is "slice-of-life misery," morbid rather
than tragic. Miller is adept at conceiving human catastrophe but does not "locate his drama in individuals of suf-
ficient complexity or stature to make the narrative
absorbing."

19   HYNES, JOSEPH A. "Attention Must be Paid. . . ." College
English, 23 (April), 574-78.
Structural difficulties, looseness in conception of
character, and uncertainty of theme betray the author's
ultimate confusion in Death of a Salesman. Reprinted:
1967.48.

20   INSERILLO, CHARLES R. "Wish and Desire: Two Poles of the
Imagination in the Drama of Arthur Miller and T. S. Eliot."
Xavier University Studies, 1 (Summer-Fall), 247-58.
A romantic where Eliot's heroes are classicists, Willy
Loman "plays endlessly with unrooted possibliity and so
allows subjectivity to become solipsistic." Willy can find
no "magic" except suicide to make his wishes come true.

21   JOHNSON, VERNON E. "Dramatic Influences in the Development of
Arthur Miller's Concept of Social Tragedy." Ph.D. dissertation, George Peabody College for Teachers. Dissertation
Abstracts, 23 (October-December), 2135-36.
Traces influence of Ibsenian, Chekhovian and expressionistic dramatic traditions in Miller's plays. Social tragedy
in Miller is a product of characters with stature and complexity "engaged in significant and vital conflicts," and
of the balance between social and personal responsibility
achieved in the plays.

22   KAEL, PAULINE. "Review of A View from the Bridge." Film
Quarterly, 15 (Summer), 27-29.
Despite good performances from Raf Vollone and Raymond
Pellegrin, the film is poorly directed. Much of the fault
is Miller's: his attempt to make a tragic hero out of a
common man; his romanticizing of the working man in a
liberal's version of the noble savage concept; and his
clumsy and tedious use of tragic inevitability.

1962

23 KAUFFMAN, STANLEY. "The Unadaptable Adapted." New Republic, 146 (February 12), 26-27.
   Brief review of film version of A View from the Bridge. Much longer than the play, and lacking a plot designed for the diffuseness of its settings, the film becomes repetitious and boring. Sidney Lumet's direction is bankrupt of style or originality of mind.

24 KNIGHT, ARTHUR. "Runaway!" Saturday Review, 45 (January 27), 28.
   The film version of A View from the Bridge has an uncomfortable mixture of different acting styles which director Sidney Lumet fails to weld together. If the performances fail to gel, "perhaps it is because the characters were mere puppets to begin with."

25 LEWIS, ALLAN. "The American Scene: Williams and Miller," in his The Contemporary Theatre. New York: Crown, pp. 286-88, 293-301.
   Compares and contrasts Miller with Tennessee Williams and Henrik Ibsen. A twentieth-century morality play in which the salesman is everyman, Death of a Salesman attempted to indict the "false values of a commercial world, but it became the personal failure of one lost soul." It has the elements of modern tragedy, but after standing on the "threshold of achievement Miller substituted his favorite father-son conflict."

26 MCANANY, S. J., EMILE G. "The Tragic Commitment: Some Notes on Arthur Miller." Modern Drama, 5 (May), 11-20.
   Compares Miller's theories of tragedy in his "Tragedy and the Common Man" (1949) and his Preface to Collected Plays (1957). The principal change is the later emphasis on unshakable commitment to a set of values.

27 MACDONALD, DWIGHT. "Films." Esquire, 57 (February), 22, 24.
   Brief review of screen version of A View from the Bridge, a film of "modest but real virtues."

28 MANDER, JOHN. "Arthur Miller's Death of a Salesman," in his The Writer and Commitment. London: Secker and Warburg (1961); Philadelphia: Dufour, pp. 138-52.
   The documentary aim of Salesman is to "study the effect of the Salesman's profession on his essential humanity and to reach certain conclusions about the quality of life conceivable within that society." However, the mixture of Freudian and Marxist methods of analysis harms the play by offering mutually gratuitous explanations of Willy's problems with family and society.

29   PRUDHOE, JOHN. "Arthur Miller and the Tradition of Tragedy."
      English Studies, 43 (October), 430-39.
          Miller's theory of tragedy emphasizes freedom of will
      realized through an Idea or Ideal which the conscience of
      his inarticulate heroes compels them to act upon. This is
      clearest in The Crucible, where the stabilized language of
      a society with stabilized beliefs is used with "precision,
      authority and beauty of style." In the modern realistic
      plays, Miller continually experiments with dramatic form
      to find contextual aids for the modern vernacular, a poor
      vehicle for the discussion of the confused values of modern
      society.

30   ROSTEN, NORMAN. "Scenarist Eyes His View from the Bridge."
      New York Times (January 21), sec. II, p. 9.
          Rosten has made virtually no significant changes, except
      to drop the narrator, in filming A View from the Bridge.
      Sequences have been cut and rearranged, but not to the
      extent of violating nuances of character.

31   ROVERE, RICHARD H. "The Conscience of Arthur Miller," in his
      The American Establishment, and Other Reports, Opinions and
      Speculations. New York: Harcourt, Brace & World,
      pp. 276-84.
          Reprint of 1957.40.

32   SHANLEY, JOHN P. "Miller's Focus on TV Today." New York Times
      (January 21), sec. II, p. 19.
          In cooperation with the American Jewish Committee's
      Institute of Human Relations, NBC will present a dramatiza-
      tion of Focus. Miller is interviewed about his views on
      television as an artistic medium and its shortcomings.

33   SOMERS, FLORENCE. "New Movies." Redbook, 118 (February), 29.
          Brief review of film version of A View from the Bridge.
      Compares it to On the Waterfront and Marty because of its
      "honesty and authenticity."

34   STEENE, BIRGITTA. "The Critical Reception of American Drama
      in Sweden." Modern Drama, 5 (May), 71-82.
          Briefly discusses Swedish reaction to Salesman and an
      Alf Sjöberg production of it. In response to the Swedish
      attitude that the play was an American tragedy, Sjöberg
      brought out its universality by making it a tragedy of
      fatherhood. The critics felt this psychological approach
      undermined the American reality of the play.

1962

35 WARSHOW, ROBERT. "The Liberal Conscience in The Crucible," in
    his The Immediate Experience. New York: Doubleday,
    pp. 189-203.
        Reprint of 1953.40.

36 WEALES, GERALD C. "Arthur Miller: Man and His Image," in his
    American Drama Since World War II. New York: Harcourt,
    Brace & World, pp. 3-17.
        Reprint of 1962.37.

37 _____. "Arthur Miller: Man and His Image." Tulane Drama
    Review, 7 (Fall), 165-80.
        Analyzes the recurrent theme of individual identity in
    conflict with the image demanded by society. While Miller's
    development of this theme is sometimes spoiled by sentimen-
    tality that accepts personal solutions to public problems
    (as in The Misfits), "sentiment and romance, if they can
    command an audience without drowning it, are not necessarily
    vices." Reprinted: 1962.36; 1967.48; 1971.43. Revised to
    include later plays in 1967.46; 1969.36. Abridged: 1973.23.

38 _____. "Theatre Without Walls," in A Time of Harvest. Edited
    by Robert E. Spiller. New York: Hill and Wang, pp. 142-43.
        Brief survey of Miller's work. His central strength is
    that his protagonists are placed "in conflict with a
    societal image by which they may be judged" and "forced to
    see themselves clearly." He is not a psychological play-
    wright in the sense that many of his contemporaries are.

39 WELLS, ARVIN R. "The Living and the Dead in All My Sons."
    Insight (Frankfurt, Germany), I: 165-74.
        The play leaves a dual impression: the individual is
    responsible to humanity, but this ideal is inadequate for
    the evaluation of human beings. Moreover, rigid idealism
    in the real world entails "suffering and waste, especially
    when the idealist is hagridden by his own ideals."
    Reprinted: 1964.82.

1963

1 ADAMCZEWSKI, ZYGMUNT. "The Tragic Loss--Loman the Salesman,"
    in his The Tragic Protest. The Hague: Martinus Nizhoff,
    pp. 172-92.
        Argues that Willy's loss of self is the source of his
    tragedy. The fact that many audiences do not find loss of
    self tragic indicates a loss of the tragic vision, which
    in itself is tragic.

2   ADLER, HENRY. "To Hell with Society," in <u>Theatre in the</u>
     <u>Twentieth Century</u>. Edited by Robert W. Corrigan. New York:
     Grove, pp. 245-72.
          Reprints 1960.1.

3   ARNOLD, MARTIN. "Artists to Appeal for Space at Fair." <u>New</u>
     <u>York Times</u> (November 18), p. 35.
          As a member of the Committee of Artists' Societies,
     Miller appeals for a special art pavillion at New York's
     World's Fair. The lack of a contemporary art pavillion,
     Miller says, "shows the world that this is a nation. . .
     without culture."

4   AUGHTRY, CHARLES E. "Arthur Miller," in <u>Modern Drama</u>. Edited
     by Charles E. Aughtry. Boston: Houghton, Mifflin,
     pp. 596-97.
          Brief introduction to <u>Death of a Salesman</u>. Short quota-
     tions from conflicting reviews of the play.

5   BARKSDALE, RICHARD K. "Social Background in the Plays of
     Miller and Williams." <u>CLA Journal</u>, 6 (March), 161-69.
          In <u>Death of a Salesman</u> and <u>A View from the Bridge</u>, the
     main characters are victims of economic determinism and
     those "political imperatives that make the society what it
     is." Their fate is determined by the social context in
     which they live and its value system. Miller's "admitted
     preoccupation with the Depression" largely determines his
     social views in these two plays.

6   BROUSSARD, LOUIS. "Everyman at Mid-Century," in his <u>American</u>
     <u>Drama</u>. Norman: Univ. of Oklahoma Press, pp. 116-21.
          Compares Elmer Rice, Thornton Wilder, T. S. Eliot,
     Robert Sherwood, Eugene O'Neill and Tennessee Williams with
     Miller. Miller differs from Eliot and Wilder most obviously
     in his neglect of God.

7   DOUGLASS, JAMES W. "Miller's <u>The Crucible</u>: Which Witch is
     Which?" <u>Renascence</u>, 15 (Spring), 145-51.
          <u>The Crucible</u> "lapses into the evil it seeks to attack"
     in reversing the usual sin of orthodoxy by its attribution
     of "diabolical malevolence to the government rather than
     the government's opposition." Excerpted 1972.19.

8   FLAXMAN, SEYMOUR L. "The Debt of Williams and Miller to Ibsen
     and Strindberg." <u>Comparative Literature Studies</u>, I (Special
     Advance Number), 51-60.

1963

In transferring it to an American milieu, Miller contin-
ues the dramatic tradition of Ibsen and Strindberg but adds
nothing to it. Documents Miller's debt to the Scandinavian
playwrights by referring to his plays and essays.

9   GANZ, ARTHUR. "The Silence of Arthur Miller." Drama Survey,
     3 (Fall), 224-37.
         Miller's eight-year silence after View from the Bridge
     was broken by The Misfits, a film whose simple but unhappy
     characters suggest Miller's recognition that the simplistic
     criticisms of modern man and society in his earlier plays
     are inadequate. Miller had failed to account for "man's
     complexities and inconsistencies and presented him as too
     easily achieving virtue," while he saw society as too easily
     tending towards corruption. Abridged: 1969.11. Excerpted
     1972.19.

10   GASSNER, JOHN. "Arthur Miller," in A Treasury of the Theatre.
     Edited by John Gassner. New York: Simon and Schuster,
     pp. 1060-62.
         Introduction to Death of a Salesman. Traces Miller's
     life and playwriting career, discusses Salesman as tragedy
     (Willy's love for Biff endows him with tragic magnitude),
     as a further statement in the cultural rebellion of the
     1920's and the social discontent of the 1930's, as realistic-
     cum-expressionistic drama, and as poetic drama.

11   GOODE, JAMES. The Story of the Misfits. Indianapolis: Bobbs-
     Merrill, 331 pp.
         A richly detailed account of the filming of The Misfits
     told in diary form and illustrated. Discusses Miller's
     part in the project, his relationship with Marilyn Monroe
     and other participants. Makes the background of the film
     perhaps more interesting than the film itself.

12   HAGOPIAN, JOHN V. "Arthur Miller: The Salesman's Two Cases."
     Modern Drama, 6 (September), 117-25.
         Abridged version of 1962.16. Reprinted: 1972.47.

13   HERBERT, EDWARD T., ed. "Eugene O'Neill: An Evaluation by
     Fellow Playwrights." Modern Drama, 6 (December), 239-40.
         Though on contemporary writers O'Neill's influence is
     not apparent, Miller regards him as a "kind of conscience
     to many writers." O'Neill "reached, strove with himself,
     insisted, struck upon issues that were worth failing at,
     knew how to tell the audience to go to hell." These qual-
     ities have always attracted Miller to him.

14 HEWES, HENRY. "Opening Up the Open Stage." Saturday Review,
    46 (August 24), 34.
        Review of the Tyrone Guthrie Theatre (Minneapolis) pro-
    duction of Salesman. Because of Hume Cronyn's dimunitive
    size and Jessica Tandy's too conscious refinement (as
    Willy and Linda Loman), "the play strikes everyone here as
    very funny." If it is true that in the original play Willy
    was described as a "little squirt," and that this was later
    changed to suit Lee J. Cobb's larger stature, it may be
    that Salesman's status as a tragedy owes much to Miller's
    decision to revise the original script.

15 HYNES, JOSEPH A. "Arthur Miller and the Impasse of Naturalism."
    South Atlantic Quarterly, 62 (Summer), 327-34.
        Though a first-rate man of the theater (no one is better
    able to construct a dilemma or project emotion), Miller is
    not yet a sufficiently mature dramatist because of his
    limited, naturalistic conception of tragedy. He fails to
    see a difference in kind between a character of sound mind
    with some freedom of choice and his own characters of weak
    mind and no freedom at all. Naturalism dictates that that
    "figure will be most memorable who appears to have had the
    smallest chance to enlist in the human race." Abridged:
    1969.11.

16 JACKSON, ESTHER MERLE. "Death of a Salesman: Tragic Myth in
    the Modern Theatre." CLA Journal, 7 (September), 63-76.
        In Salesman, Miller answers American drama's need for
    myths, or symbolic interpretations of human experience.
    His play is the "most nearly mature myth about human suf-
    fering in an industrial age." Compares Salesman with
    Classic and Romantic concepts of tragedy. Argues that
    Miller finds the roots of modern suffering in moral ignor-
    ance. Suffering is achieved through a sacrifical "Odyssey"
    culminating in death. Reprinted: 1972.47.

17 LEASKA, MITCHELL A. "Miller," in his The Voice of Tragedy.
    New York: Speller, pp. 273-78, 285.
        Like Oedipus, Willy Loman exemplifies the "tragic cir-
    cumstances precipitated by the misuse of reason in an
    individual in conflict with society" and must punish him-
    self to expiate his violation of the laws of that society.

18 MILLER, E. S. "Perceiving and Imagining at Plays." Annali
    Instituto Universiturio Orientale (Naples), 5: 5-11.
        Discusses "short time" (elapsed time of the action) and
    "long time" (flashbacks) in Death of a Salesman. Viewers

have an "outside" and "inside awareness" of Willy's life that is deliberately ambiguous and that results from such devices as the set design, staging, and Willy's talking to himself.

19   OTTEN, CHARLOTTE F. "Who Am I? A Re-investigation of Arthur Miller's Death of a Salesman." Cresset, 26 (February), 11-13.
Compares Biff Loman and Tiresias, Willy and Oedipus. Despite the manifold differences, both Oedipus Rex and Death of a Salesman are universal plays because the "question of all ages echoes in both: Who am I?" The basic problem of self-knowledge is one all of us must still face.

20   ROVERE, RICHARD H. "Arthur Miller's Conscience," in Contemporary Moral Issues. Edited by Harry K. Girvetz. Belmont, Calif.: Wadsworth, pp. 75-79.
Reprint of 1957.40.

21   SARGEANT, WINTHROP. "The Crucible." American Record Guide, 29 (March), 508-509, 599.
Discusses Robert Ward's recorded operatic version of The Crucible as belonging to the grand tradition of operatic theater, while being a true American music-drama whose "roots are imbedded in our national conscience and its history."

22   STEINBECK, JOHN. "The Trial of Arthur Miller," in Contemporary Moral Issues. Edited by Harry K. Girvetz. Belmont, Calif.: Wadsworth, pp. 72-74.
Reprint of 1957.41.

23   TAUBMAN, HOWARD. "Death of a Salesman Done in Minnesota." New York Times (July 20), p. 11.
Favorable review of Tyrone Guthrie Theatre production of Salesman, "still a compelling and significant drama" in which the Lomans serve as a "metaphor for the debased values by which so many Americans live."

24   WEST, PAUL. "Arthur Miller and the Human Mice." Hibbert Journal, 61 (January), 84-86.
Except in The Crucible, Miller deals with the "psychology of unheroic economic man hovering between isolation and community, between selfishness and dedication." His are Christian plays concerned with "sympathetic sanity." Salesman and Crucible bring to mind Mark Twain in that they

defend the "hampered decency of Huck Finn in terms of
Camus' l'homme révolté." Miller's "drama of human worry
is intended to restore us to a sense of human and humane
responsibility."

1964

1   ALLEN, HAROLD VAN. "An Examination of the Reception and Critical Evaluation of the Plays of Arthur Miller in West
Germany from 1950-1961." Ph.D. dissertation, University of
Arkansas. Dissertation Abstracts, 25 (September), 1901.
    To judge from newspapers, West German critics and audi-
ences, like their American counterparts, find A View from
the Bridge and A Memory of Two Mondays to be lesser plays
than All My Sons, Death of a Salesman and The Crucible.
Miller's themes are found to be universal as well as contemporary, though some critics are dismayed by his anti-
capitalistic criticism. Miller is seen as a socio-critical
dramatist in the tradition of Ibsen, Hauptmann and Sudermann.

2   ANON. "Saturday Evening Post to Print Miller's Plays." New
York Times (January 11), p. 15.
    After the Fall is to appear in the Saturday Evening Post.
The price for magazine rights is said to be in the "five
figure range."

3   ANON. "Facsimile of Marilyn Monroe in Miller's Play." Times
(London) (January 24), p. 8.
    Review of New York opening of After the Fall. The play
fails because of the autobiographical elements and its
explicit and insistent defense of its unsavory hero. Its
"occasional vividness and theatrical effectiveness are
expended in an unworthy cause."

4   ANON. "The Miller's Tale." Time, 83 (January 31), 54.
    Review of New York opening of After the Fall. Under-
lying the play is Miller's tormented, intellectualized
quest for self-justification, with the audience enjoined
to share his guilt and pronounce his absolution. The code
of the play, that when life seems unbearable one should
find a new woman and start anew, not only ignores duty but
"lacks all tragic sense."

5   ANON. "Marilyn's Ghost Takes the Stage." Life, 56 (February
7), 64 A.
    Brief notice of After the Fall's premiere.

1964

6   ANON. "After the Fall." Virginia Quarterly Review, 40
      (Summer), cxii.
           Review of published version of After the Fall. Despite
      its awkwardness, pretentiousness, tediousness, repetitious-
      ness and lack of humor, the play has a "crude power" and
      is acute in its psychological study of relations among
      husbands, wives and friends. And Miller's explanation of
      the paradoxes of his theme, that each of us kills the thing
      he loves and that love itself kills, is often very moving.

7   ANON. "Miller Reads New Play to Repertory Troupe." New York
      Times (August 27), p. 28.
           Accompanied by his director, Harold Clurman, Miller
      reads Incident at Vichy to members of the Lincoln Center
      Repertory Company.

8   ANON. "Guilt Unlimited." Time, 84 (December 11), 73.
           Review of New York opening of Incident at Vichy. Miller's
      moral lecture on guilt and responsibility in the case of
      the mass murder of European Jewry is faulty in stagecraft
      and even more so in logic. In proposing that the living
      atone for the dead, Miller forgets that one cannot be
      accountable for acts he was powerless to avert or affect.

9   ANON. "We are All Scum." Newsweek, 64 (December 14), 86.
           Though Harold Clurman's staging of Incident at Vichy
      manages to keep its "rhetorical gassiness from carrying it
      right out the exits," the play still resembles a "second
      rate but superficially engrossing movie about the Nazis"
      made in 1942. Nothing is dramatized, almost all is posture,
      none of the issues is grappled with, most words hang in
      mid-air like "hoarsely delivered sermons." It is unfair of
      Miller to "try to implicate us in his personal problem of
      inarticulateness and philosophical confusion."

10   AYLEN, LEO. "Miller," in Greek Tragedy and the Modern World.
      London: Methuen, pp. 248-57.
           Discusses Death of a Salesman, The Crucible, and A View
      from the Bridge in relation to Greek tragedy. Since Miller
      asks us to see his plays from the viewpoint of a hero, the
      social viewpoint of Greek tragedy is lacking. There is a
      "contradiction between the strong social purpose he believes
      in and the emotional tension of the particular situation
      he is describing." Miller has "achieved success in spite
      of, rather than because of, his medium."

11   BAXANDALL, LEE. "Arthur Miller: Still the Innocent." Encore,
      11 (May-June), 16-19.

After the Fall is flawed basically by aesthetic and
moral defects in its structure. The failure of the myths
of socialism and limitless love lead Quentin and us "into
the sterile desert of an ultra-personalist scepticism,
relativism and individualism." Miller retreats from the
question of what to do about the man who "stools" on his
friends because the play's director, Elia Kazan, is the man
in question. Reprinted: 1971.43.

12   BLAU, HERBERT. "Counterforce I: The Social Drama," in his
     The Impossible Theatre. New York: Macmillan, pp. 186-92.
        The Crucible is not the "tough" play Miller claimed.
     Compared with Dostoevsky, Melville or Shakespeare, Miller
     fails to "drive below partisanship to a judgment of anti-
     social action from which none of us could feel exempt."
     The Crucible neither jeopardizes nor extends our principles;
     "no play is deeper than its witches." Reprinted: 1969.10.
     Abridged: 1971.43; 1972.19.

13   BLOOM, LYNNE G. and CAROL Z. ROTHKOPF. "The Crucible": A
     Commentary. Study Master Series. New York: American
     R.D.M. Corporation, 50 pp.
        A study guide that analyzes plot structure and character-
     ization and gives biographical information, study questions
     and a bibliography.

14   BRAHMS, CARYL. "Marilyn, Dolly and Dylan." Spectator, 212
     (February 14), 213.
        Review of New York production of After the Fall. "Almost
     perfectly directed" by Elia Kazan, the play is arresting
     mainly because Miller's apologia for the breakup of his
     marriage to Marilyn Monroe becomes an apologia for her.
     The dramatization of Monroe's guilt or innocence in the
     matter is in "hideously bad and bitter taste," though
     Miller writes sparsely and often superbly for her.

15   BRUSTEIN, ROBERT. "Arthur Miller's Mea Culpa." New Republic,
     150 (February 8), 26-28, 30.
        After the Fall is a "three-hour breach of taste," a
     "confessional autobiography of embarrassing explicitness,"
     a "spiritual striptease while the band plays mea culpa."
     Worse, the play is dull and shapeless since Miller is too
     close to his material to dramatize it effectively. Perhaps
     director Elia Kazan was purposely undermining the play.
     Miller's self-consciousness is a form of dishonesty that
     conceals a misogynistic strain and self-justification in
     the apparent remorse. Reprinted: 1965.13.

1964

16   _____. "Muddy Track at Lincoln Center." New Republic, 151
      (December 26), 26-27.
          Review of Lincoln Center production of Incident at Vichy.
      Though Harold Clurman's production almost transcends the
      limitations of the writing, the play suffers from outdated
      and half-understood ideas, "noisy virtue and moral flatu-
      lence." Reprinted: 1965.14.

17   CALTA, LOUIS. "After the Fall Is Sought Abroad." New York
      Times (February 8), p. 15.
          Seventeen foreign countries have acquired performance
      rights to After the Fall, and eleven more are negotiating
      for them. Miller and his family are in Paris for a three-
      month stay.

18   CHAPMAN, JOHN. "After the Fall Overpowering." New York Daily
      News (January 24).
          After the Fall is "do-it-yourself psychoanalysis" on the
      part of a man seeking the truth about himself, God, and the
      "relations between two persons when each is a separate
      being." The acting is brilliant and the "clarity of the
      drama is due not only to Miller but to Elia Kazan's staging
      and direction." Reprinted: 1964.50.

19   _____. "Arthur Miller Is No Chekhov in Revival of The
      Crucible." New York Daily News (April 7).
          In revival and with the political steam gone, The
      Crucible seems a "juvenile and stereotyped exercise in
      dramatics, an awkwardly written dramatic thesis on the too-
      obvious evils of Puritan witch-hunting." Reprinted:
      1964.51.

20   CLURMAN, HAROLD. "Arthur Miller: Theme and Variations."
      Theatre: The Annual of the Repertory Theater of Lincoln
      Center, 1: 13-22.
          Though After the Fall is the first of Miller's plays
      to emphasize his personal life and to concern itself largely
      with marital relationships, it is an extension of earlier
      themes and a reaffirmation through reversal. The "auto-
      criticism" not only exposes Miller but liberates him to
      continue writing free of "false legend and heavy halo."
      Reprinted: 1969.10. Abridged: 1973.23.

21   COHEN, NATHAN. "Hollow Heart of a Hollow Drama." National
      Review, 16 (April 7), 289-90.
          Though Elia Kazan's direction is an eloquent effort to
      save the play, After the Fall is a "badly designed and
      hollow dramatic structure." The gap between conception and
      execution, arrogance of aim and pettiness of achievement,

is largely attributable to the confusion or hypocrisy in
the character of Quentin, who says he is a failure while
spending three hours in self-vindication. The play confirms the decline in Miller's capabilities evident nine
years earlier in A View from the Bridge.

22 CRIST, JUDITH. "The Crucible More Fiery than Ever." New York
     Herald Tribune (April 7), p. 14.
          Using the revised script of 1958, director Jack Sydow
     gives audiences the finest production of The Crucible in
     New York to date. It is a play that "touches the heart as
     it fascinates the mind," one that "seethes with passion,
     sparkles with dramatic tensions and glows with simple
     humanity, even as it preaches a powerful sermon for our
     times." Reprinted: 1964.51.

23 DRIVER, TOM F. "Arthur Miller's Pilgrimage." Reporter, 30
     (February 27), 46, 48.
          After the Fall "lacks aesthetic distance" and "that
     freshness of tone which is the mark of authentic personal
     discovery." Despite fine acting and direction, "the play
     seems soft, if not vacant, as its core."

24 FREEDLEY, GEORGE. "After the Fall." Library Journal, 89
     (April 1), 1620-21.
          Brief mention of Viking edition of After the Fall,
     "unquestionably Miller's greatest play."

25 FUNKE, LEWIS. "Robert Whitehead Looks Forward." New York
     Times (December 27), sec. II, p. 1.
          It is anticipated that Miller will withdraw After the
     Fall and Incident at Vichy from the Lincoln Center Repertory
     Company in the wake of the departure of Robert Whitehead
     as producing director at the Center.

26 GANZ, ARTHUR. "Arthur Miller: After the Silence." Drama
     Survey, 3 (Fall), 520-30.
          Though flawed by looseness of structure, After the Fall
     is Miller's laudable attempt to encompass the complexities
     of guilt for the first time. "Since the analysis of subtle
     states of mind is not an area in which Miller has previously
     distinguished himself, it is hardly surprising that his
     first attempt to enter it should be less than triumphant."
     Our estimate of the play depends on whether or not we share
     Quentin's belief in his own impulse to genuine evil and in
     universal guilt.

1964

27   GASSNER, JOHN. "Broadway in Review." <u>Educational Theatre Journal</u>, 16 (May), 177-79.
        The real dimensions of <u>After the Fall</u> are smaller than those of the author's claims in his "structure and sententious reflections on the events and in the extensiveness of the production." Basically, the play is a small private drama inflated into a large public one. It is the "lumpy raw material for two or three plays exposed on the stage too soon." Reprinted: 1968.26.

28   . "New American Playwrights: Williams, Miller and Others," in <u>On Contemporary Literature</u>. Edited by Richard Kostelanetz. New York: Avon Books, pp. 48, 55, 62.
        Abridged version of 1949.54.

29   GELB, BARBARA. "Question: 'Am I My Brother's Keeper?'" <u>New York Times</u> (November 29), sec. II, pp. 1, 3.
        Though the episode on which <u>Incident at Vichy</u> is based had been in Miller's mind since 1950, his recent attendance at the Nazi murder trials in Frankfurt so sharpened his viewpoint about guilt and responsibility that he was able to turn out a final draft in three weeks upon his return. In an interview Miller discusses his recent plays, future writing plans, and domestic life.

30   GILMAN, RICHARD. "Getting It off His Chest, But Is It Art?" <u>Chicago Sun Book Week</u> (March 8), pp. 6, 13.
        Though its "public life is a triumph of propaganda and publicity," <u>After the Fall</u> is a "disastrous failure." The autobiographical elements remain untransformed from "chaos and impenetrability" into form and definition, it lacks structural focus, its rhetoric is vague and absurdly pretentious. The play reveals "Miller's desperate attempt to live up to his artificial position as a playwright of passion and ideas." His "intellectual shortcomings and verbal inadequacy have never been more flagrantly exhibited." Reprinted: 1971.17. Abridged: 1976.19.

31   . "Still Falling." <u>Commonweal</u>, 79 (February 17), 600-601.
        Review of Lincoln Center premier of <u>After the Fall</u>. Miller has failed to transform the raw material of his life into art. Thus the play is no drama at all, but a mixture of repellent self-justification and sophomoric revery about meaning, an internal bull-session that has only gossip-column interest. Elia Kazan's staging is the "quintessence of artiness." Reprinted: 1971.17. Abridged: 1976.19.

32 GOYEN, WILLIAM. "Arthur Miller's Quest for Truth." New York
    Herald Tribune Magazine (January 19), p. 35.
        Interview with Miller, who discusses repertory companies,
    Lincoln Center Theater, playwriting, and After the Fall.
    The play unifies three themes through Quentin: man in
    relation to his society, man in relation to his God, and
    man in relation to himself.

33 HASCOM, LESLIE. "After the Fall: Arthur Miller's Return."
    Newsweek, 63 (February 3), 49-52.
        Gossipy account of rehearsals, autobiographical elements
    ("he should have told it to Gerold Frank"), and Miller's
    career. His "impassioned pity" for the desperation of
    ordinary men tempts them to "crawl close," but Miller,
    believing he can help nobody, has built up a front of
    aloofness.

34 HEWES, HENRY. "Quentin's Quest." Saturday Review, 47
    (February 15), 35.
        Though the size of its concerns is impressive, Elia
    Kazan's staging admirable, and Jo Mielziner's "open stage
    theatre a beauty," After the Fall suffers from the audi-
    ence's divided attention between the real story of Marilyn
    Monroe and Maggie as a part of Quentin's experience. The
    play is a "fine source book for an intensively searching,
    but as yet not consistently dramatic play." Reprinted:
    1969.11.

35 _____. "Waiting Periods." Saturday Review, 47 (December 19),
    24.
        The theme of Incident at Vichy is that it is human to
    "want to get rid of anyone who is someone else and there-
    fore a threat to our own selves." The play is mostly an
    illustrated essay better suited to the "precisely controlled
    close-up medium of the motion picture." Despite director
    Harold Clurman's encouraging the actors to "infuse their
    arguments with passion," the characters are unconvincing.

36 HOGAN, ROBERT. Arthur Miller. Pamphlets on American Writers,
    No. 40. Minneapolis: Univ. of Minnesota Press, 48 pp.
        Interweaves analysis of Miller's work (including early
    radio plays) with biography. Miller's real significance,
    in a time of eclectic and experimental theater, is his
    embodiment of the "austere tragic spirit" of Sophocles,
    Racine and Ibsen. Miller constantly attempts to give "indi-
    vidual man his reason for existence, personal significance
    and morality," while centering his plays around the conflict
    between the ideal and the real. Up to View from the Bridge,

1964

Miller sees a new social morality as the answer to individual disintegration in modern society, but <u>After the Fall</u>
signals a recognition that this answer was simplistic. His
position in twentieth-century drama is "both secure and
high." Excerpted 1972.19; 1973.23.

37   JOHNSON, ROBERT GARRETT. "A General Semantic Analysis of
      Three of Arthur Miller's Plays: <u>Death of a Salesman</u>, <u>The
      Crucible</u>, and <u>All My Sons</u>." Ph.D. dissertation, University
      of Denver, 1963. <u>Dissertation Abstracts</u>, 24 (June), 5610.
          Analyzes the plays according to principles of general
      semantics set forth by Alfred Korzybski to "discover if a
      conceptual framework based upon a knowledge of structure,
      symbolic processes, and consciousness of abstracting might
      supply a systematic method" for play analysis.

38   KAZAN, ELIA. "Look, There's the American Theatre." <u>Tulane
      Drama Review</u>, 9 (Winter), 61-83.
          Interview. Kazan discusses staging, casting, acting in
      <u>After the Fall</u>. The controversy generated by the play is
      good for the theatre, and because of Miller the "theatre
      will be a little bolder" in future.

39   KERR, WALTER. "<u>Incident at Vichy</u>." <u>New York Herald Tribune</u>
      (December 4), p. 12.
          Review. Miller seems to wish the audience to feel
      oppressed with guilt rather than freshly informed about the
      "folly, gullibility, malice and perverse blindness that
      conspired to help the Nazi regime do what it did." The
      audience may feel guilty also at finding parts of the play
      tedious. Miller's play is an "essay in moral responsi-
      bility" that ignores the "physical energy of incident and
      the tangible, small truths of human character." Reprinted:
      1964.52.

40   _____. "Miller's <u>After the Fall</u>." <u>New York Herald Tribune</u>
      (January 24), pp. 1, 11.
          <u>After the Fall</u> is comparable to a confessional which
      Miller enters as penitent but emerges as priest. This
      "tricky quick change constitutes neither an attractive nor
      persuasive performance." The play fails not because of
      its materials but because there is no "imaginative hand
      molding this clay, making something new, independent, com-
      plete and self-assertive of it." Miller lacks distance
      from his subject. Thus Quentin's search is "verbal, pon-
      tifical, rhetorical, rather than concrete and carved out of
      bone." Reprinted: 1964.50. Expanded: 1969.21.

41   LAWRENCE, S. A. "The Right Dream in Miller's Death of a Sales-
     man." College English, 25 (April), 547-49.
          Both society and Willy Loman are responsible for the
     salesman's death. Society has lost touch with values--
     freedom, individuality, personality, and most of all, love--
     that should not be relegated to the personal sphere or
     family unit. Willy persists in believing in love and that
     there is a link between love and success. "He is destroyed
     to the extent that both he and society fail to acknowledge
     [love's] demands."

42   LEWIS, THEOPHILUS. "After the Fall." America, 110 (March 7),
     332.
          Brief review of play, emphasizing autobiographical
     elements.

43   LEYBURN, ELLEN DOUGLAS. "Comedy and Tragedy Transposed."
     Yale Review, 53 (Summer), 555-57.
          Rather than being a tragic figure, Willy Loman's self-
     deception, physical defects, and overheartiness of manner
     "identify him with a long line of aging comic butts who
     have tried to convince an unbelieving world and themselves
     that they are 'well-liked.'"

44   LOUGHLIN, RICHARD L. "Tradition and Tragedy in All My Sons."
     English Record, 14 (February), 23-27.
          Discusses parallels between All My Sons and biblical
     story of Cain and Abel, ancient Greek epics, and medieval
     morality plays.

45   MCCARTEN, JOHN. "Miller on Miller." New Yorker, 39 (February
     1), 59.
          Review of New York premier of After the Fall. The play
     is "transparently autobiographical, too long, desultory and
     garrulous," with "otiose or mystifying flights of rhetoric"
     and an unsettling lack of concern for the chronology of
     other characters' involvement with Quentin.

46   _____. "The Theatre: Easy Doesn't Do It." New Yorker, 40
     (December 12), 152.
          Despite Harold Clurman's capable direction, Incident at
     Vichy is lethargic in exposition, didactic, lacking in
     dramatic flair, and stilted in its language.

47   MCCLAIN, JOHN. "Arthur Miller's After the Fall." New York
     Journal American (January 24).
          Despite the "overwhelming cast" and the "consistently
     authoritative direction," After the Fall is pretentious,

1964

too long and lacking in taste. Structurally, it is "less
a play than a series of episodes with very little progression in the character of Quentin." Reprinted: 1964.50.

48   _____. "Lincoln Center's 'Wish Fulfillment.'" New York
Journal American (December 4).
    Review of Incident at Vichy. Though the play is "not
very theatrical and takes quite a time to get going, the
writing is first class and the performances exceptional."
It is Miller's best writing because "one is caught even in
the most static moments on stage." Reprinted: 1964.52.

49   _____. "Superb Repertory." New York Journal American (April
7).
    The direction, sets and cast for The Crucible's revival
"give the play an impact and importance beyond the range
of the original." If Miller's case against the judiciary
was ridiculously patent and his insinuation that time had
not improved matters unacceptable, the play is seen now to
have strong merits qua play, with no "implications beyond
the inability of man to face up to his most terrible
errors." Reprinted: 1964.51.

50   MARLOWE, JOAN and BETTY BLAKE, eds. "After the Fall." New
York Theatre Critics' Reviews, 25 (February 3), 374-78.
    Reprints New York Critics reviews: Chapman (1964.18);
Kerr (1964.40); McClain (1964.47); Nadel (1964.58);
Taubman (1964.77); Watts (1964.81).

51   _____. "The Crucible." New York Theatre Critics' Reviews,
25 (April 7), 295-98.
    Reprints New York Critics' reviews: Chapman (1964.19);
Crist (1964.22); McClain (1964.49); Nadel (1964.59);
Tallmer (1964.72); Taubman (1964.76).

52   _____. "Incident at Vichy." New York Theatre Critics'
Reviews, 25 (December 14), 116-19.
    Reprints reviews of New York critics: Kerr (1964.39);
McClain (1964.48); Nadel (1964.57); Taubman (1964.74);
Watt (1964.79); Watts (1964.80).

53   MEYER, RICHARD D. and NANCY MEYER. "Setting the Stage for
Lincoln Center." Theatre Arts, 48 (January), 12-16, 69.
    An account of the establishment, acting company, and
opening-year operations of Lincoln Repertory Center in New
York, with emphasis on After the Fall as a centerpiece.
Discusses form and emotional complexity in After the Fall.

1964

Elia Kazan, the director, believes the play is "one of the truly great plays with which he has come in contact."

54 MILLER, JONATHAN. "Broken Blossoms." New York Review of Books, II (March 5), 4-5.
Review of After the Fall. The play is pretentious and too long, the product of a "sound, but essentially minor talent." The self-righteous outcry of a prurient public against the "Marilyn" part draws attention away from the boring inadequacy of the play. Resembling a pumped up video-dilemma by Reginald Rose, it exemplifies the "uneasy yet intimate alliance between the Thirties Left and the slick commercial liberalism of Broadway and television drama."

55 MILLER, JORDAN Y. "Myth and the American Dream: O'Neill to Albee." Modern Drama, 7 (September), 190-98.
Miller attempts in Salesman to demonstrate the potential disaster of the American Dream, whereas in reality he has merely pointed up Willy's erroneous approach. The Dream at its best lives next door, in the person of young Bernard, the ideal success-image.

56 MOSS, LEONARD. "Arthur Miller and the Common Man's Language." Modern Drama, 7 (May), 52-59.
Miller's penchant for voicing ethical and socially relevant abstractions causes stylistic problems. The desire to articulate substantive truth sometimes restricts his talent for expressing inward urgency through colloquial language. The dialogue is most telling when it works by implication rather than explication. His writing attains its greatest power, and the language of his common man becomes emotionally resonant, when there is a well-proportioned interplay between idiomatically authentic, emotionally intense, and ethically meaningful styles. Abridged: 1969.11. Reprinted: 1972.47.

57 NADEL, NORMAN. "Miller Calls World as Witness." New York World Telegram and Sun (December 4).
Review of Incident at Vichy. Miller's play "transmutes human statistics back into persons" and its single incident seems for a while to "embrace everyone, everywhere." It is "no aloof, academic and impersonal discussion." Though a consummate craftsman, Miller's "primary stature is to be found in a towering idealism that is strengthened rather than undermined by his awareness of men's failings, including his own." Reprinted: 1964.52.

113

1964

58   _____. "Miller Play One of Inward Vision." New York World
        Telegram and Sun (January 24).
             After the Fall is a "beautiful, remarkable play" that
        advances theater as O'Neill and Strindberg did before. A
        "powerful and portentous drama that arouses the audience
        and enriches the season," it is a "somber, funny, tragic,
        and terrifying triumph of purposeful introspection."
        Reprinted: 1964.50.

59   _____. "Miller's Crucible Re-enacted Recalls Sickness of the
        Land." New York World Telegram and Sun (April 7).
             Though the sickness of McCarthyism has diminished, The
        Crucible has not. In this revival, its "timelessness is
        eloquently affirmed." It remains a "warning, a good, a
        rock-ribbed durable drama." Reprinted: 1964.51.

60   NOVICK, JULIUS. "Incident at Vichy." Nation, 199 (December
        21), 504.
             Too often the play emphasizes ideology at the expense
        of dramaturgy. It only occasionally catches the sound of
        human speech, tending instead toward abstractness, senten-
        tiousness, and self-consciousness. "In overvaluing himself
        as thinker and stylist, Mr. Miller neglects his greatest
        gift, which is precisely for dramaturgy in the best sense:
        for creating meaning through action."

61   POPKIN, HENRY. "After the Fall." Vogue, 143 (March 15), 66.
             Review of New York opening of After the Fall. The "real
        shocker" is that the play's "purpose is to absolve Quentin
        of any responsibility for anything that happens to others."
        Quentin is a "poltroon whose main aim in life is passing
        the buck." The play is seriously marred by the many point-
        ers that direct the audience to wrong interpretations.

62   _____. "Arthur Miller's The Crucible." College English,
        26 (November), 139-46.
             The parallels between the Salem of 1692 and the U.S. of
        1953 are imperfect and Miller has had to "adulterate
        Proctor's innocence" to create a specious kind of Aristo-
        telian flaw in him. Thus The Crucible falls short as a
        play of ideas and as a tragedy, though it succeeds in
        furnishing exciting crises in the lives of people in whom
        we have been made to take an interest. Reprinted: 1965.48.
        Abridged: 1972.19.

63   PRICE, JONATHAN R. "Arthur Miller: Fall or Rise?" Drama,
        73 (Summer), 39-40.

1964

As Miller's first breakaway from American themes, <u>After the Fall</u> will "outlive the clamour of its success." The play represents Miller's first successful fusion of the psychological and sociopolitical elements which were in conflict in his earlier plays.

64 PRIDEAUX, TOM. "A Desperate Search by a Troubled Hero." <u>Life</u>, 56 (February 7), 648-65.
    Review of premier of <u>After the Fall</u>. Miller is not guilty of bad taste in inviting a comparison between the heroine and Marilyn Monroe, whose exposure is for once integrated with serious philosophical ideas. Miller evidently believes Monroe's tragic example can serve to better the human condition.

65 QUASIMODO, SALVATORE. <u>The Poet and the Politician</u>. Translated by Thomas G. Bergin and Sergio Pacifici. Carbondale: Southern Illinois University Press, pp. 148-51, 160-61.
    <u>Death of a Salesman</u> is a "chronicle and memory of a man multiplied by infinite men." The play is a lesson in style for recent European dramatists. Miller brings back "the character" into the theatre, an element from which dramatists after Pirandello had increasingly withdrawn. In <u>The Crucible</u> Miller reveals a "natural imagination," though his creative instinct often strays into melodrama. The "secret" of the play is its surprisingly good construction, an indication that Miller has entered the "tradition of the great Anglo-Saxon theatre."

66 ROBERTS, JAMES L. <u>"Death of a Salesman": Notes</u>. Lincoln, Nebraska: Cliff's Notes, 71 pp.
    Summarizes and comments on <u>Salesman</u> scene by scene. Analyzes characters, structure, motifs, themes, style and includes discussion questions.

67 ROGOFF, GORDON. "Theatre." <u>Nation</u>, 198 (February 10), 153-54.
    Review of Lincoln Center premier of <u>After the Fall</u>. Miller offers reportage rather than detachment and compassion in what resembles a young author's autobiographical first novel rather than a mature artist's play. "Cerebral pornography is a shabby substitute for real, transmuted experience." Adopting Miller's "enervating nostalgia" and "antiseptic, frigid harshness," Elia Kazan's production is a "drifting, almost featureless performance."

68 SHELDON, NEIL. "Social Commentary in the Plays of Clifford Odets and Arthur Miller." Ph.D. dissertation, New York University, 1963. <u>Dissertation Abstracts</u>, 24 (January), 3018-19.

1964

        Shows the relationship of Miller's to Clifford Odets' plays in their commentary on the significant social issues of the Depression.

69   SIMON, JOHN. "Theatre Chronicle." <u>Hudson Review</u>, 17 (Summer), 234-36.
        <u>After the Fall</u> is flawed by the megalomania and hypocrisy of its author as reflected in Quentin. Miller lacks the imagination to digest, transpose and transubstantiate the givens of his life. Abridged: 1969.11.

70   SONTAG, SUSAN. "Going to Theater (and the Movies)." <u>Partisan Review</u>, 31 (Spring), 284-87.
        A sermon on being "tough with oneself," <u>After the Fall</u>'s argument is as "soft as mush." It insists on "dealing with big social and moral themes, but is sadly wanting in both intelligence and moral honesty." It fails dramatically because it does not present an action so much as ideas about action.

71   STEENE, BIRGITTA. "Arthur Miller's <u>After the Fall</u>." <u>Moderna Sprak</u>, 58: 446-52.
        Compares <u>After the Fall</u> with Strindberg's <u>To Damascus</u>. Similarities of form, ideas, and personal background of the playwrights are discussed. Miller "fails to fuse form and character" because his play serves primarily as a "private catharsis."

72   TALLMER, JERRY. "He Who Says No." <u>New York Post</u> (April 7).
        No longer a "metaphor of political outrage" as in 1953, <u>The Crucible</u> has gained in stature. Jack Sydow's direction gives the play a "trajectory and cumulative force" it never had before. <u>The Crucible</u> says "No, not only to witch hunters, who come and go, but to every betrayal of the self." Reprinted: 1964.51.

73   TAUBMAN, HOWARD. "A Cheer for Controversy." <u>New York Times</u> (February 2), sec. II, p. 1.
        <u>After the Fall</u> is Miller's maturest play because it "seeks truth without bitterness," whereas in <u>Salesman</u> Willy cannot "accept the responsibilities of his own frailties and failures." Dismissing as nonsense the deprecation of the play on the ground that it is autobiographical, Taubman blames director Kazan for the overly long and intense scenes of Maggie's disintegration and the sexual experience of Quentin and Maggie.

74 _____. Incident at Vichy." New York Times (December 4),
p. 44.
    Review of New York opening of Incident at Vichy. Miller's
"moving, searching play is one of the most important of our
time; it returns the theater to greatness." The play is a
"thundering cry of anguish and warning that might issue
from the heart of a prophet." Reprinted: 1964.52.

75 _____. "Inquiry Into Roots of Evil." New York Times
(December 20), sec. II, p. 3.
    Compares Incident at Vichy with Robert Lowell's Benito
Cereno and Hannah Arendt's study of the banality of evil,
Eichmann in Jerusalem, in that Miller uses an incident as
a "point of departure for a moral inquest that has the most
searching pertinence for man today or any time."

76 _____. "Return of The Crucible." New York Times (April 7),
p. 30.
    In a National Repertory Theater production, The Crucible
proves it is still a "stirring dramatization of an idea and
a commitment that bears continual reaffirmation." Miller
must be given credit for tackling a subject of this order
at a time when silence was easier, and for the skill and
passion with which he makes it vivid for any time.
Reprinted: 1964.51.

77 _____. "Theater: After the Fall." New York Times (January
24), p. 18.
    Review of New York premiere. Miller's "distillation of
the remembrance of things past," After the Fall is a
"pain-wracked drama" and the playwright's most mature play.
Elia Kazan's staging is "unfaltering in its perception and
orchestration." None of the actors is less than compelling.
Reprinted: 1964.50; 1973.2.

78 THOMPSON, HOWARD. "After the Fall Bought for Film." New York
Times (June 27), p. 14.
    Screen rights to After the Fall have been bought for a
reported $500,000 by Carlo Ponti and Ira Steiner. Sophia
Loren and Paul Newman will co-star. Miller, who will write
the film script, says the play will have to be "completely
reconceived" technically.

79 WATT, DOUGLAS. "Incident at Vichy." New York Daily News
(December 4), p. 64.
    Review of New York opening of Incident at Vichy. The
play is outdated, despite its theme that all mankind bears
guilt for the persecution of the Jews by the Nazis. Though

1964

there are "flurries of strong language and bits of contrived theatrics," the play is mostly "philosophical clap-
trap." Reprinted: 1964.52.

80   WATTS, RICHARD. "Arthur Miller Looks at the Nazis." New York
      Post (December 4).
          Review of Incident at Vichy, hardly a major Miller work
      but "continuously absorbing" and a sign that he is "getting
      back into his stride as a playwright of ideas." Yet there
      is nothing new in Miller's treatment of the hackneyed, if
      always relevant, subject of Nazi race savagery. Reprinted:
      1964.52.

81   _____. "The New Drama by Arthur Miller." New York Post
      (January 24).
          Though the power and passion of his earlier plays are
      present in After the Fall, the play is a "disappointing
      and self-indulgent kind of personal apologia." The "air
      of self-exculpation" causes discomfort, but several scenes
      are striking and powerful, and Jason Robards as Quentin is
      brilliant. Reprinted: 1964.50.

82   WELLS, ARVIN R. "The Living and the Dead in All My Sons."
      Modern Drama, 7 (May), 46-51.
          Reprint of 1962.39.

                              1965

1   ABIRACHED, ROBERT. "Allez à Aubervilliers." Le Nouvel Obser-
      vateur, 27 (May 20), 32-33.
          Review of French production of Death of a Salesman. The
      French audience can recognize itself in Willy Loman. The
      play is a modern tragedy in that it "shows the unbearable
      tension that is created between a human being and the
      society that molds him, until the moment when the breakdown
      occurs, bringing to light a terrible truth indeed."
      Reprinted (in English): 1972.47.

2   ANON. "Waiting to Be Exterminated." Life, 58 (January 22),
      39-40.
          Brief notice of premiere of Incident at Vichy.

3   ANON. "Miller Declares Pravda 'Twisted' Play." New York
      Times (February 2), p. 30.
          A Pravda review of Incident at Vichy implied that the
      Communist character had made the sacrifice rather than the
      Austrian, according to Miller in a Moscow interview.

4   ANON. "All Too Easy to Resist." <u>Times Literary Supplement</u>
        (February 4), p. 89.
            Review of published version of <u>After the Fall</u>. Miller
        is at the "disadvantage of writing at a time when tradi-
        tional categories have broken down." While the theme of
        <u>After the Fall</u> is "unassailable," the method of presenta-
        tion "makes the flesh creep." It is "insensitivity on the
        grand scale to use the image of the Auschwitz chimney" to
        help the hero back into a happy marriage.

5   ANON. "The Directors." <u>Newsweek</u>, 65 (March 15), 93.
            Review. Under Ulu Grosbard's direction the revival of
        <u>A View from the Bridge</u> is an "almost wholly satisfying
        theatrical experience, if not a revelatory one." The play
        suffers from a "basic failure of vision, a muddled grasp
        of how psychic action relates to existential truth, and an
        insufficiency of language rich enough to support its theme,"
        but its sensual reality and potential physical life give
        it stage viability.

6   ANON. "<u>Incident at Vichy</u>." <u>Booklist</u>, 61 (April 15), 779.
            Brief review of the play as an "effective succinct com-
        mentary on the Nazi treatment of Jews."

7   ANON. "<u>Incident at Vichy</u>." <u>Choice</u>, 2 (May), 166.
            More objective in character delineation than <u>After the
        Fall</u>, <u>Incident at Vichy</u> illustrates the "genius for
        motivating action and dialogue evidenced in <u>Death of a
        Salesman</u> and <u>The Crucible</u>." It marks Miller's return as
        one of the theatre's finest practitioners.

8   ANON. "Miller Sees Pen Growing Mightier." <u>New York Times</u>
        (July 6), p. 30.
            Report of Miller's presidential address to P.E.N. con-
        gress in Yugoslavia. He believes writers are increasing in
        political and social influence because of the dissemina-
        tion of culture through mass communications, especially
        television.

9   ANON. "PEN Pals." <u>Newsweek</u>, 66 (July 26), 92.
            An account of annual congress of International PEN (a
        writer's association of playwrights, poets, essayists,
        editors and novelists) at Dubrovnik, Yugoslavia. Miller
        was named new president of the association.

10 ANON. "Arthur Miller Spurns Invitation by Johnson." <u>New York
        Times</u>, <u>International Edition</u> (September 28), sec. II, p. 2.

1965

Acknowledging that the Arts and Humanities Act "surely
begins a new and fruitful relationship between the American
artists and their government," Miller nevertheless declines
an invitation from President Johnson to witness the signing
of the bill because of his opposition to Johnson's Vietnam
War policy.

*11   BANERJEE, CHINMOY. "Arthur Miller: The Prospect of Tragedy."
       English Miscellany (St. Stephen's College, Delhi), 3: 66-76.
       Cited in Hayashi (1976.7).

12   BAXANDALL, LEE. "Arthur Miller's Latest." Encore, 12 (March-
       April), 19-23.
          Incident at Vichy concerns the irrationality of men and
       their cruel subterfuges, even toward those they love. The
       characters are based on a close reading of Bettelheim,
       Fromm, Arendt and other analysts of the phenomenon of indif-
       ference to and thus complicity in cruelty. The play is
       relevant to the mass cruelty of Vietnam, the Congo and
       Mississippi, and marks an ethical advance for Miller in
       that it does not end in the martyrdom of an innocent victim
       but in LeDuc's decision to save himself, thereby acknowledg-
       ing both his guilt and his responsibility to act in a man-
       ner beneficial to the world.

13   BRUSTEIN, ROBERT S. "Arthur Miller's Mea Culpa," in his
       Seasons of Discontent. New York: Simon & Schuster,
       pp. 243-47.
       Reprint of 1964.15.

14   _____. "Muddy Track at Lincoln Center," in his Seasons of
       Discontent. New York: Simon and Schuster, pp. 259-63.
       Reprint of 1964.16.

15   CHIARI, J. "Drama in the U.S.A.," in his Landmarks of Con-
       temporary Drama. London: Herbert Jenkins, pp. 146-57.
          Extended analysis of Death of a Salesman, A View from
       the Bridge and After the Fall. A "confusion of aims" in
       Salesman mars its wholeness and prevents it from being the
       play it might have been, whereas View is Miller's "most
       original play and his nearest and most successful approach
       to tragedy." Compares After the Fall with O'Neill's Long
       Day's Journey Into Night, and finds Miller's play lacking
       in sensibility. The "mnemonic psychicodrama" is given
       "skillful production with an impressionistic background,"
       but it remains gimmicky and without definite dramatic
       structure.

16   CLURMAN, HAROLD. "Director's Notes: <u>Incident at Vichy</u>."
      <u>Tulane Drama Review</u>, 9 (Summer), 77-90.
          Preliminary notes before the making of the "director's
      book." First impressions of the themes and characters of
      <u>Incident at Vichy</u>. Reprinted: 1969.10. Abridged: 1973.23.

17   CURTIS, PENELOPE. "<u>The Crucible</u>." <u>The Critical Review</u>.
      No. 8, pp. 45-58.
          Despite the rationality of Miller's notes and his attempt
      to discredit belief in evil forces, the Court scenes in
      <u>The Crucible</u> show that it is a play about a community pos-
      sessed by evil forces. In creating the dramatic illusion
      of a quasi-impersonal force, communicated through hysteria
      from one person to another, the "Court scenes make an
      extraordinary discovery about the potentialities of the
      stage." Reprinted: 1971.43; 1972.19.

18   DONOGHUE, DENIS. "The Human Image in Modern Drama." <u>Lugano</u>
      <u>Review</u>, 1 (Summer), 167-68.
          Concerned with tribal sin and personal expiation, <u>A</u>
      <u>View from the Bridge</u> recognizes that "we live through the
      paradox of determinism and freedom." Eddie Carbone allows
      himself to be "fully known through human relationships,
      time, place and the reality of passion, as distinct from
      sensible men--the rest of us--who settle for a safe half."

19   EPSTEIN, ARTHUR D. "A Look at <u>A View from the Bridge</u>." <u>Texas</u>
      <u>Studies in Literature and Language</u>, 7 (Spring), 109-22.
          Miller's revision of <u>A View from the Bridge</u> into two
      acts rather than one and his omission of the commentator
      weaken the play. Though Miller's statements about <u>View</u>
      reveal his uncertainty as to the intended audience response
      to its hero, Miller "clearly feels Eddie Carbone is a tragic
      figure because, in the intransigence of his actions, there
      is an implicit fidelity to the self" and to his own beliefs,
      no matter how perverse.

20   EPSTEIN, LESLIE. "The Unhappiness of Arthur Miller." <u>Tri-</u>
      <u>Quarterly</u>, 1 (Spring), 165-73.
          <u>After the Fall</u> and <u>Incident at Vichy</u> are "destroyed
      by a failure of self-understanding and a lack of courage"
      in facing "Quentin-Miller's guilt, which springs from the
      way in which creative activity uses, manipulates and even-
      tually objectifies people." Compares Quentin with Hamlet
      and Miller with Ibsen.

21   ESSLIN, MARTIN. "Team Work." <u>Plays and Players</u>, 12 (March)
      32-33.

1965

> Lawrence Olivier's production of The Crucible shows that "a political play can remain artistically valid and dramatically viable for a long time" if it is written with sincerity and has "three dimensional human beings as characters."

22   FALLACI, ORIANA. "A Propos of After the Fall." World Theatre, 14 (January), 79, 81.
>   Interview. Miller rails against critics of After the Fall, the "story of a man trying to find out why he is alive" and the "best play I have ever written."

23   FERGUSON, FRANCIS. "A Conversation with Digby R. Diehl." Transatlantic Review, 18 (Spring), 119-20.
>   After the Fall has moral fervor and sincerity, but the author lacks sophistication and "awareness of what had happened in the world before his play." In this "sensational but pretentious" play one cannot accept Quentin as a universal specimen of contemporary man, because Miller's attitude towards his material is one of "wilful myopia," of refusing to "relate it to a more general human vision."

24   FERON, JAMES. "Miller in London to see Crucible." New York Times (January 24), p. 82.
>   Miller comments on a variety of topics related to his plays and life in an interview on a visit to London to see Olivier's production of The Crucible and to arrange a production of Incident at Vichy, also in London.

25   FREEDLEY, GEORGE. "Incident at Vichy." Library Journal, 90 (February 15), 892.
>   Brief notice of Viking edition of the play.

26   GARDNER, R. H. "Tragedy of the Lowest Man," in his The Splintered Stage. New York: Macmillan, pp. 122-34.
>   Salesman cannot be an attack on the American Dream or system, since Bernard is proof of its effectiveness; nor is Willy a Lear of the middle classes, since he defies respect and seems to have always suffered from pathological delusions rather than "false dreams." The play succeeds because of Miller's technical skill in creating patterns of meaning of much broader scope than Tennessee Williams is able to suggest.

27   GROSS, BARRY EDWARD. "Peddler and Pioneer in Death of a Salesman." Modern Drama, 7 (February), 405-10.
>   Willy's ideal of manly success is embodied in his brother, the enterprising pioneer, Ben; yet he is capable only of

being a peddler like his father. Only at the end are
peddler and pioneer combined, when Willy barters his existence for a legacy and penetrates the unknown territory of
death. Reprinted: 1972.47.

28   GRUEN, JOSEPH. "Portrait of the Playwright at Fifty." New
     York (October 24), 12-13.
        Interview. Miller discusses the process of writing, the
     themes in his plays, After the Fall, his refusal to witness
     the signing of the Arts and Humanities Act because of oppo-
     sition to President Johnson's Vietnam policy, and the
     "emotional journalism" of the young, off-Broadway play-
     wrights. Reprinted: 1968.31.

29   HALBERSTAM, DAVID. "Polish Students Question Miller." New
     York Times (February 17), p. 36.
        Report of guest lecture to American literature class at
     University of Warsaw while visiting Poland to talk to
     writers and producers and watch rehearsals of After the Fall.
     Miller is popular in Poland because his plays are not
     filled with purely American nuances, and their recurrent
     social themes are acceptable to the government.

30   HUFTEL, SHEILA. Arthur Miller: The Burning Glass. New York:
     Citadel; London: W. H. Allen, 256 pp.
        Sympathetic, detailed analyses of Miller's work and
     dramatic theory through Incident at Vichy. An English
     critic, Huftel surveys critical reaction to both European
     and American productions. The basis of Miller's social
     drama is the "gradual and remorseless crush of factual and
     psychological conflict"; the basis of his character's
     heroism is their unwisdom or lack of practicality; the
     "spine in his plays is the fundamental need to know," and
     the question of guilt and innocence. Includes an analysis
     of "Bridge to a Savage World," Miller's film script on
     juvenile delinquency for the New York City Youth Board;
     Miller's letters to Huftel; photographs of productions; and
     lists of casts. Excerpted: 1969.11; 1972.19.

31   KENNEDY, C. E. "After the Fall: One Man's Look at His Human
     Nature." Journal of Counseling Psychology, 12 (Summer),
     215-17.
        After the Fall is useful in facilitating the communica-
     tion and introspection of some college students. On the
     verge of re-entry into the real world, Quentin is like the
     college student entering the world of the graduate. Both
     are concerned with commitment, with process of choice, with

the search for authenticity and with the tasks of dealing
with responsibility and guilt. Also, the language is in
the introspective counselor-counselee style.

32 KILBOURN, WILLIAM. "Theatre Review: After the Fall."
    Canadian Forum, 44 (March), 275-76.
        Like Death of a Salesman, After the Fall is a play of
    and about consciousness, as well as individual conscience
    on trial. The action is objectively seen and realized
    through vividly alive characters. The nervous obsession
    with the play as a roman à clef is probably an escape from
    the painful truth of the play's terrible but real questions.

33 LENOIR, JEAN-PIERRE. "Paris Critics Cold to After the Fall."
    New York Times (January 25), p. 21.
        Nine of the first ten reviews by Paris critics of the
    French version of After the Fall are completely negative.
    Luchino Visconti's production is censored almost as much as
    the play.

34 LEWIS, ALLAN. "Arthur Miller," in his American Plays and Play-
    wrights of the Contemporary Theatre. New York: Crown,
    pp. 35-53, 195, 242, 243, 257.
        Discusses After the Fall at length and Salesman, The
    Crucible and Incident at Vichy briefly. While the first
    half of After the Fall is a "towering achievement," the
    second half lacks the artistic objectivity that would enable
    audiences to empathize with Quentin. However, had the play
    been written by someone else, or had audiences not been
    familiar with Marilyn Monroe, it "might have been regarded
    as an unusual and provocative experience."

35 LEWIS, THEOPHILUS. "Incident at Vichy." America, 112
    (January 23), 147-49.
        Review of New York début. Discusses main themes of play,
    concludes that it has "timeless universal values."

36 LUFT, FRIEDRICH. "Arthur Miller's Death of a Salesman:
    Hebbel-Theater (Berlin)," in his Stimme der Kritik-
    Berliner Theater seit 1945. Velber bei Hannover: Friedrich
    Verlag, pp. 82-85.
        Death of a Salesman is an elegy on failure, a "beautiful
    play with the particular melody of contemporary poetry."
    The Berlin production is almost better than the one in New
    York because it takes greater pains to familiarize its
    audience with what is already familiar to Americans.
    Reprinted (in English): 1972.47.

37   MARTIN, ROBERT ALLEN. "The Major Plays and Critical Thought
      of Arthur Miller to the <u>Collected Plays</u>." Ph.D. disserta-
      tion, University of Michigan. <u>Dissertation Abstracts</u>, 26
      (November), 2755.
          Compares Miller's plays with his essays on drama to show
      the relationship between theory and practice. While he is
      moving toward thematic complexity and structural simplicity
      in the plays, Miller's theory is shifting from social issues
      to an emphasis on individual consciousness.

38   MEYER, RICHARD D. and NANCY MEYER. "<u>After the Fall</u>: A View
      from the Director's Notebook." <u>Theatre: The Annual of the
      Repertory Theater of Lincoln Center</u>, 2: 43-73.
          An examination of Elia Kazan's director's notebook for
      <u>After the Fall</u>, with excerpts and linking commentary by the
      authors. Kazan's intention was to "anchor each abstraction
      of the play to something tangible which could be recognized
      by the audience and immediately understood."

39   MIELZINER, JO. "Designing a Play: <u>Death of a Salesman</u>," in
      his <u>Designing for the Theatre</u>. New York: Bramhall House,
      pp. 23-63.
          Traces Mielziner's involvement as set designer for
      <u>Salesman</u> from first reading of the script to opening night.
      Includes sketches. Abridged: 1967.48.

40   MILES, THOMAS O. "Three Authors in Search of a Character."
      <u>Personalist</u>, 46 (Winter), 65-72.
          Compares portraits of modern man in Aldous Huxley's
      <u>Brave New World</u>, Albert Camus' <u>Exile and the Kingdom</u> and
      Miller's <u>Death of a Salesman</u>. Willy's familiar plight is
      that he "senses himself contradicted by the nature of the
      culture around him" but cannot continue his own metamor-
      phosis at the same rate that the culture is changing.

41   MORLEY, SHERIDAN. "Miller on Miller." <u>Theatre World</u>, 61
      (March), 4.
          Interview. Miller affirms that Olivier's London pro-
      duction of <u>The Crucible</u> is the best he has seen "because
      the characters are approached as human beings" and the
      English actors attack the language in a manner Americans
      cannot.

42   NICHOLS, LEWIS. "Politics." <u>New York Times Book Review</u> (May
      23), p. 8.
          The French oppose Miller's nomination as International
      President of P.E.N. (an association of poets, editors, and
      novelists) by nominating Miguel-Angel Asturias.

1965

43 NOURSE, JOAN T. Arthur Miller's "Death of a Salesman" and
    "All My Sons." New York: Monarch Press, 121 pp.
         Brief survey of Miller's life and work. Plot analyses,
    analyses of major characters, commentary, bibliography,
    and review questions and answers for each play are included.

44 _____. "Arthur Miller's The Crucible," "A Memory of Two
    Mondays," "A View from the Bridge," "After the Fall,"
    "Incident at Vichy." New York: Monarch Press, 96 pp.
         Brief survey of Miller's life and works through After
    the Fall. There are plot analyses, analyses of major char-
    acters, commentary, and review questions and answers for
    each play.

45 OLIVER, EDITH. "The Theatre: Off Broadway." New Yorker, 40
    (February 6), 94.
         Review of expanded version of A View from the Bridge,
    directed by Ulu Grosbard. Bridge is Miller's "most forth-
    right and least annoying play," despite his habit of assign-
    ing universal guilt for individual dirty tricks and his use
    of the remotely connected lawyer who muses on the importance
    or universality of the fussy narrative. "If the play never
    attains the stature of classical tragedy, it is still an
    effective and exciting melodrama."

46 PHILLIPS, JOHN and ANNE HOLLANDER. "The Art of the Theatre:
    I." Paris Review, 9 (Winter-Spring), 74.
         In an interview, Lillian Hellman criticizes Miller for
    "cashing in" on Marilyn Monroe and himself in After the
    Fall, though she admits he was being tolerant in the play
    of those who betrayed their friends, as well as those who
    did not: "Two sides to every question and all that rot."

47 POPKIN, HENRY. "Arthur Miller: The Strange Encounter," in
    American Drama and Its Critics. Edited by Alan Downer.
    Chicago: Univ. of Chicago Press, pp. 218-39.
         Reprint of 1960.24.

48 _____. "The Crucible," in Scholarly Appraisals of Literary
    Works Taught in High Schools. Edited by Stephen Dunning
    et al. Champaign, Ill.: National Council of Teachers of
    English, pp. 110-17.
         Reprint of 1964.62.

49 _____. "Incident at Vichy." Vogue, 145 (January 15), 27.
         Review of New York opening. Incident at Vichy is a com-
    petent production but "at this late date, any new play

about the Nazis needs more than this ritualized discovery
of evil in a haze of facile small talk."

50 RAHV, PHILIP. "Arthur Miller and the Fallacy of Profundity,"
    in his The Myth and the Powerhouse. New York: Farrar,
    Straus and Giroux, pp. 225-33.
        Review of Incident at Vichy. Rather than the "callow
    subjectivity" of After the Fall, Incident at Vichy suffers
    from an "overstrain of intellectual capacity." The direc-
    tor, Harold Clurman, however, succeeds in negotiating the
    "hazards of the author's ideological ambition and senten-
    tiousness of language." The surprise ending is a "melo-
    dramatic contrivance," hopefully attributable more to
    "intellectual confusion than theatrical opportunism."
    Reprinted: 1969.29. Abridged: 1974.19.

51 RANALD, MARGARET LOFTUS. "Death of a Salesman: Fifteen Years
    After." Comment: a New Zealand Quarterly, 6 (August),
    28-35.
        The "confusions of vision, of language and style" make
    Salesman less than satisfying. The "stage carpentry and
    contrivances" now seem more evident and less new, while some
    scenes seem "thin in their essence." Though the play is
    still moving and pathetic, it has been made to bear too
    much. Rejects Willy as a representative modern tragic
    hero, asks whether our age can produce a "play that can
    fully express the pity, the terror and the resultant purga-
    tive joy, of the human condition."

52 S., F. "New Shows Reviewed." Theatre World, 61 (March), 8.
        Review of Laurence Olivier's National Theatre (London)
    production of The Crucible. With the fading of the polit-
    ical parallels, the play emerges as a "rich piece of drama
    in its own right in which the development of individual
    characters is more apparent." Olivier's production is
    "justifiably inclined towards melodrama."

53 SHEED, WILFRID. "Revival of a Salesman." Commonweal, 81
    (February 19), 670-71.
        Despite the "cheapjack universalizing, the sociological
    gospel-singing, the terrible flatness of characterization,"
    A View from the Bridge succeeds because of the unmistakable
    flavor of the basic Miller family and the "haunted Miller
    house" of his "Brooklyn plays." Reprinted in 1971.38.
    Abridged: 1973.23.

54 SIEGEL, PAUL N. "The Drama and the Thwarted American Dream."
    Lock Haven Review, 7: 52-62.

1965

> Miller is among leading American dramatists since World
> War I who have returned to the motif of the thwarted Amer-
> ican dream. Discusses relevant symbolism in Salesman.

55 SONTAG, SUSAN. "Theatre." Vogue, 146 (August 15), 51-52.
    Compares John Osborne's Inadmissible Evidence with
    After the Fall, a play it "strikingly resembles."

56 TAUBMAN, HOWARD. "Theater: Miller Revival." New York Times
    (January 29), p. 24.
    Ten years after its introduction on Broadway, A View
    from the Bridge still blazes with the elementary intensity
    of Italian opera. Though it does not rise to tragedy, it is
    anything but a negligible achievement. It tells its "agon-
    ized story of a man on an emotional rack in the burning
    character and confrontations of drama naked and unashamed."

57 WILLETT, RALPH W. "The Ideas of Miller and Williams."
    Theatre Annual, 22: 31-40.
    The ideas and attitudes of Miller and Williams are simi-
    lar, though neither is truly original. Miller takes too
    many sides, which leads to incoherence and "defeats his
    end, the social theatre that will teach us how to live."
    Miller's belief that every person can be his own great man
    harks back to the romanticism of Emerson, and his interest
    in individualism and agrarianism place him firmly in the
    American grain also.

58 YOUNG, B. A. "Crucible Staged by Olivier." New York Times
    (January 20), p. 35.
    Sir Laurence Olivier's triumphant and stunning produc-
    tion of The Crucible at London's National Theater shows the
    play has lost none of its old power, even though the polit-
    ical events that sharpened its initial impact have faded.

59 ZOLOTOW, SAM. "Lincoln Center Troupe to Drop Three Dramas
    from Repertory." New York Times (January 1), p. 10.
    In a dispute over the operation of Lincoln Center
    Repertory Theater, Miller withdraws After the Fall and
    Incident at Vichy from the repertory company.

1966

1 ANON. "After the Fall Seen at Paris American Church." New
   York Times (February 1), p. 26.
   The Studio Theatre of Paris is presenting a second Paris
   production of After the Fall. Gordon Heath, the black
   actor-singer, is the director.

2   ANON. "Arthur Miller Has Hepatitis." New York Times (January
        20), p. 29.
            In Brighton for the pre-London run of Incident at Vichy,
        Miller is hospitalized with hepatitis.

3   ANON. "Arthur Miller: P.E.N., Politics and Literature."
        Publisher's Weekly, 190 (July 18), 32-33.
            Report of Miller's first address as presiding officer of
        an international P.E.N. congress. Affirming that to
        "universalize culture is our ultimate aim," Miller argues
        that the "integral beauty or perfection of literature in
        itself is subordinate to its relevance to the survival and
        prestige of the social presumptions in which it was brought
        forth."

4   ANON. "Incident at Vichy in London Premiere." New York Times
        (January 27), p. 28.
            Summary of mostly disappointing reviews of London pro-
        duction of Incident at Vichy.

5   BLY, ROBERT. "The Dead World and the Live World." Sixties,
        8 (Spring), 2-7.
            Like Robert Lowell and Saul Bellow, Miller "brings us
        news of the human mind." Nature and the universe are miss-
        ing from his plays. In After the Fall, Miller reaches for
        characters that are mentally extreme, having given up on
        ordinary salesmen.

6   BRASHEAR, WILLIAM R. "The Empty Bench: Morality, Tragedy and
        Arthur Miller." Michigan Quarterly Review, 5 (Fall),
        270-78.
            Uses After the Fall and Nietzsche's Birth of Tragedy to
        argue that Miller is a moral and social dramatist rather
        than a tragedian. The play is an objectification of an
        individual's intellectual and moral evolution, whereas the
        tragedian is the supreme subjective artist because he re-
        jects the epistemological fallacy of positing a reassuring
        objective world of "things", i.e. of matter, ideas,
        societies, values, morals, and language itself.

7   BRYDEN, RONALD. "Dead Ernest." New Statesman, 71 (February
        4), 170.
            Review of London production of Incident at Vichy. What
        is the "peculiar curse on Miller's talent which prevents
        his plays from rising to their themes" but which suggests
        rather the "short-sighted pebble lens of mere earnestness?"
        Answer: in Vichy he sees guilt mainly as an obstacle to

1966

innocence, and instant saintliness arising from martydom
as a short cut to guiltlessness. In a play about human
weakness, no character has the weakness one would expect
in his or her situation.

8   CARLISLE, OLGA and ROSE STYRON. "The Art of the Theatre: II."
      Paris Review, 10 (Summer), 61-98.
            Interview. Miller discusses writing fiction versus
      drama, his beginnings, his relationship with his father,
      the younger dramatists, Russia, Lincoln Center, method
      acting, television, the American success ethic, critics,
      O'Neill, and Zefferelli's Italian production of After the
      Fall.

9   CASTY, ALAN. "Post-Loverly Love: A Comparative Report."
      Antioch Review, 26 (Fall), 399-411.
            Compares Saul Bellow's Herzog, Federico Fellini's 8½
      and After the Fall in their treatment of the quest for
      love and the emotional destructiveness of the intellectual's
      drive toward abstraction, a theme foreshadowed in Nathaniel
      Hawthorne's work. After the Fall is weakened in its memory
      scenes by a "programmatic conception of the material" that
      lacks the control which an "exactly defining perspective"
      would bring.

10 FRANK, STANLEY. "A Playwright Ponders a New Outline for TV."
      TV Guide, 14 (October 8), 7-8, 10-11.
            Interview. Miller proposes that each American television
      network devote one hour each week to "creative programming"
      to transform television into an "authentic art form on a
      par with the theater and the movies." He also discusses
      Salesman's durability and the reasons for its popular and
      critical success on television.

11 GOULD, JEAN R. "Arthur Miller," in her Modern American Play-
      wrights. New York: Dodd, Mead, pp. 247-63.
            Biographical and critical survey. Like Robert Sherwood
      before him, Miller is America's public conscience, popular
      because he mingles "common speech with democratic idealism,
      poetic expression and an ancient people's capacity for
      understanding the anguish of the soul."

12 JAMES, STUART B. "Pastoral Dreamer in an Urban World." Denver
      Quarterly, 1 (Autumn), 45-57.
            Through Willy Loman, Miller "romanticizes the role of
      the past in American history," but his subjectivity mars
      the play and prevents a "more accurate evaluation of the
      present."

13   KOPPENHAVER, ALLEN J.   "The Fall and After: Albert Camus and
     Arthur Miller." Modern Drama, 9 (September), 206-209.
          Examines similarities and differences between Albert
     Camus' The Fall and After the Fall.

14   KRACHT, FRITZ ANDRE. "Rise and Decline of U.S. Theatre on
     German Stages." American-German Review, 32 (June-July)
     13-15.
          Plays like The Crucible and Death of a Salesman were
     successful in postwar Germany because of their shock value.
     They revealed a different America from that portrayed by
     the official American "re-education" program in Germany.

15   LAMBERT, J. W. "Plays in Performance." Drama, 80 (Spring),
     20-21.
          In Incident at Vichy, the writing betrays Miller's pas-
     sion about his subject. The characters remain types rather
     than people, the dialogue editorializes, the mechanics of
     his anecdote are not easily credible. Passion cannot be
     conveyed in plain words, "only in resonances which are
     totally absent from his dialogue."

16   LASK, THOMAS. "How Do You Like Willy Loman?" New York Times
     (January 30), sec. II, p. 23.
          Review of record albums of Death of a Salesman and A
     View from the Bridge. Though Willy Loman is "scarcely the
     stuff of tragedy," he represents all those "who are trapped
     by false values, but who are so far on in life that they do
     not know how to escape them." (The album brings back Lee J.
     Cobb and Mildred Dunnock, two principals of the original
     production.) View is the revised 1965 version. Ulu
     Grosbard's direction of both albums is excellent.

17   MOSS, LEONARD. "Biographical and Literary Allusion in After
     the Fall." Educational Theater Journal, 18 (March), 34-40.
          Miller invokes literary sources (the Bible, the works of
     Albert Camus, his own plays) as well as autobiographical
     sources in After the Fall to support and authenticate his
     themes of human inconstancy and the disintegration and
     reintegration of self-confidence. In his life as well as
     his work he finds that "self-knowledge offers the only
     tenable alternative to self-defeat."

18   MURRAY, EDWARD J. "Point of View in After the Fall." CLA
     Journal, 10 (December), 135-42.
          The faulty structure, lack of tension and irony in
     After the Fall can be attributed to Miller's mistaken use
     of Quentin's point of view for the play. Miller is tempted

1966

into windy generalizations, and the drama, despite its
serious and important theme, comes to resemble an "old-
fashioned thesis play" that vitiates and makes irrelevant
its central concern. In other words, it fails in its "continuing attempt to reduce a multitude of differences to a
single formula."

19 _____. "Structure, Character and Theme in the Plays of Arthur
Miller." Ph.D. dissertation, University of Southern
California. Dissertation Abstracts, 27 (October), 1061A-62A.
A critical study whose aim is to establish Miller as the
only dramatist other than Tennessee Williams "worthy to be
mentioned with Eugene O'Neill." When Miller's plays fail,
it is attributable to his didactic tendency. The Crucible
and Incident at Vichy are not thesis plays, however, but
"philosophical melodrama." See 1967.36 for published
version.

20 NOLAN, PAUL T. "Two Memory Plays: The Glass Menagerie and
After the Fall." McNeese Review, 17: 27-38.
Compares and contrasts Tennessee Williams' The Glass
Menagerie with After the Fall as "memory plays," a new
genre of psychological drama which, unlike the dream play
and expressionistic drama, is a "projection of the con-
scious mind and concerned only with that action that is
understood and retained in the mind of the protagonist."

21 PARKER, BRIAN. "Point of View in Arthur Miller's Death of a
Salesman." University of Toronto Quarterly, 35 (January),
144-57.
The "blurred line between realism and expressionism"
in Salesman provides a more complex dramatic excitement
than is found in later plays, where Miller uses the technique more skillfully. And in keeping close to actual
observation, the play weighs American values more accurately
than Miller's subsequent analyses suggest. Reprinted:
1969.10.

22 ROTH, MARTIN. "Sept-d'un-coup." Chicago Review, 19: 108-11.
Since Miller's sensibility is lyrical rather than dramatic, Incident at Vichy, like his other plays, is concerned with the shriek or lyric poem that precedes drama.
Thus it fails as drama, allegory and psychoanalytic symposium. The murder of six million Jews remains a pain-knotted
experience in which Miller wallows publicly.

23   WHITMAN, ROBERT F. "The Nature and Kinds of 'Reality' in
     Drama," in his The Play-Reader Handbook. Indianapolis:
     Bobbs-Merrill, pp. 31-32, 46-49, 61-62, 208.
          Discusses expressionistic devices in Salesman which
     represent directly and visually what supposedly lies beneath
     the surface of Willy's consciousness. The Crucible rises
     above the contemporary political parallel largely because
     the "existence of the parallel suggests that the situations
     and personal qualities involved are not limited to any
     particular historical era."

24   WILLIAMS, RAYMOND. "From Hero to Victim," in his Modern
     Tragedy. Stanford, Calif.: Stanford University Press;
     London: Chatto & Windus, pp. 103-105.
          Though the false society Miller depicts is seen as alter-
     able, merely to live in it is to be its victim. In After
     the Fall the false society of torture and betrayal can no
     longer even be opposed because it is part of one's own
     desires.

                            1967

1   ANON. "Arthur Miller," in Contemporary Authors. Edited by
     James E. Ethridge and Barbara Kopala. Vols. 1-4. Detroit:
     Gale Research, pp. 665-66.
          Brief summary of Miller's life and career with comments
     by Miller and his critics. Selected bibliography.
     Expanded: 1969.1.

2   ANON. "At Another Distance." Times Literary Supplement
     (November 30), p. 1125.
          Review of I Don't Need You Any More. Some stories seem
     too "plotty" and play-like, while others are "pure anecdote."
     "A Search for a Future," however, "eloquently combines the
     compelling themes" of the collection as a whole.

3   ANON. "I Don't Need You Any More." Choice, 4 (July-August),
     532.
          The short story collection "shows Miller favorably in
     another medium and dimension." A wide range of humanity,
     diverse subject matter and stylistic excellence characterize
     the book.

4   ANON. "International." Akron Beacon Journal (March 16),
     sec. E, p. 5.
          Reports comments of Georgy Kapralov, Russian critic, on
     Moscow rehearsals for Incident at Vichy and After the Fall.

                            133

1967

> Though Miller is one of the few American writers who defends humanism and democracy, he suffers from the illusion that the "contradictions of America can be solved within the framework of bourgeois society."

5   ANON. "P.E.N. Congress Urges Release of Writers." New York Times (August 1), p. 33.
    In Abidjan (Ivory Coast) Miller is re-elected president of the International P.E.N. Club.

6   ANON. "Playwrights in Print." Time, 89 (March 10), 102.
    Though not in the same class as his plays, the stories in I Don't Need You Any More are concise and unified around that "incessant search for identity so common to American writers."

7   ANON. "Writers Appeal on Soviet Jews." New York Times (May 21), p. 12.
    Miller signs letter, drafted by Robert Penn Warren, urging Soviet writers to use their influence in restoring Jewish cultural institutions in Russia.

8   BENTLEY, ERIC. "The American Drama, 1944-1954," in his The Theatre of Commitment. New York: Atheneum, pp. 35-40.
    The Crucible misses "the essence of our political situation," though it "hits on a wish-fulfilling fantasy" and "soothes the bad conscience" of the quasi-liberals of Miller's generation.

9   BIGSBY, C. W. E. "The Fall and After: Arthur Miller's Confession." Modern Drama, 10 (September), 124-36.
    After the Fall is a "revolt against the simplistic responses of the dramatists of the 30's and 40's to social questions not fully understood" and Miller's attempt to tie up the "ends left dangling by his earlier plays." It is an unsatisfactory play because Miller "fails to establish the credibility of his protagonist."

10 BONE, LARRY E. "Arthur Miller's I Don't Need You Any More." Library Journal Book Review. New York: Bowker, p. 674.
    Reprint of 1967.11.

11 _____. "I Don't Need You Any More." Library Journal, 92 (February 1), 596.
    Brief notice. Reprinted: 1967.10.

12   BUITENHUIS, PETER. "Arthur Miller: The Fall from the Bridge."
      Canadian Association for American Studies Bulletin, 3
      (Spring-Summer), 55-71.
          In After the Fall Miller therapeutically tackled the
      American and individual dream of innocence and "stripped it
      away to reveal the nightmare of unrelatedness and guilt at
      its centre." Putting aside its oft-noted limitations, the
      play is Miller's King Lear, in which he strips himself of
      normative theories of social behavior and gives us the "poor
      forked animal facing the elements of his own psychology."

13   CALLAHAN, ELIZABETH AMIDON. "The Tragic Hero in Contemporary
      Secular & Religious Drama." Literary Half-Yearly, 8
      (January-July), 42-49.
          Discusses The Crucible and T. S. Eliot's Murder in the
      Cathedral as Aristotelian tragedies.

14   CHARYN, JEROME. "Arthur Miller Off Stage." Book World,
      (February 12), pp. 4, 17.
          The title story in I Don't Need You Any More is a master-
      piece whose child hero grows up to be Quentin in After the
      Fall. Regardless of whether Miller's plays are in or out
      of fashion in any particular year, his "short stories will
      not easily go out of style."

15   COEN, FRANK. "Teaching the Drama." English Journal, 56
      (November), 1136-39.
          Compares All My Sons with Ibsen's The Master Builder as
      a practical exercise in critical analysis for high school
      students.

16   COOK, RODERICK. "I Don't Need You Any More." Harper's, 234
      (March), 136.
          The stories do "nothing either way for Miller's reputa-
      tion as a Great American Author." The story "The Misfits"
      is better than the movie based on it, possibly because the
      character called Roslyn, played by Marilyn Monroe in the
      movie, never actually appears.

17   ERICSON, RAYMOND. "Arthur Miller, Italian Style." New York
      Times (October 15), sec. II, p. 19.
          Announcement of forthcoming Philadelphia production of
      Renzo Rossellini's Italian opera Uno Sguardo del Ponte,
      based on A View from the Bridge.

18   FENDER, STEPHEN. "Precision and Pseudo Precision in The
      Crucible." Journal of American Studies, 1 (April), 87-98.

1967

The language of the Salemites reveals an absence of any consistent moral or ethical outlook and a "complete disjunction between their theory and the facts of human action." After destroying their phony language, Proctor reconstructs a speech in which words are related to their lexis. Reprinted: 1971.43.

19   FREEDMAN, MORRIS. "Bertolt Brecht and American Social Drama," in his The Moral Impulse. Carbondale: Southern Illinois University Press, pp. 107-14, passim.
     Contrasts Bertolt Brecht and Miller as writers of epic theatre. Though Miller attempts to transcend the particular and achieve the universal in epic style, his early plays have the appearance or gesture of thought and idea rather than the actuality. At the same time they lack Brecht's massive authenticity.

20   FRENCH, PHILIP. "The Old Miller Stream." New Statesman, 74 (November 10), 651.
     Review of Coventry production of After the Fall. Though Leonard Schach's production is exemplary, the play is banal. One would not object to the autobiographical element if Miller had made something of the important themes: "guilt, personal and social responsibility, loss of innocence, the need to curb our instinctive compulsion to destroy." The play proves once again that one wallow does not make a summa.

21   GOLDMAN, ARNOLD. "I Don't Need You Any More." Listener, 78 (November 2), 580.
     Some recent stories in this collection are very distinguished, with none of the narrative awkwardness of Miller's first published fiction, Focus. There is a little too much admiration for the "doggedly irrepressible, if shabby soul, getting on with a bad job but retaining a characteristic sense of wonder."

22   GOULD, JACK. "Arthur Miller's High Pitched The Crucible." New York Times (May 5), p. 79.
     Review of television adaptation of The Crucible. The camera fragments the cumulative frenzy, reminding the viewer that the play is "less a drama than a narrative tract--important, but cold and remote."

23   HALSTEAD, WILLIAM P., ed. "Arthur Miller Talks." Michigan Quarterly Review, 6 (Summer), 153-84.

A question and answer session with students at the University of Michigan. Miller discusses the state of the American theatre, audiences, critics, Lincoln Center and other matters.

24 HANDLIN, OSCAR. "I Don't Need You Any More." Atlantic, 219 (March), 143.
Brief notice. Occasionally, Miller "deals with the family tensions that elicit his best writing," but there are "few dramatic elements in the stories, despite his prolific work for the stage."

25 HAYASHI, TETSUMARO. "Arthur Miller: The Dimension of His Art and a Checklist of his Published Works." Serif, 4 (June), 26-32.
Emphasizes minor works because "few know what he has written in addition to Death of a Salesman and a few other plays."

26 HILL, PHILIP G. "The Crucible: A Structural View." Modern Drama, 10 (December), 312-17.
Refutes George Jean Nathan's criticisms of The Crucible, especially the charge that the courtroom climax comes too early in the play. The central action is internal and sustained to its logical conclusion at the end of the play. In a competent performance, therefore, the real climax occurs when Proctor rips up his confession, after which a quick denouement brings us to a satisfactory and stunning conclusion. Reprinted: 1972.19.

27 HUBBARD, E. D. and PATRICIA TRUELSON. "Death of a Salesman": A Critical Commentary. Study Master Series. New York: American R.D.M. Corporation, 59 pp.
A study guide that analyzes plot structure and characterization and gives biographical information, study questions and bibliography.

28 HUGHES, ALLEN. "Opera from Play by Miller Is Given." New York Times (October 19), p. 56.
Review of Uno Sguardo del Ponte, Renzo Rossellini's Italian opera based on A View from the Bridge. The old-fashioned score lacks the strength and intensity of the production, the performance, and the original play.

*29 HUTTAR, CHARLES. Arthur Miller. New York: Everymans Library.

1967

30   KOVEN, STANLEY. "I Don't Need You Any More." Commonweal, 85
      (March 17), 686-87.
          Miller's intention in his short stories of "shifting his
      distance toward or away from the terrible heat at the center
      of the stage" renders them ineffective. He works best when
      "nearest the hot center." Too often in this collection we
      find the "author and ourselves receding until the event, or
      the crisis behind it seems only a blur." The craftsmanship
      is flabby, the soothsaying "a bunch of furry dilemmas."

31   LASK, THOMAS. "18 Leading Poets and Writers Give Reading
      Stressing Peace." New York Times (November 13), p. 60.
          In New York, Miller and others participate in "Poets for
      Peace," a reading sponsored by the Fellowship of Reconcil-
      iation. Miller reads a "lengthy prose comment" asking "Why
      kill a nation [Vietnam] no one hates?"

32   ____. "Mr. Miller Offstage." New York Times (March 18),
      p. 27.
          At their best, the stories in I Don't Need You Any More
      make a striking impact and will enhance Miller's standing
      as a writer. Despite his tendency to squeeze too much
      "meaning" into them, the stories successfully cover a "large
      segment of the country of the mind."

33   LONG, MADELEINE J. "Sartrean Themes in Contemporary American
      Literature." Ph.D. dissertation, Columbia University.
      Dissertation Abstracts, 28 (October), 1439A.
          Applies pertinent themes of Jean-Paul Sartre to Death
      of a Salesman.

34   MOSS, LEONARD. Arthur Miller. Twayne's United States Authors
      Series. New York: Twayne, 160 pp.
          Focuses on Miller's technical resources—dialogue styles,
      narrative conventions, symbolic devices, and structural
      principles—in the plays to show that he is more concerned
      with the "psychological consequences of fanatic self-
      assertion" than registering indignant protests against in-
      justice or a society that teaches the wrong values. Miller
      is at his best when visualizing the causal complexity of
      personal motives. Ironically, in so doing he comes closest
      to fulfilling his ambition to write coherent social drama;
      though the effort to unify social and psychological per-
      spectives is the source of his failures as well as his
      accomplishments as a dramatist. Includes chronology, bio-
      graphical chapter, bibliography. Excerpted: 1972.19;
      1973.23.

35   MOTTRAM, ERIC. "Arthur Miller: The Development of a Political
      Dramatist in America," in American Theatre. Stratford
      Upon Avon Studies, No. 10. Edited by J. R. Brown and
      Bernard Harris. London: Edward Arnold, pp. 127-61.
          Critical survey of plays through Incident at Vichy. In
      deference to his audiences and backers, Miller's early plays
      stop short of advocating revolutionary social change. They
      are not tragedies but "plays of partial awakening to fate
      before a conclusion in suicidal waste." The later plays
      place the burden of guilt and decision increasingly on the
      individual rather than enriching the social and political
      context of his actions. This leads to nihilism in After
      the Fall and Incident at Vichy. Reprinted: 1969.10.
      Excerpted: 1972.19; 1973.23.

36   MURRAY, EDWARD. Arthur Miller, Dramatist. New York: Ungar,
      186 pp.
          Detailed explications and analyses of structure, dia-
      logue, character and theme in Miller's principal plays
      through Incident at Vichy. Refutes charges that Miller's
      characters are too schematized and that Salesman and View
      from the Bridge are "split" structurally and thematically.
      Though there is no smooth line of development in the plays,
      they are thematically related. The Crucible and Incident
      at Vichy are morality or philosophical dramas, not to be
      confused with thesis plays like All My Sons. If Miller is
      rejected because he lacks a metaphysic or theology of crisis,
      then some of the most vital playwrights of the modern the-
      ater must likewise be rejected. Excerpted: 1972.19;
      1976.19.

37   OBERG, ARTHUR K. "Death of a Salesman and Arthur Miller's
      Search for Style." Criticism, 9 (Fall), 303-11.
          A stylistically clichéd language, based on New York
      Jewish speech that rises to a peculiarly American idiom,
      reveals the disparities between Willy Loman's aspirations
      and reality. Miller constantly seeks to go beyond a
      "limited realism and a confining prose" to find an "un-
      usually expressive speech" with which to overcome the lack
      of an "established and available idiom" in America.
      Reprinted: 1972.47.

38   RAYMONT, HENRY. "Harriet De Onis Gets Book Prize." New York
      Times (May 9), p. 44.
          Lewis Galantiere, retiring president of the P.E.N. Club's
      American Center, announces Miller's recent re-election in
      London to another two-year term as president of P.E.N.
      International.

1967

39 SHEFFER, ISAIAH. "I Don't Need You Any More." New Leader,
      50 (June 5), 24.
          The "variety, skill and feeling" with which these stories
      are written "keeps alive the faith that whatever his recent
      troubles in the theater, Miller is not finished yet."
      "Fitters Night" is the best of the stories, followed by
      "The Misfits" and "The Prophecy."

40 STINTON, JOHN J. "Structure in After the Fall: the Relevance
      of the Maggie Episodes to the Main Themes and the Christian
      Symbolism." Modern Drama, 10 (December), 233-40.
          In dismissing After the Fall, critics confuse Miller's
      questionable taste with bad art. In fact the play is not
      structurally weak or inchoate; the second act is tightly
      connected to the first. Quentin (Act I) and Maggie (Act
      II) share guilt and are also Christ-victim figures; more-
      over, Act II develops or further presents other themes
      developed in Act I.

41 TROWBRIDGE, CLINTON W. "Arthur Miller: Between Pathos and
      Tragedy." Modern Drama, 10 (December), 221-22.
          Miller's seriousness of purpose commits him to attempt-
      ing tragedies; yet pathos, the arch-enemy of tragedy, is
      often the result. Pathos settles for an oversimplified
      vision that has no power over us. Whereas in earlier plays
      fate took the form of political, social or economic forces,
      in View from the Bridge Eddie struggles with himself, with
      a passion he cannot understand or control. Miller's new
      concept of tragedy is employed most successfully in After
      the Fall.

42 TYNAN, KENNETH. "American Blues: the Plays of Arthur Miller
      and Tennessee Williams, Excerpts from Curtains," in The
      Modern American Theatre. Edited by Alvin B. Kernan.
      Englewood Cliffs, N.J.: Prentice-Hall, pp. 34-44.
          Reprints 1954.12.

43 VINCE, THOMAS L. "I Don't Need You Any More." Best Sellers,
      26 (March 1), 436.
          While the title story is "singularly dull," "Monte
      Sant'Angelo" and "Lowe" are well done. The stories might
      have turned out better if done by a writer of lesser repu-
      tation, but then they would probably he overlooked.

44 WAGER, WALTER, ed. The Playwrights Speak. New York:
      Delacorte, pp. 1-24.

Interview. Miller discourses on the process of play-
writing, critics, and audiences, concentrating on background,
themes and technique of <u>Incident at Vichy</u>.

45   WAKEMAN, JOHN. "Story Time." <u>New York Times Book Review</u>
      (April 2), p. 4.
         <u>I Don't Need You Any More</u> is "exact, humane, knowledgeable
      writing, free of affectation and self-congratulation, its
      many successes honestly earned." The sociological preoccu-
      pations of the plays are absent. Miller sees life less
      simply than he did, a view that is a handicap in the theater.

46   WEALES, GERALD C. "Arthur Miller," in <u>The American Theater
      Today</u>. Edited by Alan S. Downer. New York: Basic Books,
      pp. 85-98.
         Revision of 1962.37. Includes later plays. Reprinted:
      1969.10.

47   _____. Introduction, in <u>Arthur Miller, "Death of a Salesman"</u>:
      <u>Text and Criticism</u>. Viking Critical Library. New York:
      Viking, pp. vii-xx.
         Discusses basis for selection of essays accompanying the
      text, reviews reception and criticism of the play, and
      addresses familiar questions such as whether <u>Salesman</u> is a
      tragedy or a social play, the roles of Biff and Linda, and
      the ending.

48   _____, ed. <u>Arthur Miller, "Death of a Salesman"</u>: <u>Text and
      Criticism</u>. Viking Critical Library. New York: Viking,
      426 pp.
         Reprints and excerpts from 1949.31; 1949.33; 1949.35;
      1949.39; 1949.40; 1949.50; 1949.52; 1949.53; 1949.58;
      1949.71; 1949.82; 1951.22; 1957.46; 1958.9; 1958.17;
      1959.20; 1959.26; 1960.11; 1960.12; 1962.19; 1962.37;
      1965.39.

49   ZIMMERMAN, PAUL. "Offstage Voices." <u>Newsweek</u>, 69 (February
      27), 92.
         Miller seems to relax in short fiction, since there is
      less at stake for him, but proves himself in <u>I Don't Need
      You Any More</u> an effective handler of the form, at least in
      the handful of stories that "blend insight and outlook."
      Reprinted: 1969.11.

1968

1   ANON. "Newman and Miller Named Delegates to Convention."
    New York Times (July 10), p. 43.
        A supporter of the presidential candidacy of Senator
    Eugene McCarthy, Miller is named a Connecticut delegate to
    the Democratic National Convention to take place in August
    1968 in Chicago.

2   ANON. "Notes and Comments." New Yorker, 43 (January 13), 19.
        Criticizes Miller's attack on the majority of Americans
    who will neither deny nor affirm the insanity of America's
    role in the Vietnam War. The country is "racked by genuine
    controversy" and asking people simply to "stand up and be
    counted is a step of limited value."

3   ANON. "Old Scores." Times Literary Supplement (October 10),
    p. 1154.
        Review of published version of The Price. With similar-
    ities to Salesman, it is Miller's most Ibsenite piece to
    date in the sense of the past influencing the present. The
    collision between the different lifestyles of Gregory
    Solomon and the Franz clan is sidetracked by the less
    interesting duel between the Franz brothers, with its
    fallacious "narcissistic assumption that life cannot go on
    until the conscience is clean."

4   ANON. "The Price." Time, 91 (February 16), 76-77.
        Review of New York opening of The Price. In this
    "vintage 1930's drama," Miller sermonizes on his favorite
    themes of guilt, responsibility and the way society imposes
    its image of identity on each of us. The challenging ideas
    are merely described rather than dramatized, in contrast to
    Death of a Salesman, in which Willy's fate has "anguishing
    impact because of the subtly manipulated flashbacks."

5   ANON. "Solzhenitsyn Plea Sent to Podgorny." New York Times
    (August 15), p. 14.
        With others, Miller signs a letter by Rolf Hochhuth to
    Nikolai V. Podgorny, Soviet head of state, pleading for the
    ban on the works of Aleksandr Solzhenitsyn in Russia to be
    lifted.

6   BARNES, CLIVE. "Arthur Miller's The Price." New York Times
    (February 8), p. 37.
        Review of New York opening of The Price. It is "engros-
    sing, entertaining, superbly theatrical, and complies with

the classic unities," but the story itself is over "before
the play begins." The details of the story are clumsy, the
language doubtful. The play is "good but not serious
theater." Reprinted: 1968.40.

7   _____. "Reappraisal of The Price." New York Times (October
     30), p. 39.
        A second viewing of The Price confirms the first impres-
     sion that it is "absolutely engrossing theater" and
     "unquestionably one of Miller's two or three best plays."

8   BARNETT, GENE A. "The Theatre of Robert Bolt." Dalhousie
     Review, 48 (Spring), 17-18.
        Compares Bolt's The Flowering Cherry with Death of a
     Salesman. Willy is a "more universal symbol of a dreamer
     and his inability to make his dream come true" than Jim.

9   BARTHEL, JOAN. "Arthur Miller Ponders The Price." New York
     Times (January 28), sec. II, pp. 1, 5.
        Miller is interviewed on the "new" theater, the theme of
     The Price ("an outgrowth of Death of a Salesman"), the dif-
     ficulties in casting and staging the play, his assessment
     of his career, and his role in the Vietnam protest movement.

10   BATES, BARCLAY W. "The Lost Past in Death of a Salesman."
     Modern Drama, 11 (September), 164-72.
        Growing up in a transitional period in American history,
     Willy finds no suitable identity. Publicly he is the glad-
     handed salesman, but privately he is four anachronisms:
     archetypal cherisher of the pastoral world; pre-industrial-
     revolution artisan; ham-handed outlaw frontiersman; and
     dutiful patriarchal male transmitting legacies from fore-
     bears to progeny.

11   BENTLEY, ERIC. "The Innocence of Arthur Miller," in his What
     Is Theatre? New York: Atheneum, pp. 62-65.
        Reprint of 1953.12.

12   BERMEL, ALBERT. "Right, Wrong and Mr. Miller." New York
     Times (April 14), sec. II, pp. 1, 7.
        Miller's plays are popular "because they do not rub the
     spectator's weaknesses or trouble him." If they dealt with
     characters who remained fallible to the end, rather than
     turning into exemplary figures, the spectator would be up-
     set, knowing the play was really about himself. The theme
     of The Price suggests Miller has not grown as a playwright
     but is still teaching kindergarten maxims. See 1968.20 for
     Harold Clurman's response.

1968

13   BIGSBY, C. W. E. "Arthur Miller," in his Confrontation and
      Commitment. London: MacGibbon & Kee; Columbia: University
      of Missouri Press, pp. 26-49.
          Miller revived the American theatre by "deflecting drama
      away from its role as dramatized case-book." His progres-
      sion from All My Sons to After the Fall is a logical one,
      leading from demonstrations that a man "is limited to his
      own possibilities" to attempts to "define the full nature
      of the human situation which must be faced."

14   BLIQUEZ, GUERIN. "Linda's Role in Death of a Salesman."
      Modern Drama, 10 (February), 383-86.
          Linda does not support Willy so much as she supports his
      dream of success. He is a victim of her ambition as well
      as his own. She is objectively the proof of her husband's
      ability as provider, and subjectively the negation of it.
      Reprinted: 1972.47.

15   BORDERS, WILLIAM. "Democrats Begin Hartford Battle." New
      York Times (June 22), p. 19.
          At a meeting of the resolutions committee of the Connec-
      ticut Democratic Party Convention, Miller offers a resolu-
      tion calling for cessation of the American bombing of North
      Vietnam and asking that all parties to the war enter nego-
      tiations aimed at peace.

16   BRONSON, DAVID. "An Enemy of the People: A Key to Arthur
      Miller's Art and Ethics." Comparative Drama, 2 (Winter),
      229-47.
          Extended comparison of Miller's adaptation of Ibsen's
      An Enemy of the People with the original. Miller's later
      work in After the Fall and The Price shows a new complexity
      of thought that goes beyond the simplifications of his
      adaptation.

17   BRUSTEIN, ROBERT. "The Unseriousness of Arthur Miller." New
      Republic, 158 (February 24), 39-41.
          Review of New York premiere of The Price. Though solemn
      and determined, the play is not serious because it is
      divorced from the concerns of modern audiences. It is a
      memory play that deals with the same quasi-autobiographical
      family situation rooted in the 1930's that Miller has dealt
      with in several other plays. It is escapist in that it
      gives us "merely the appearance of significance behind
      which nothing meaningful is happening." Reprinted: 1969.9.
      Abridged: 1976.19.

1968

18   CALTA, LOUIS. "Miller Defends Theme of Price." New York
      Times (March 5), p. 32.
           Miller responds to Robert Brustein's contention that
      The Price is divorced from current problems. The point of
      the play is that "certain things cannot be justified" on a
      quid-pro-quo basis, and Walter's behavior "was more repre-
      sentative of a kind of way most people in this country act,
      rather than Victor, the cop." However, Miller refuses to
      be a journalist in the theater.

19   CHAPMAN, JOHN. "The Price Absorbing, Splendidly Acted." New
      York Daily News (February 8).
           Review. Though there is little "action" in The Price,
      the play is spellbinding in its intensity. The actors are
      perfectly suited to their roles, and Ulu Grosbard's direc-
      tion contributes significantly to the impact of the play.
      Reprinted: 1968.40.

20   CLURMAN, HAROLD. "The Merits of Mr. Miller." New York Times
      (April 21), sec. II, pp. 1, 7.
           Defends Miller and The Price against charges levelled by
      Albert Bermel [New York Times (April 14), sec. II, pp. 1,
      7. See 1968.12]. While Miller's determination to "hold
      fast to a traditional morality" is unfashionable, this
      "resistance to our souls' sloth defines his signal contri-
      bution to the American theater of our day." Reprinted:
      1969.10. Abridged: 1973.23.

21   ____. "Theatre." Nation, 206 (February 26), 281-83.
           Review of Broadway premiere of The Price. The play is a
      dialogue between the idealistic and the pragmatic, or the
      ethical and the efficient, as represented by the two
      brothers. It is a tension in Miller and in American society.
      In this, as in his other plays, however, plot devices and
      characters do not measure up to the scope of his intentions.

22   COHEN, MARSHALL. "The Sins of the Sons." Atlantic, 221
      (June), 120-22.
           Review of New York opening of The Price. The themes and
      techniques are familiar, "the audience--liberal, middle-
      aged, affluent--is the one that wept over Willy Loman and
      found Proctor a political hero." But The Price has differ-
      ent psychological assumptions, humor, and some disinterested,
      if unsustained, moral analysis.

23   COOKE, RICHARD P. "Restoration of Miller." Wall Street
      Journal (February 9).

1968

Review. The Price is a "first rate evening of theater," and a play about "real people, real issues and, above all, real illusions." Miller's theme is that "fine motives are often self-delusion, and though praiseworthy in themselves, hold no patent of absolute truth." Reprinted: 1968.40.

24 CORRIGAN, ROBERT W. "The Achievement of Arthur Miller." Comparative Drama, 2 (Fall), 141-60.
    If the conflict in Miller's early plays grew out of a crisis of identity, that of the later ones concerns the crisis of generativity or otherness. "The identity crisis is a crisis of consciousness; the generativity crisis is one of conscience." Writing with a moral earnestness and a sense of moral responsibility rarely equalled in the modern theatre, Miller continually demands from it more than the despair which seems its dominant tone. Reprinted: 1969.10; 1973.8. Excerpted: 1973.9; 1973.23.

25 DOWNER, ALAN S. "Old, New, Borrowed and (a Trifle) Blue: Notes on the New York Theatre, 1967-1968." Quarterly Journal of Speech, 54 (October), 203-206.
    Review of New York production of The Price, "a revival in which Miller returns to and revitalizes that quintessential American family, the Lomans." Written with economy, but not miserliness, it is concerned with ultimate things, not the faddish or evanescent. It goes "beyond the tragic catastrophe to the maturity of understanding and acceptance."

26 GASSNER, JOHN. "The Lincoln Center Repertory Company: After the Fall," in Dramatic Soundings. New York: Crown, 708 pp., passim.
    Pages 547-72 reprint 1964.27. Excerpted: 1976.19.

27 GIANAKARIS, C. J. "Absurdism Altered: Rosencrantz and Guildenstern Are Dead." Drama Survey, 7 (Winter), 52-58.
    Discusses Miller's contention (see 1968.9) that avant-garde, absurdist theater is negative, sophomoric, and deals with the superficial ironies of existence. Argues that Tom Stoppard's Rosencrantz and Guildenstern Are Dead is an answer to Miller's position, since it "reconciles the disparities between drama anchored in personal social responsibility and that pledged to the stripping of hackneyed illusions underlying much of current life."

28 GILL, BRENDAN. "The Theatre: In the Wilderness." New Yorker, 43 (February 17), 99.

In The Price, Miller's Puritan relish for hellfire invites us to believe that what ails us is past cure but that the unexamined life is not worth living. The lesson of this latest jeremiad is that we are all but the sum of our self-deceptions, dating back to birth and perhaps beyond.

29 GILROY, HARRY. "A Million Sales for Willy Loman." New York Times (March 8), p. 36.
    Miller receives gold copy of the title page of Death of a Salesman from Viking Press to celebrate the sale of the millionth copy of the play. On The Price, chastises American critics for misunderstanding the play, considers Victor Franz an antithesis of Willy Loman but a descendant of John Proctor, and argues that Walter Franz is the "real, integral dropout."

30 GOTTFRIED, MARTIN. "The Price." Women's Wear Daily (February 8).
    Review. Though Miller still has a "strength, an ease with the language, a dedication to reason, and an ability to create striking characters," The Price is "old-fashioned, carelessly written and displays Miller as a slackening artist." The familiar discussion in Miller of the responsibility of one human being to another in a family situation is "overcomplicated for the wrong reasons and its genuine subtleties are oversimplified." The Price is, "in a real way, a failure in logic." Reprinted: 1968.40.

31 GRUEN, JOSEPH. "Portrait of the Playwright at Fifty," in his Close Up. New York: Viking, pp. 58-63.
    Reprint of 1965.28.

32 HEWES, HENRY. "Used People." Saturday Review, 51 (February 24), 38.
    The Price is entertaining, memorable, and searching theatre, despite its inconclusiveness and the eventual tiresomeness of the brothers' confrontation.

33 KANFER, STEFAN. "Miller Plays Variations on Salesman." Life, 64 (March 8), 18.
    The Price is retrogressive, half-Ibsen, half-Yiddish theater. Miller cannot always rely on a minor character like Gregory Solomon to rescue him and must find a dramatically viable way out of the forties and into the sixties.

34 KERR, WALTER. "Mr. Miller's Two New Faces." New York Times (February 18), sec. II, pp. 1, 3.

1968

Review of New York opening of The Price. In the character of Gregory Solomon, Miller reveals a "becoming strain
of wry kindliness," but there is a new uncertainty in the
play as a whole. The play's lack of a real ending is a
dramatic defect but "makes the author rather more troubled
and human" than before. Reprinted: 1968.40; 1969.21.

35   KLOTEN, EDGAR. "Miller in Hartford." Drama Criticism, 11:
48-49.
Review of Hartford, Connecticut, production of A View
from the Bridge. It is a "stunning, and corrosive" play
that "stimulates a kind of modern purgation--a realization
of the complexity of the human condition."

36   KOENIG, RICHARD E. "Arthur Miller's The Price." Catholic
World, 207 (May), 74-75.
Review of Broadway premier. Finds The Price a fine and
absorbing work, a "modern morality play thinly disguised
as drama." Victor Franz is the most sympathetic of the
three principal characters, though he could not accept his
"right" choice and paid the price of destructive hatred of
self and brother.

37   KROLL, JACK, "The Crucible." Newsweek, 71 (February 19), 104.
Review of New York premier of The Price. A typical
Miller play in its preoccupation with the family ("Miller's
perennial crucible") and in its combination of undoubted
talents with horrendous faults. Its power comes from
Miller's "insight into the dynamics and dialects of guilt,"
but its flaw is that in letting his own life into the
debate on guilt, he "settles for half-measures rather than
driving straight for the breaking point," as do Strindberg,
Dostoevski, Kafka, and even O'Neill.

38   "Letters on The Price." New York Times (May 12), sec. II,
p. 5.
Nine letters to the editor on the Bermel-Clurman dialogue regarding The Price and Miller's merits and shortcomings as a playwright. See 1968.12; 1968.20.

39   LEWIS, THEOPHILUS. "The Price." America, 118 (March 30),
422-23.
Review of New York debut of play. Though Miller leaves
unanswered the question of moral responsibility his play
raises (the price Walter pays for filial negligence), it is
exciting drama.

40 MARLOWE, JOAN and BETTY BLAKE, eds. "The Price." New York
      Theatre Critics' Reviews, 29 (February 8), 334-35, 352-54.
        Reprints New York critics' reviews: Barnes (1968.6);
      Chapman (1968.19); Cooke (1968.23); Gottfried (1968.30);
      Kerr (1968.34); Watts (1968.55).

41 MONAGHAN, CHARLES. "Arthur Miller as Gnostic." National
      Review, 20 (May 21), 511-12.
        Summarizes New York critics' reviews of The Price, which
      is Miller's variation on the Gnostic theme that knowledge
      guarantees salvation. In The Price, knowledge leads to
      unhappiness ever after. Because of Gregory Solomon, it is
      Miller's best play since Salesman.

42 NELSON, BENJAMIN. "Avant-Garde Dramatics from Ibsen to
      Ionesco." Psychoanalytic Review, 55: 505-12.
        Credits Miller and others with establishing sexual
      pathology and perversion as familiar elements in drama.
      Miller, Williams, Albee are Freudians, whereas Ibsen and
      Strindberg were proto-Freudians, and Beckett, Ionesco, and
      Genêt post-Freudians.

43 PALMER, TONY. "Artistic Privilege." London Magazine, 8 (May),
      47-48.
        Plot summary of The Price.

44 RAINES, MARY B. "The Price." Library Journal, 93 (April 15),
      1649-50.
        In this "powerful, compassionate play, Miller has dis-
      sected the frailties of man with consummate artistry."
      Reprinted: 1968.45.

45 _____. "The Price," in Library Journal Book Review. New
      York: Bowker, p. 656.
        Reprint of 1968.44.

46 RAYMONT, HENRY. "Roundup of Writers in Prague Reported."
      New York Times (August 31), pp. 1, 2.
        Commenting on the "shocking news" reports received by
      the American Center of P.E.N. that Soviet intelligence
      agents were holding in detention and beating Czech writers,
      Miller announces his intention to gather signatures from
      American writers for an appeal to the Soviet Government and
      the Union of Soviet writers on behalf of their Czech
      colleagues.

47 RICHARDSON, JACK. "Theater Chronicle." Commentary, 45 (April),
      74-76.

1968

Where Miller's earlier plays strove to make the mundane appear profound, The Price pretends to nothing. Unlike Chekhov and O'Neill, who find articulation in all human life and bring it to the stage without inventing a false dramatic coherence, Miller simply "provides a dilemma and some epitaphs for his characters in a language that is never precise or startling." We are left only with the author's heavy insistence that a meaningful question about life is being asked.

48 SIMON, JOHN. "Settling the Account: The Stage." Commonweal, 87 (March 1), 655-56.
    As before, Miller's model in The Price is Ibsen, but whereas Ibsen's plays concern themselves with the present as well as the past, The Price merely looks backward and "argues about what really happened back then." The play is improbable, awkward in construction, plastic in characterization, a "well-meaning, respectable, middlebrow anachronism."

49 _____. "Theatre Chronicle." Hudson Review, 21 (Summer), 322.
    Review of The Price. The play is characterized by a "relentless retrogression," an "obsessive dredging up of the same family trauma found in most of Miller's plays." Miller is even looking backward technically and ideologically: neither the style nor the socio-political aspect is relevant to our time. Abridged: 1974.19.

50 STAMBUSKY, ALAN A. "Arthur Miller: Aristotelian Canons in the Twentieth Century Drama," in Modern American Drama. Edited by William E. Taylor. Deland, Fla.: Everett/ Edwards, pp. 91-115.
    Finds Miller's plays lacking as Aristotelian tragedies and Miller's tragic theories (found mainly in his "Tragedy and the Common Man") lacking in a real understanding of the class concept of tragedy. Thus "his attempts to derive classical connotations from his tragedy of the common man are abortive." Miller's strength as a dramatist "lies in his understanding of and compassion for human beings in their most personal relationships." His weakness is the "extreme intellectualism," expressed almost without his realizing it, in the plays.

51 STANDLEY, FRED L. "An Echo of Milton in The Crucible." Notes and Queries, n.s. 15 (August), 303.
    Giles Corey's plea for "more weight," as great stones are placed on his chest, is similar to a passage in John Milton's "Another on the Same," on the death of a university mail carrier. See 1969.15.

52 STREIKER, LOWELL D. "Sons and Brothers." <u>Christian Century</u>,
    85 (March 27), 405-406.
        Review of Broadway premier of <u>The Price</u>. Miller's best
    play in many years, <u>The Price</u> heightens the audience's self-
    knowledge by showing that each of us "chooses his role and
    must play it until the destroying end." The choice is free,
    but once made all freedom is lost.

53 TAUBMAN, HOWARD. "<u>The Price</u> in Tel Aviv." <u>New York Times</u>
    (October 19), sec. II, p. 29.
        Discusses changes in characterization in Hebrew produc-
    tion of <u>The Price</u>. Since other characters are made Jewish,
    Gregory Solomon has an "undeclared yet understood mutuality
    of origins with them," and since Solomon does not steal the
    show as in New York, the play "takes on more shapeliness."

54 THERESE, SISTER MARIAN. "Miller in Princeton." <u>Drama
    Criticism</u>, 11: 49-51.
        Review of Princeton, New Jersey, production of <u>The
    Crucible</u>. Both as "an existential tragedy and a social
    protest drama fraught with contemporary significance,"
    <u>Crucible</u> fails in this production. The director's opinion
    is that, because of weak dialogue, actors must "put a great
    deal of depth into these lines to achieve characterization."
    In repertory theater, insufficient rehearsal time and the
    actors' inexperience often make this difficult.

55 WATTS, RICHARD. "Conflict Between Two Brothers." <u>New York
    Post</u> (February 8).
        Review. <u>The Price</u> lacks dramatic power because although
    it is "serious, intense, thoughtful," with "conscientious
    ruminations and excellent acting," it lacks an "effective
    resolution and steady interest." The price each man must
    pay for his course in life remains vague. The play is most
    interesting when the "enlivening character" of Gregory
    Solomon is on stage. Reprinted: 1968.40.

56 WEALES, GERALD. "The Song of Solomon." <u>Reporter</u>, 38 (March
    21), 42, 44.
        Despite echoes of Miller's earlier plays, <u>The Price</u>
    "belongs with his recent plays as an examination of guilt
    and the attempt to escape it." Though Miller sometimes
    veers toward soap opera with his ponderous characters and
    .situations, the play is redeemed by Gregory Solomon, who
    is not only the funniest character Miller has created, but
    a dramatic image (as Victor's true father) as well.

1968

57   WEATHERBY, W. J.   "Messengers or Actors." The Guardian
     (Manchester) (February 17), p. 7.
         Review of New York production of The Price. A fine
     play but Miller manqué. Ever since The Misfits Miller has
     failed to push to the bottom of his dramatic situations.
     He "strains to be reasonable at the expense of the wildness
     of the spirit," and so the ending does not seem Miller's
     true ending.

58   WILLIAMS, RAYMOND.   "Arthur Miller," in his Drama from Ibsen
     to Brecht. London: Chatto & Windus, pp. 267-76.
         A critical survey of Miller's plays through After the
     Fall. Discusses Miller's debt to Ibsen, Marxist alien-
     ation, and German expressionism. The common thread in his
     plays is the breaking and destruction of a man through
     guilt. With After the Fall, Miller moved to the alterna-
     tive or Tennessee Williams tradition in the American Theater
     of the "direct exposure of inarticulate private feeling."

1969

1   ANON.   "Arthur Miller," in Two Hundred Contemporary Authors.
     Edited by Barbara Harte and Carolyn Riley. Vols. 1-4.
     Detroit: Gale, pp. 189-91.
         Updates 1967.1.

2   ANON.   "15 Americans Meet Soviet Group in Rye." New York
     Times (January 21), p. 3.
         Miller participates in fifth Dartmouth Conference of
     U.S. and Soviet citizens aimed at arms limitation and the
     "expansion of exchanges in many fields."

3   ANON.   "The Price Acclaimed by Critics in London." New York
     Times (March 6), p. 36.
         Summary of unanimously laudatory reviews of London pro-
     duction of The Price.

4   ANON.   "The Price Will Close." New York Times (January 14),
     p. 36.
         After 425 performances, the original New York production
     of The Price will close. It will be produced in London in
     February 1969.

5   ANON.   "16 Western Intellectuals Score Soviet Attacks on
     Solzhenitsyn." New York Times (December 5), p. 47.
         Miller signs letter to the Soviet Government condemning
     the expulsion from Russia of Aleksandr Solzhenitsyn.

6   BERGERON, DAVID M. "Arthur Miller's The Crucible and Nathaniel
    Hawthorne: Some Parallels." English Journal, 58 (January),
    47-55.
        Whereas Salesman is a "low tragedy," The Crucible is a
    "high" or classical tragedy. If Willy is the typical figure
    of modern drama, John Proctor is the "sort who for centuries
    has engendered responses of admiration from the audience."
    Discusses parallels in setting, characters, and themes
    between The Crucible and Hawthorne's The Scarlet Letter.

7   BLUMBERG, PAUL. "Sociology and Social Literature: Work
    Alienation in the Plays of Arthur Miller." American
    Quarterly, 21 (Summer), 310 (supplement).
        Miller's plays broaden our perspective of work alien-
    ation, a subtheme in Miller's preoccupation with contempor-
    ary man's "alienation from a sense of community or
    relatedness to others."

8   BROWN, FRANCES. "Miller Opens P.E.N. Congress in France."
    New York Times (September 16), p. 43.
        Miller opens thirty-sixth international congress of the
    P.E.N. Club, appealing to young writers to "make it apparent
    that the writer belongs to the street and not to the power."

9   BRUSTEIN, ROBERT. "The Unseriousness of Arthur Miller" and
    "The Memory of Heroism," in his The Third Theatre. New
    York: Knopf, pp. 103-106, 242-44.
        Reprints 1960.8; 1968.17.

10 CORRIGAN, ROBERT W., ed. Arthur Miller: A Collection of
    Critical Essays. Englewood Cliffs, N.J.: Prentice-Hall,
    176 pp.
        Reprints: 1953.40; 1959.26; 1960.13; 1960.28; 1964.12;
    1964.20; 1965.16; 1966.21; 1967.35; 1967.46; 1968.20;
    1968.24.

11 CURLEY, DOROTHY NYREN and MAURICE KRAMER and E. F. KRAMER,
    eds. Modern American Literature. Library of Literary
    Criticism. Fourth edition. New York: Ungar, pp. 338-45.
        Reprints excerpts from 1960.23: (1947.38; 1947.44;
    1949.41; 1949.51; 1949.54; 1949.71; 1949.73; 1949.83;
    1953.24; 1953.30; 1955.26; 1957.40); and 1960.24; 1963.9;
    1963.15; 1964.34; 1964.56; 1964.69; 1965.30; 1967.49.

12 CZIMER, JOZSEF. "Price and Value." New Hungarian Quarterly,
    10 (Winter), 169-74.
        Review of Budapest production of The Price, with dis-
    cussion of Miller's reputation in Hungary, his themes, and
    the difficulties encountered in staging the play.

1969

13   DEKLE, BERNARD. "Arthur Miller," in his <u>Profiles of Modern</u>
     <u>American Authors</u>. Rutland, Vt.: Tuttle, pp. 147-53.
         Brief sketch of Miller's life and career through <u>After</u>
     <u>the Fall</u>. The main strength of Miller's writing "lies in
     the authenticity of his characterization." Abridged:
     1973.23.

14   EVANS, RICHARD I. <u>Psychology and Arthur Miller</u>. Dialogues
     with Notable Contributors to Personality Theory, Vol. 5.
     New York: Dutton, 136 pp.
         Three extensive interviews with Miller on "The Writer
     as Creator," "The Writer and Psychology," and "The Writer
     and Society."

15   FERRIS, OLIVER H.P. "An Echo of Milton in <u>The Crucible</u>."
     <u>Notes and Queries</u>, n.s. 16 (July), 268.
         Rejects <u>The Crucible</u>'s implied indebtedness to Milton
     (<u>see</u> 1968.51) as "ridiculous." Miller's attribution to
     Corey of the phrase "more weight" is based on historical
     research.

16   FUNKE, LEWIS. "Stars Help Miller Film TV Antiwar Allegory."
     <u>New York Times</u> (November 17), p. 58.
         An account of the filming on Miller's Connecticut estate
     of <u>The Reason Why</u>, a one-act script intended for television,
     starring Eli Wallach and Robert Ryan. Miller concedes that
     the play is somewhat autobiographical, and that the war in
     Vietnam had a part in his writing it.

17   GENTLEMAN, DAVID. "<u>In Russia</u>." <u>New Statesman</u>, 78 (December
     5), 826.
         An unromantic, neutral book about Russia, Miller's
     essay accompanying Inge Morath's photographs is a "most
     penetrating and convincing picture of both the good and
     bad aspects of an artist's life in such a society."

18   HAYASHI, TETSUMARO. <u>Arthur Miller Criticism, 1930-1967</u>.
     Metuchen, N.J.: Scarecrow, 149 pp.
         The first attempt at a "comprehensive bibliography,"
     this work also "attempts to include all of the known pub-
     lished and unpublished works of Miller." Revised: 1976.7.

19   HAYMAN, RONALD. "Arthur Miller Talks About His Play." <u>Times</u>
     (London) (February 15), p. 19.
         Interview. Miller discusses the origin of the character
     of Gregory Solomon in <u>The Price</u>, his interest in the play
     in finding "what it takes to be a person who refuses to

adopt the sex-and-success motives of the society," the role
of the past in the play and his unfinished work--some fifty
plays and "more poetry than most of the poets write."
Expanded: 1970.14.

20   HEILMAN, ROBERT B. "Salesmen's Deaths: Documentary and Myth."
     Shenandoah, 20 (Spring), 20-28.
        Detailed comparison and contrast of Death of a Salesman
     with Eudora Welty's story "The Death of a Traveling
     Salesman."

21   KERR, WALTER. "The View from the Mirror" and "The Other
     Arthur Miller," in his Thirty Plays Hath November. New
     York: Simon and Schuster, pp. 214-20.
        Expands 1964.40. Reprints 1968.34.

22   MACEY, SAMUEL L. "Non-heroic Tragedy: A Pedigree for American
     Tragic Drama." Comparative Literature Studies, 6 (March),
     1-19.
        Examines the influence of European "non-heroic tragedy"
     on the American tragedies of Miller, Williams and O'Neill.
     Briefly discusses Death of a Salesman, A View from the
     Bridge, After the Fall.

23   MAINI, DARSHAN S. "The Moral Vision of Arthur Miller," in
     Indian Essays in American Literature. Edited by Sujit
     Mukherjee and D.V.K. Raghavacharyulu. Bombay: Popular
     Prokashan, pp. 85-96.
        General survey of Miller's thought, touching on such
     varied topics as the roots of his morality, the universality
     of his plays, his Depression background, the political ele-
     ments in his plays, sex and sin, and Marxism.

24   MARTIN ROBERT A. "Arthur Miller: Tragedy and Commitment."
     Michigan Quarterly Review, 8 (Summer), 176-78.
        Interview. Miller discusses After the Fall, his con-
     cept of tragedy, and agrees that at the end of the play
     Quentin is like John F. Kennedy in that he is an "idealist
     without illusions."

25   _____. "The Creative Experience of Arthur Miller: An Inter-
     view." Educational Theater Journal, 21 (October), 310-17.
        Miller discusses his nondebt to Ibsen, the origins of
     his plays, the autobiographical elements in After the Fall,
     and the Jewishness of his characters, among other matters.

26   NIGHTINGALE, BENEDICT. "Family Sores." New Statesman, 77
     (March 14), 384.

1969

Review of London opening of The Price. It is hard to believe the "spiritual transformation" Miller calls for in his play is "possible or even desirable." The "lies and failures of his characters" and the "dreary world of negatives" they inhabit are what define them. "Family sores can only be profitably scratched for so long."

27   PARTRIDGE, C.J. Death of a Salesman. Oxford: Blackwell, 57 pp.
Written for British school, college and university students, this study of Salesman includes discussion questions and class projects, in addition to the social and dramatic context of the play. The "crucial factors" in the play are Willy's personal intensity, which is both a strength and a weakness, and the resultant dramatic intensity.

28   PORTER, THOMAS E. "Acres of Diamonds and the Long Shadow of the Law," in his Myth and Modern American Drama. Detroit: Wayne State Univ. Press, pp. 127-52, 177-99.
Miller denounces the American success myth in Salesman but fails to find any real substitute for it. Because the audience cannot solve this dilemma either, it becomes involved in Willy's sufferings. The Crucible explores attitudes responsible for the failure of court trial ritual, which embodies the opposition between two American ideals: the need for law and law enforcement, and the right of the minority to dissent.

29   RAHV, PHILIP. "Arthur Miller and the Fallacy of Profundity," in his Literature and the Sixth Sense. Boston: Houghton Mifflin, pp. 385-91.
Reprint of 1965.50.

30   RAYMONT, HENRY. "Miller Refuses Greek Book Plan." New York Times (July 3), p. 29.
Miller refuses to allow his works to be published in Greece until the "repressive" policies of Greece's military regime are ended.

31   _____. "P.E.N. Congress May Discuss Censorship of Soviet Writers." New York Times (August 12), p. 36.
In his capacity as international president of P.E.N., Miller urges extensive debate on the conditions in Russia that led to the defection of the Soviet author, Anatoly Kuznetsov.

1969

32 RENO, RAYMOND H. "Arthur Miller and the Death of God."
    Texas Studies in Literature and Language, 11 (Summer),
    1069-87.
        Miller's plays constitute a sprawling treatment of a
    single theme, the death of God. Each play is a revision
    of an earlier dramatic version of the theme, and a further
    step in the dismantling of the Christian myth.

33 SALISBURY, HARRISON E. "In Russia." New York Times Book
    Review (December 14), pp. 1, 57.
        Miller and Inge Morath capture the contradictions of
    Russia, something Miller is well suited to do since he has
    "known persecution and harassment in his own country."
    Because Miller understands himself and America well, he can
    "judge accurately what he saw in Russia."

34 SHENKER, ISRAEL. "Arthur Miller Adjusting The Price for
    London." New York Times (February 15), p. 20.
        Miller visits the set of The Price to socialize and sug-
    gest improvements before the opening of the London production.

35 _____. "Arthur Miller Expresses Criticism of the Soviet
    Literary Scene." New York Times (August 17), p. 26.
        Summary of Miller's report on the situation of the writer
    in Russia which will be published in Harper's magazine in
    September, and later in book form as In Russia.

36 WEALES, GERALD C. "Williams and Miller," in his The Jumping
    Off Place. New York: Macmillan, pp. 14-23.
        Revision of 1962.37.

37 WEST, CONSTANCE C. "The Use of Persuasion in Selected Plays
    of Arthur Miller." Ph.D. dissertation, University of
    Minnesota, 1968. Dissertation Abstracts, 29 (April), 3718A.
        A rhetorical analysis of Miller's plays, with emphasis
    on Death of a Salesman and The Crucible, to assess his use
    of persuasive methods.

38 WHITEHEAD, ROBERT. "Preface," in Psychology and Arthur Miller.
    By Richard I. Evans. New York: Dutton, pp. xi-xvii.
        In the context of Evans' interviews with Miller
    (1969.14), discusses the writer's sense of the psychological
    motivations of his work. Miller did not consciously realize
    After the Fall might be construed as a play about Marilyn
    Monroe until he had worked on it for eighteen months.

39 WINEGARTEN, RENEE. "The World of Arthur Miller." Jewish
    Quarterly, 17 (Summer), 48-53.

1970

Review of The Price for English readers. Gregory Solomon
is the "first positive symbol of that dignity and self-
respect which his earlier characters found only in death";
another new note is the idea of life as a farce, symbolized
by the laughing record. Miller's most mature work since
The Crucible, The Price stresses the precariousness of
American society. Summarizes Miller's career and his reputation in England versus America; criticizes the lack of a
"larger dimension" in all Miller's plays but The Crucible
and perhaps The Price. "The scale of a play alters when it
is a man's immortal soul to be lost, rather than his innocence, righteousness or self-respect."

<u>1970</u>

1   ANON. "Brandeis Lauds Two Generations in Arts Awards." <u>New
York Times</u> (May 18), p. 38.
        Miller receives a Creative Arts Award from Brandeis
University for "eloquent and stirring statements--in drama,
story and social action."

2   ANON. "The Chemistry of Travel." <u>Times Literary Supplement</u>
(January 22), p. 76.
        Miller's essay in <u>In Russia</u> asks accurate, disturbing,
probing questions, despite the fact that "no visitor to the
Soviet Union can expect a better time than an acceptable
playwright."

3   ANON. "Teacher Is Backed in Stand on Pledge." <u>New York Times</u>
(February 23), p. 24.
        Miller and more than two dozen residents of Roxbury,
Connecticut, sign a statement protesting the suspension of
a teacher who refused to say the Pledge of Allegiance with
her classes.

4   BATES, MERETE. "<u>Death of a Salesman</u> in Bolton." <u>The Guardian</u>
(Manchester) (April 1), p. 8.
        Review of Octogon Theatre, Bolton, England, revival of
<u>Salesman</u>. The play is difficult to produce because the
"sense of brute push and tensions is never quite as strong
in England" and because of the shifting time sequences.

5   BERGMAN, HERBERT. "The Interior of a Heart: <u>The Crucible</u>
and <u>The Scarlet Letter</u>." <u>University College Quarterly</u>,
15 (May), 27-32.
        Discusses similarities and differences between <u>The
Crucible</u> and <u>The Scarlet Letter</u>. In the pluralistic

twentieth century the violation of an individual's sense
of self is the greatest sin, whereas in "Hawthorne's order
the sin is adultery and the lie of its concealment."

6   BIGSBY, C.W.E. "What Price Arthur Miller?: An Analysis of
    The Price." Twentieth Century Literature, 16 (January),
    16-25.
         After the Fall and The Price penetrate beyond the "bland
    facade of success" and the "social and psychological ration-
    alizations" of Miller's earlier plays, to examine his "guilt
    as a survivor" of the persecution of Jews in World War II.
    With some of his personal ghosts laid in After the Fall,
    Miller could "maintain the tension between determinism and
    freedom" in The Price and create a character like Gregory
    Solomon.

7   BURG, VICTOR. "The Arthur Millers in Russia." Christian
    Science Monitor (January 8), p. 17.
         Review of In Russia. Miller's essay accompanying Inge
    Morath's photographs is a "nonsequential series of encoun-
    ters with other writers and the country itself" that is
    "strictly personal and concernedly honest."

8   DRIVER, TOM F. "Arthur Miller: Portrait of a Playwright."
    Saturday Review, 53 (July 25), 35.
         Review of Benjamin Nelson's book (see 1970.17). Argues
    that what makes Salesman is not Willy's character, or story,
    or the image of Brooklyn in the play, but the "way all
    these serve to provide the actor with grist for his mill."
    It is the performances of actors (Robinson, Cobb, Dunnock,
    Marshall, Kennedy, Gray) that "comprise the substance of
    Miller's stage and screen career." Nelson fails to address
    Miller's theatricality. Abridged: 1974.19.

9   EISINGER, CHESTER E. "Focus on Death of a Salesman," in
    American Dreams, American Nightmares. Edited by David
    Madden. Carbondale: Southern Illinois University Press,
    pp. 165-74.
         Salesman romanticizes the rural-agrarian American dream
    and is ambiguous about the business-success American dream.
    Miller is unwilling or unable to take a firm position with
    respect to American culture. Loman's failure is not to be
    equated with America's. Abridged: 1976.19.

10 EPSTEIN, ARTHUR D. "Arthur Miller's Major Plays: A Critical
    Study." Ph.D. dissertation, Indiana University. Disserta-
    tion Abstracts International, 30 (May), 4983 A.

1970

Traces theme of the individual's relationship to himself
and to his world in Miller's plays. The latest play, The
Price, suggests there "is no solution to the tension between
the need for fidelity to the self and responsibility to
others." A balance of conflicting forces may be obtained,
though, through a self-definition that permits reliable
assessment of responsibility to self and others.

11 FLANAGAN, JAMES K. "Arthur Miller: A Study in Sources and
Themes." Ph.D. dissertation, University of Notre Dame.
Dissertation Abstracts International, 30 (May), 4984A.
Examines the relationship between Miller's life and
literary works as manifested in three basic themes: family,
society, and women. Includes works difficult to obtain
because of Miller's stringent conditions upon their use."

12 GROSS, THEODORE L. "Arthur Miller," in Representative Men.
Edited by Theodore L. Gross. New York: Free Press,
pp. 276-77.
Brief introduction, discussing Miller's views of tragedy
and the typical Miller hero.

13 GWERTZMAN, BERNARD. "Soviet Asks Tight Ideology Curb." New
York Times (November 24), p. 3.
In order to "prevent the shadow of liberalism from
obscuring the clarity of ideological positions," Miller's
plays have been removed from the Russian theatre repertoire.
Miller's book In Russia, it is implied, may have been partly
responsible for the ban.

14 HAYMAN, RONALD. Arthur Miller. London: Heinemann; New York:
Ungar, 1972, 141 pp.
Discusses plays through The Price, gives dates and casts
of original productions, expands a London Times interview
with Miller (see 1969.19). Miller's social plays "analyze
in terms of process," asking how something came to be the
way it is. He appears old-fashioned because he "assumes
that memory does not change the past and that events have
causal connections." Argues that Miller is the "most
Sartrean of contemporary dramatists," though he is inferior
as a thinker and his plays are intellectually inferior to
his writings about them. It is difficult for him to articulate his ideas in drama because he avoids intellectual
heroes. Finally, the unconscious personal subject of his
plays is slightly different from their ostensible social
subject.

15 MARTIN, ROBERT A. "Arthur Miller and The Meaning of Tragedy."
    Modern Drama, 13 (May), 34-39.
        Interview. Miller discusses changes in his conception
    of tragedy, and the meaning of After the Fall.

16 MURTHY, V. RAMA. "Death of a Salesman," in his American
    Expressionistic Drama. Delhi: Doaba House, pp. 73-96.
        An introductory survey of Miller's plays through The
    Price, with emphasis on Death of a Salesman. Brief bio-
    graphical sketch and selected bibliography.

17 NELSON, BENJAMIN. Arthur Miller: Portrait of a Playwright.
    New York: McKay; London: Peter Owen, 336 pp.
        A close analysis of Miller's plays and career through
    The Price. Miller's strengths are a concern with human
    destiny that transcends politics and economics, a challeng-
    ing belief in man's ability to exercise responsibility, and
    a meticulous craftsmanship. Adverse criticism of his
    didacticism and polemicism fails to recognize that the
    "gulf between pamphleteering and playwriting is, most of
    the time, bridged by works that are stunning dramatic
    achievements." Includes selected bibliography.

18 REEVE, F. D. "In Russia." Book World (January 4), p. 11.
        Review. The book is superficial, pretentious, and arty,
    tries for too much, and is erroneous in its comparisons
    between Russia and the U.S. Its virtues are its sincerity
    and candor. Miller believes what Western liberals want to
    believe about Russia, ignoring facts such as the continuing
    repression of intellectuals. Finally, the book is drab and
    serious, lacking any of the ebullience and humor of Russian
    life.

19 ROBOTHAM, JOHN S. "In Russia," Library Journal, 95
    (February 1), 496.
        Describes contents of In Russia, "one of the most inter-
    esting of Russian travel books." Reprinted: 1970.20.

20 _____. "In Russia," in Library Journal Book Review. New
    York: Bowker, p. 316.
        Reprint of 1970.19.

21 SCHRAEPEN, EDMOND. "Arthur Miller's Constancy: A Note on
    Miller as a Short Story Writer." Revue des Langues
    Vivantes, 36: 62-71.
        The themes of "I Don't Need You Any More" and "The
    Prophecy" are similar to those of Miller's plays. "The

1970

Prophecy" in particular has common elements with <u>After the Fall</u> and the earlier <u>All My Sons</u> and <u>Death of a Salesman</u>.

22   SIDORSKY, DAVID. "Miller Disputed on Solzhenitzyn." <u>New York Times</u> (December 26), p. 16.
       Disputes Miller's opinion (<u>New York Times</u>, December 10, 1970) that Solzhenitzyn "confined his attacks to Stalin." In <u>The First Circle</u> he attacks many aspects of the current regime and Western fellow-travellers as well.

23   UNGAR, HARRIETT. "The Writings of and About Arthur Miller: A Check List, 1936-1967." <u>Bulletin of the New York Public Library</u>, 74 (February), 107-34.
       A selective "bio-bibliography" limited to materials in English and Western European languages written from a literary point of view.

24   WHITE, SIDNEY HOWARD. <u>Guide to Arthur Miller</u>. Merrill Guides. Columbus, Ohio: Charles E. Merrill, 47 pp.
       Survey of Miller's major accomplishments and life through <u>The Price</u>. Devoting half his pages to <u>Salesman</u>, White discusses tragic elements, Miller's debt to Ibsen, and form in the plays. Miller is both an intellectual and an artist whose idealistic search for self-understanding recalls the Greek commandment to "know thyself."

25   WILLIS, ROBERT J. "Arthur Miller's <u>The Crucible</u>: Relevant for All Times." <u>Faculty Journal</u> (East Stroudsburg, Pa., State College), 1: 5-14.
       Because it "points up the split between the private life of a man and his public social life," there is contemporary relevance in <u>The Crucible</u>. The slogan "America, love it or leave it" presents a choice akin to Proctor's between neglecting conscience and truth in order to live or upholding conscience and truth and dying. Similarly, Miller's theme that "there are individuals dedicated to evil, who, under the guise of doing good, knowingly condemn their fellow men" is universal.

1971

1   ANDERSON, ROBERT <u>et al</u>. "Repression in Brazil." <u>New York Times</u> (April 24), p. 28.
       A letter, signed by Miller and others, protesting the arrest and political harassment of the Brazilian theatrical director, Augusto Boal, after his return to Brazil from a U.S. visit.

162

1971

2   ANON. "Notes on People." New York Times (December 9), p. 59.
        Miller is elected to the American Academy of Arts and
    Letters, a fifty-member "inner body" of the 250-member
    National Institute of Arts and Letters.

3   ASHLEY, FRANKLIN B. "The Theme of Guilt and Responsibility
    in the Plays of Arthur Miller." Ph.D. dissertation,
    University of South Carolina, 1970. Dissertation Abstracts
    International, 31 (April), 5349A.
        Examines the central character in each of Miller's seven
    major plays to show development of his major themes: that
    "man cannot divorce himself from the rest of humanity" and
    that "guilt is universal."

4   ATKINSON, BROOKS. "A Theater of Life." Saturday Review, 50
    (February 25), 53.
        Compares Tennessee Williams and Miller as short story
    writers in The Knightly Quest and I Don't Need You Any More.
    While "The Misfits" is a "little masterpiece of impromptu
    life," Miller's collection will not enhance his reputation.

5   BARNES, CLIVE. "Miller Version of An Enemy of the People."
    New York Times (March 12), p. 26.
        Review of Lincoln Center revival of Miller's adaptation
    of Ibsen's An Enemy of the People. One of Miller's best
    plays, it is not really intended as a realistic or an
    ecological drama. More than Ibsen's original, it deals
    with issues rather than people. Miller is "at his best
    in the confrontation between the two brothers; at his
    worst in conveying the atmosphere and essence of Ibsen's
    original."

6   BENTLEY, ERIC. "Arthur Miller," in Thirty Years of Treason.
    Edited by Eric Bentley. New York: Viking, pp. 791-825.
        Excerpts from Miller's appearance before the House
    Committee on Un-American Activities, June 21, 1956.
    Preface discusses Miller's left-wing involvement and after-
    math of Congressional hearing.

7   BLEICH, DAVID. "Psychological Bases of Learning from Litera-
    ture." College English, 33 (October), 32-45.
        Bleich's individual experience and teaching experience
    with Death of a Salesman confirm the view that literature
    instructs by letting the reader rediscover a personally
    known "moral" learned earlier from a close adult. If
    literary enjoyment is to contribute to an individual's
    growth process, there must be at least an emotional or
    intraphysical moral, if not a religious one.

1971

8   CALTA, LOUIS. "Miller Has a New Play for Broadway." <u>New
     York Times</u> (September 9), p. 50.
          Miller's <u>The Creation of the World and Other Business</u>
     will open in January or February 1972. Described by
     Miller as a "catastrophic comedy," it was begun a year
     earlier together with a "play on the Depression and contem-
     porary America as seen through the perspective of the last
     40 years."

9   CLURMAN, HAROLD. "Biographical Notes and Editor's Introduc-
     tion," in <u>The Portable Arthur Miller</u>. Edited by Harold
     Clurman. Viking Portable Library. New York: Viking,
     pp. vii-xxv.
          A critical survey of Miller's output through <u>The Price</u>
     by the director of national companies of several Miller
     plays. Miller's plays are poetic in "conception and inten-
     sity," though not in language. It is the poetry of the
     "impassioned moralist" seeking to convey not so much a
     thought as an "emotion which goes beyond the factual mate-
     rial employed." His appeal to Europeans is based not only
     on his criticism of America but his "vigorous, optimistic
     moral concern, which is one of the most enduring contribu-
     tions of our American heritage."

10   _____. "An Enemy of the People." <u>Nation</u>, 212 (March 29),
     411-12.
          Review of revival of Miller's adaptation of Ibsen's <u>An
     Enemy of the People</u>. Objects to the adaptation being con-
     sidered anything but Ibsen's play.

11   COHN, RUBY. "The Articulate Victims of Arthur Miller," in
     her <u>Dialogue in American Drama</u>. Bloomington: Indiana
     University Press, pp. 68-96.
          Discusses dialogue in Miller's plays. If O'Neill was
     the first American playwright to convey a feeling of
     observed life rather than books read in his dialogue,
     Miller furthers the feeling through "dignified, uneducated
     characters who articulate functionally in dramatic context."
     Abridged: 1974.19.

12   FREEDMAN, MORRIS. "The Jewishness of Arthur Miller," in his
     <u>American Drama in Social Context</u>. Carbondale: Southern
     Illinois University Press, pp. 43-58.
          Though Miller's career is an archetype of the mid-century
     Jewish intellectual hero, his plays are ethnically anony-
     mous. In 1930's liberal fashion Miller is arguing both that
     Jews should not be discriminated against and that there are
     no Jews, only undifferentiated Americans.

13 FUNKE, LEWIS. "By Arthur Miller." New York Times (February
    7), sec. II, pp. 1, 22.
        Miller is reported to be writing a play on the Great
    Depression, a subject he had attempted before in unpub-
    lished plays. Studs Terkel's Hard Times is said to have
    given Miller "a new spur to a full-scale treatment of the
    subject."

14 _____. "Miller--Before the Fall." New York Times (October
    3), sec. II, pp. 1, 8.
        Miller denies that his comic success with Gregory
    Solomon in The Price made him decide to write his full-
    length comedy, The Creation of the World and Other Business.
    He assures readers that his untitled play, for which Studs
    Terkel's Hard Times provided impetus, has not been abandoned.

15 GEISINGER, MARION. "Arthur Miller," in her Plays, Players,
    & Playwrights. New York: Hart, pp. 591-600, passim.
        Plot outlines and brief comments on Miller's plays.

16 GILL, BRENDAN. "Bad Old Days." New Yorker, 47 (March 20),
    93-94.
        Review of Lincoln Center production of Miller's adapta-
    tion of Ibsen's An Enemy of the People. While Stockman
    and his brother are played very well, Miller's translation
    is "ugly and inaccurate."

17 GILMAN, RICHARD. "Still Falling" and "Getting It off His
    Chest, But Is It Art?," in his Common and Uncommon Masks.
    New York: Random House, pp. 152-55, 156-59.
        Reprints of 1964.30; 1964.31.

18 GOTTFRIED, MARTIN. "An Enemy of the People." Women's Wear
    Daily (March 15).
        Review of revival of Miller's adaptation of Ibsen's
    An Enemy of the People. The revival is "dull and pointless"
    because relevance (water pollution and the suppression of
    truth by political and business interests) is not "reason
    enough to do a play"; because it "confuses political-
    social interest with theater value"; because Miller's
    adaptation "overloads the original with message at the cost
    of artistic qualities"; and because the original is "not of
    lasting value anyway." Reprinted: 1971.30.

19 GOULD, JACK. "Miller's The Price." New York Times (February
    4), p. 71.
        Review of television adaptation of The Price. The
    "tight focus of the camera captured superbly the agony of

1971

the two brothers," and the production benefited also from
a perfect cast, including George C. Scott, Colleen Dewhurst,
and David Burns.

20   GWERTZMAN, BERNARD.   "Jews in Soviet Are Warned Against Espous-
ing Zionism." New York Times (February 20), pp. 1-2.
Miller and others are criticized in an Isvestia article
for participating in a Brussels conference of Jewish organi-
zations to draw attention to the situation of Jews in the
Soviet Union.

21   HARRIS, LEONARD.   "An Enemy of the People." New York Theatre
Critics' Reviews, 32 (March 22), p. 337.
Television review of Miller's adaptation of Ibsen's An
Enemy of the People. The play and production lack subtlety,
though it is an "exciting fire-eating tract and a cathartic."
The audience is "cleansed of its indignation" and can return
to its "daily rounds of compromise."

22   HARROW, KENNETH J.   "The Transformation of the Rebel: A
Comparative Study of the Works and Development of Albert
Camus, Arthur Miller, and Ignazio Silone." Ph.D. dissertation, New York University, 1970. Dissertation Abstracts
International, 31 (June), 6609A-10A.
Compares Miller's thematic development with that of
Silone and Camus as all three writers changed from "rebels
to mature humanists." All My Sons is a stylistic watershed
for Miller and represents his "last attempt at totally committed theatre." After rejecting Communist ideology, Miller
attempts in his middle period to "construct an ethic
founded on rebellion and community." In the more recent
plays, "characterized by the psychological crisis of guilt
and unproductivity," concern for political action is replaced
by the need to act in good faith and to accept man's inevitable guilt as a way to authentic relationships.

23   HAYMAN, RONALD.   "Arthur Miller: Between Sartre and Society."
Encounter, 37 (November), 73-79.
Miller's plays now seem old-fashioned because he assumes
that the past does not change in remembering, and that it
is possible to write meaningfully about casual connections
between events. His social commitment makes him "the most
Sartrean of living dramatists," as does his concern with
individual freedom and resistance to mass conformity of
thought. Abridged: 1976.19.

24   HEATON, C. P. "Arthur Miller on <u>Death of a Salesman</u>." <u>Notes</u>
      <u>on Contemporary Literature</u>, 1 (January), 5.
          Quotes Miller's responses to questions on <u>Salesman</u> from
      students at Florida State University.

25   KALEM, T. E. "Moral Pollution." <u>Time</u>, 97 (March 22), 41.
          New York revival of Miller's adaptation of Ibsen's <u>An</u>
      <u>Enemy of the People</u>. Though in 1950, when Miller adapted
      the play, he was concerned with McCarthyism, today's audi-
      ences are more interested in its ecological aspects. By
      reducing Ibsen's emphasis on Stockman's Coriolanus complex,
      Miller shirks the issue of when or whether majority rule
      may be abrogated by a single individual and turns Stockman
      into a "pioneer spirit of the purely ethical life."
      Reprinted: 1971.30.

26   KROLL, JACK. "The People No." <u>Newsweek</u>, 77 (March 22),
      114-15.
          Review of New York revival of <u>An Enemy of the People</u>,
      Miller's adaptation of Ibsen's play. Where the original is
      rooted in Ibsen's "dark intransigence," Miller's version is
      a "vague, all purpose polemic" for any ideological crisis.
      Miller blunts the force of much of Ibsen's argument, espe-
      cially its criticism of the masses, by scaling it down to
      liberal moralizing. Reprinted: 1971.30.

27   LAVI, GAY HEIT. "Children of Civilization Fall Together: A
      Study of Style and Language in the Plays of Arthur Miller."
      Ph.D. dissertation, University of Pittsburgh. <u>Dissertation</u>
      <u>Abstracts International</u>, 32 (September), 1518A.
          Traces Miller's growing pessimism that leads him to
      "accept compromise in a fallen world." Emphasizes themes
      and problems of expression, methods of characterization,
      poetic approach to narrative, and use of mythological super-
      structures to lend themes universal significance. Analysis
      shows <u>Death of a Salesman</u> and <u>After the Fall</u> to be early
      and late peaks of Miller's development.

28   LEOPOLD, VIVIAN RUTH. "Man and Society in the Plays of Arthur
      Miller." Ph.D. dissertation, New York University. <u>Disser-</u>
      <u>tation Abstracts International</u>, 32 (November), 2833A.
          Finds that Miller's concern for the individual in rela-
      tion to society, as expressed in his essays, is reflected
      in his plays also, from the earliest unpublished efforts
      through <u>The Price</u>. Miller's essays "establish the theme
      that man can adapt to a rapidly changing technological
      civilization and retain his identity, if he understands his
      propensities toward creation and destruction, and learns to
      curb his destructive tendencies."

1971

29   LEWIS, ALLAN. "Death of a Salesman," in his The Contemporary
      Theatre. Second edition. New York: Crown, pp. 341-42,
      348-56.
           Though Salesman was "designed to indict the false values
      of a commercial world, it became the personal failure of
      one lost soul." Miller stood on the threshold of modern
      tragedy, then "substituted his favorite father-son con-
      flict." Miller's dilemma is revealed in the later plays,
      where no blame can be fixed nor any choice be absolute.

30   MARLOWE, JOAN and BETTY BLAKE, eds. "An Enemy of the People."
      New York Theatre Critics' Reviews, 32 (March 22), 334-37.
           Reprints of New York critics' reviews; Gottfried
      (1971.18); Kalem (1971.25); Kroll (1971.26); Melloan
      (1971.31); Watt (1971.40); Watts (1971.41).

31   MELLOAN, GEORGE. "The Theater." Wall Street Journal (March
      15).
           Review of revival of Miller's adaptation of Ibsen's An
      Enemy of the People. The play's topicality lies not only
      in its ecological theme but also in the deeper theme of
      Ibsen's challenge of the principle of majority rule. A
      "central issue of 1971 is whether the nation's leaders
      can or should obey the mandate of a silent majority." The
      fact that the play must be discussed in political as well
      as dramatic terms suggests its polemical nature. Polemicism
      inevitably sacrifices dramatic credibility. This problem
      is sharpened by Miller's "stripping the play to barer essen-
      tials and applying modern vernacular to the dialogue."
      Reprinted: 1971.30.

32   NEWMAN, EDWIN. "An Enemy of the People." New York Theater
      Critics' Review, 32 (March 22), p. 337.
           Television review of revival of Miller's adaptation of
      Ibsen's An Enemy of the People. This production stresses
      the melodrama of the original too much, and though water
      pollution is a topical subject, it is "treated too boldly,
      almost innocently." Some of Miller's language is neither
      of our time nor Ibsen's. The "effect is incongruous."

33   NOVICK, JULIUS. "Arthur Miller: Does He Speak to the
      Present?" New York Times (February 7), p. 17.
           Review of television productions of A Memory of Two
      Mondays and The Price. A "gentle, lyrical, Chekhovian
      evocation of the past with a special unpretentious charm,"
      the former is a neglected play that it is good to see
      again. The Price seems to "be written out of an impulse
      long since exhausted," with "colorless characters and stilted
      dialogue."

34 PARTRIDGE, C. J. The Crucible. Notes on English Literature.
    Oxford: Blackwell, 87 pp.
       Analyzes The Crucible from the standpoint of tragedy and
    the conflicts between men and between women. Gives social
    and political background (of both seventeenth and twentieth
    centuries). Aimed primarily at British high school, college
    and university students, the study includes discussion
    questions, research projects and a brief bibliography.

35 PINSKER, SANFORD. "'The End of the Tether': Joseph Conrad's
    Death of a Sailsman." Conradiana, 3: 74-76.
       Finds similarities between the plight of Henry Whalley
    in Conrad's "The End of the Tether" and that of Willy Loman
    in Death of a Salesman.

36 RAYMONT, HENRY. "Miller and Freed Brazilian Discuss New Satire
    Genre." New York Times (June 25), p. 16.
       Miller meets with Augusto Boal, a leading Brazilian
    stage director whose plays won him a prison sentence on
    "charges of defaming his Government." They discuss Boal's
    "newspaper theater," in which actors read contradictory
    reports from the same newspaper to satirize official
    propaganda.

37 SCANLAN, THOMAS M. "The American Family and Family Dilemmas
    in American Drama." Ph.D. dissertation, University of
    Minnesota, 1970. Dissertation Abstracts International, 32
    (September), 1529A.
       Sensing the completeness of O'Neill's treatment of the
    American family, Miller attempted to move to new ground by
    emphasizing the social context; but his efforts to "connect
    his protagonists with some larger redeeming social order
    are dramatically unrealized." Recently, however, Miller
    has "fully explored the familial relations which are his
    materials," though he does not advance the subject much
    beyond O'Neill's achievement. One chapter on Miller.

38 SHEED, WILFRID. "A View from the Bridge," in his The Morning
    After. New York: Farrar, Straus & Giroux, pp. 168-71.
       Reprint of 1965.53.

39 VOS, NELVIN. "The American Dream Turned to Nightmare: Recent
    American Drama." Christian Scholar's Review, 1 (Spring),
    200-201.
       ·In All My Sons and Death of a Salesman the "repudiation
    of money-seeking fathers by their sons culminates in the
    father's self-destruction." Both plays are "powerful images
    of the seemingly inherent destruction within the American
    Dream."

1971

40   WATT, DOUGLAS. "Enemy of the People Given Vibrant Revival."
      Daily News (March 12).
          Review of revival of Miller's adaptation of Ibsen's An
      Enemy of the People. Whereas in 1950, when Miller's adap-
      tation was first presented, it appeared his target was
      McCarthyism, the play now speaks to environmentalist con-
      cerns. The adaptation remains "fluent and forceful."
      Reprinted: 1971.30.

41   WATTS, RICHARD. "Ibsen's Strong Man Alone." New York Post
      (March 12).
          Review of revival of Miller's adaptation of Ibsen's An
      Enemy of the People. Miller's version contains "all the
      force and moral fury of the original" and is a "dramatic
      work of great interest and distinguished stature." The
      play has a new timeliness, since it deals with the current
      topic of pollution. Reprinted: 1971.30.

42   WEALES, GERALD. "Introduction," in Arthur Miller: "The
      Crucible:" Text and Criticism. Edited by Gerald Weales.
      Viking Critical Library. New York: Viking, pp. ix-xvii.
          Argues that critics have paid too much attention to the
      polemics of The Crucible and too little to its dramatic
      virtues. Miller's insistence on the validity of his re-
      search and the assumption of some people that artists are
      sources of information are to blame. The Crucible avoids
      specific historical parallels because Miller wanted it to
      "outlast the moment"; anyone with a "touch of conscience,
      a hint of political interest, a whisper of moral concern"
      will be drawn to the play.

43   _____, ed. Arthur Miller, "The Crucible": Text and
      Criticism. Viking Critical Library. New York: Viking,
      484 pp.
          Reprints 1953.1; 1953.7; 1953.8; 1953.12; 1953.25;
      1953.28; 1953.39; 1953.40; 1954.4; 1954.7; 1955.31;
      1955.34; 1955.35; 1957.40; 1957.46; 1960.17; 1962.37;
      1964.11; 1964.12; 1965.17; 1967.18.

44   WILLETT, RALPH. "A Note on Arthur Miller's The Price."
      Journal of American Studies, 5 (December), 307-10.
          In its treatment of tensions between two brothers and
      their father, The Price is similar to They Too Arise
      (1938), All My Sons and Death of a Salesman. Despite hints

of the world's absurdity, The Price is rarely more pene-
trating in its insights than the previous plays. In trans-
cending nihilism, Miller has not gone beyond romantic
individualism, nor acknowledged that "opportunities for
mutuality and community still exist."

1972

1   AILEY, ALVIN et al. "Dismissal of Kirov Dancer." New York
    Times (June 19), p. 32.
        Miller and others sign letter protesting the dismissal
    of the Jewish dancer, Valery Panov, from the Kirov State
    Dance Theater following his decision to emigrate to Israel.

2   ANON. "Miller's Play Closes Dec. 16." New York Times
    (December 8), p. 37.
        The New York production of The Creation of the World and
    Other Business will close after twenty performances.

3   ANON. "Writers Seek to Bar Jailing of Ginzburg." New York
    Times (February 14), p. 26.
        Miller and forty others issue statements opposing the
    jailing of Ralph Ginzburg on a conviction of mailing obscene
    materials nine years earlier. Miller points out that "a
    man is going to prison for publishing and advertising stuff
    a few years ago which today would hardly raise an eyebrow
    in your dentist's office."

4   BARNES, CLIVE. "Arthur Miller's Creation of World." New
    York Times (December 1), p. 28.
        Review of New York opening of The Creation of the World
    and Other Business. A "victory of craft over artistry and
    of mind over matter," Creation "has the air of a comic
    strip version of Genesis." While it carefully avoids pre-
    tentiousness, the writing "varies surprisingly between
    Shavian dialectic" and the humor of The Flintstones. The
    play is neither intellectually nor dramatically gripping.

5   _____. "Miller's Crucible." New York Times (April 28),
    p. 36.
        Generally favorable review of Lincoln Center revival of
    The Crucible. It is Miller's best play, and, if he seems
    too self-confident about his own morality, the "play still
    does have a moral force and great dramatic impact."

6   _____. "New York Notebook." Times (London) (May 13),
    p. 10.

1972

Review of Lincoln Center revival of The Crucible, a play
that "shows Miller at his best" yet lacks any "concept of
the theater as a mystery." His voice is "always crisp,
cold, and effective" yet lacking in poetry. Miller is contrasted to Tennessee Williams on both counts.

7   BETTENHAUSEN, ELIZABETH A. "'Forgiving the Idiot in the House':
     Existential Anxiety in Plays by Arthur Miller and Its Impli-
     cations for Christian Ethics." Ph.D. dissertation, Univer-
     sity of Iowa. Dissertation Abstracts International, 32
     (June), 7076A.
          Paul Tillich's contention that "the anxiety of emptiness
     and meaninglessness is characteristic of this century" is
     supported by the existential anxiety of the characters in
     All My Sons, Death of a Salesman, After the Fall, Incident
     at Vichy and The Price. In Miller's plays the anxiety of
     guilt and condemnation is as strong as that resulting from
     emptiness and meaninglessness.

8   BLADES, LARRY T. "Williams, Miller, and Albee: A Comparative
     Study." Ph.D. dissertation, St. Louis University, 1971.
     Dissertation Abstracts International, 32 (February), 4600A.
          Examines thematic relationships. Each dramatist's
     typical protagonist is intensely aware of reality rather
     than illusion-ridden, and each has a deep sense of guilt
     and need for atonement. Heterosexual relationships, com-
     monly unsatisfactory, are examined, as well as the inoper-
     able family situations they produce. Each playwright's
     conception of a socially relevant theatre, and his con-
     frontation with the theatre of the absurd, is discussed.

9   BUCKLEY, TOM. "In the Beginning Miller's Creation. ..." New
     York Times (December 5), pp. 49, 67.
          Interviews with Miller, Harold Clurman (the director),
     and others involved, on reasons for Creation's failure.
     Lack of communication between Clurman and the actors, in-
     sufficient rehearsal time to perfect the acting style
     required, unprofessional behavior of actors, and the un-
     finished state of the play are cited, among other reasons.

10   _____. "Miller Takes His Comedy Seriously." New York Times
     (August 29), p. 22.
          Interview with Miller at start of rehearsals for The
     Creation of the World and Other Business. Miller discusses
     his penchant for seeing comedies, his attempts to write one,
     the writing of Creation, the delay in its production, his
     own religious beliefs, and the youthful audience he hopes
     his play will appeal to.

11   CALTA, LOUIS. "Clurman Quits Creation." New York Times
      (October 17), p. 35.
           On Miller's birthday and the opening date in Washington,
      Harold Clurman is reported to have quit as director of The
      Creation of the World and Other Business because of "dif-
      ferences of opinion over its interpretation."

12   _____. "Play by Miller Due on Broadway." New York Times
      (May 19), p. 19.
           The cast, producer and director of The Creation of the
      World and Other Business, to open November 16 on Broadway,
      are announced.

13   CLARITY, JAMES F. "Notes on People." New York Times (May 31),
      p. 37.
           Miller donates "original manuscript of a new play sched-
      uled for production this fall" to a fund-raising auction
      for the Fellowship of Reconciliation, which is dedicated to
      nonviolent solutions to problems of keeping peace.

14   CLURMAN, HAROLD. "The Crucible." Nation, 214 (May 15),
      636-37.
           Review of revival at Lincoln Center. With the passage
      of time, the real theme of The Crucible emerges as the
      mutual responsibility of all individuals to each other and
      to "that truth within us which we hold most worthy." The
      language of the play is "formal and pristine," and its
      structure "tight, steady and clean as the 17th-century New
      England which is its scene."

15   CORRY, JOHN. "Intellectuals in Bloom at Spring Gathering."
      New York Times (May 18), p. 49.
           As a newly elected member, Miller attends annual awards
      ceremonies of the Academy of Arts and Letters and the
      National Institute of Arts and Letters. He says that the
      ceremonies are "an attempt to get some communication
      between people in the arts."

16   EMERY, FRED. "The Meeting of St. George and the Godfather."
      Times (London) (November 6), p. 12.
           Miller states that, in running against Richard Nixon for
      the U.S. Presidency, George McGovern is auditioning for the
      wrong part. "We are not casting the Moses to lead us out
      of the desert but the chief officer of a bank in which we
      are all depositors." McGovern "lacks the touch of larceny
      we enjoy in our leaders."

1972

17   ESSLINGER, PAT. <u>Barron's Simplified Approach to Arthur Miller</u>.
      Woodburg, N.Y.: Barron's Educational Series.
        Biographical sketch, critical survey and study guide of
      the plays through <u>The Price</u>.

18   FERRES, JOHN H. "Still in the Present Tense: <u>The Crucible</u>
      Today." <u>University College Quarterly</u>, 17 (May), 8-18.
        <u>The Crucible</u> has contemporary appeal because it is con-
      cerned with the right to dissent when conscience demands
      it, and with self-actualization through an individual's
      search for identity. Also, it is ambivalent about heroism
      and reminds Americans that the blessings of their Puritan
      heritage are mixed. Expanded: 1972.19, with addition of
      biographical sketch.

19   _____, ed. <u>The Crucible: A Collection of Critical Essays</u>.
      Twentieth Century Interpretations. Englewood Cliffs, N.J.:
      Prentice-Hall, 122 pp.
        Reprints and excerpts from 1953.24; 1953.28; 1960.15;
      1960.28; 1961.50; 1963.7; 1963.9; 1964.12; 1964.36;
      1964.62; 1965.17; 1965.30; 1967.26; 1967.34; 1967.35;
      1967.36; 1972.18.

20   FIELDS, B. S. "Death of a Salesman." <u>Twentieth Century</u>
      <u>Literature</u>, 18 (January), 19-24.
        Briefly reviews arguments for and against the tragic
      nature of <u>Salesman</u>, and interpretations of Willy's charac-
      ter. Argues that Willy's suicide is an appropriate catas-
      trophe for the play since his tragic crime was to make his
      sons morally and socially impotent.

21   FLEMING, WILLIAM P. "Tragedy in American Drama: The Tragic
      Views of Eugene O'Neill, Tennessee Williams, Arthur Miller,
      and Edward Albee." Ph.D. dissertation, University of
      Toledo. <u>Dissertation Abstracts International</u>, 33 (July)
      308A.
        In Miller's uniquely American tragedies the tragic hero
      is characterized by "the desire to solve a problem, the
      will to withstand any obstacle, and the confidence to
      sacrifice himself, if need be, for the cause."

22   GILL, BRENDAN. "For the Prosecution." <u>New Yorker</u>, 48 (May 6),
      54-56.
        Review of revival of <u>The Crucible</u> at New York's Lincoln
      Center. The play succeeds "not because it poses portentous
      spiritual questions, but because it is a well-told story
      about sexual rivalry and vengeance; these are great themes
      and nothing else matters a straw."

23   _____   "Here Come the Clowns." <u>New Yorker</u>, 48 (December 9), 109.
      Review of <u>The Creation of the World and Other Business</u>. Though the first two acts are coherent and intermittently funny, the third is an "incoherent assortment of debates." As the title suggests, one of the "great myths by which we live is reduced to Miller's schoolboy level of foolery."

24   GOTTFRIED, MARTIN.   "<u>The Creation of the World and Other Business</u>." <u>Women's Wear Daily</u> (December 4).
      Review. Miller has chosen a "foolish project for his tremendous talent." The play is "coy, fake, fatuous biblicism laced with night school wisdom." Its humor is "forced and clumsy." Since it aims at "intellectualism on paper rather than viability on stage," the characters are not characters in their own rights but given increasingly to "observational flatulence." Miller has been in trouble "ever since he turned his attentions from social problems to philosophical ones." Reprinted: 1972.44.

25   _____.   "<u>The Crucible</u>." <u>Women's Wear Daily</u> (May 1).
      Review of revival of <u>The Crucible</u>. A "true classic, powerful and heroic," the play has a "subtle and broad meaning" and shows that the dismissal of Miller as a "message-carrying, unimaginatively naturalistic ibsenite is unfair." In writing declamatory speeches Miller risks bombast, in taking moral stands he risks smugness, in stating a philosophy he risks sophomorism. He runs the risks but comes through with the prize: "true manliness and proof of the existence of intelligence." Reprinted: 1972.45.

26   GREENFIELD, JOSH.   "Writing Plays is Absolutely Senseless, Arthur Miller Says, 'But I Love It. I Just Love It.'" <u>New York Times Magazine</u> (February 13), pp. 16-17, 34-39.
      Interview with Miller, "one of those rare celebrity writers who has gracefully made the transition from the limelight back to the desklamp." Miller discusses his writing methods, his dislike of directing, his opinions of Elia Kazan, Harold Clurman, Women's Liberation, the contemporary theater, the new "mythological" trend in his plays, fiction as compared to playwriting, the current political scene, and his reputation in the future.

27   GUSSOW, MEL.   "Black <u>Salesman</u>." <u>New York Times</u> (April 9), p. 69.
      Review of Baltimore all-black production of <u>Death of a Salesman</u>. Since the play confronts universals, the

1972

        Lomans could be black; and in fact the play becomes an "insightful drama about the superimposition of white standards on repressed black people."

28   HARRIS, LEONARD. "The Creation of the World and Other Business." New York Theater Critics Reviews, 33 (December 1), 154.
        Television review. Creation is not Miller's best work, but it is not pompous and provides many chuckles. To say something new about the issues Miller takes up is very difficult. It is an "amusing minor play."

29   _____. "The Crucible." New York Theatre Critics Reviews, 33 (April 28), 298.
        Television review of revival of The Crucible. Though "stuffy and bombastic" in parts, the play's strength and anger overwhelm these flaws. In addition to the experience of Miller and others in the McCarthy era, The Crucible speaks of the "collusion and persecution and courage of France in the 1940's and of America now."

30   HEWES, HENRY. "Distal and Proximal Bite." Saturday Review, 55 (May 20), 62.
        Review of a "very respectable revival of a significant American drama," The Crucible. The play passionately poses a question as relevant for the Vietnam experience as for the McCarthy experience: which is more important, respect for the truth or respect for authority?

31   HUGHES, CATHARINE. "Picking Up the Pieces." America, 127 (December 30), 570.
        Review of New York opening of The Creation of the World and Other Business. The play is portentous, superficial, not very funny, and "more interesting in its aspirations than successful in their realization."

32   JANSON, DONALD. "Ginzburg Begins 3-Year Term for 1963 Obscenity Conviction." New York Times (February 18), p. 16.
        In a New York Times advertisement protesting Ralph Ginzburg's sentence, Miller argues that the "same court should now close down 90% of the movies now playing. . . . Compared to the usual run of entertainment in this country, Ginzburg's publications are on a par with the National Geographic."

33   KALEM, T. E. "Adam and Evil." Time, 100 (December 11), 122.
     Review of New York opening of The Creation of the World
     and Other Business, a "sad and embarrassing event" indi-
     cating a decline of Miller's powers or a temporary lapse
     at least. The cast does all it can to buoy things up, but
     the muddled reasoning, lack of guiding purpose and deli-
     catessen humor sink it like a stone. Reprinted: 1972.44.

34   _____. "The Ethos of Courage." Time, 99 (May 15), 59.
     This revival of The Crucible is the "finest production
     of a play ever mounted at Lincoln Center's Vivian Beaumont
     Theater." Miller's answer to the universally recurring
     question of the individual conscience versus any form of
     tyranny is that the "currency of conscience has only one
     backing--a man's lifeblood." Reprinted: 1972.45.

35   KAUFFMANN, STANLEY. "The Creation of the World and Other
     Business." New Republic, 167 (December 23), 26, 35.
     Review of New York production. The play was evidently
     written by a "writer starving for subject matter, anxious
     to keep busy," who masked his desperation by treating a
     classic subject comically, "as though he had just managed
     to find time, in the midst of a busy schedule, for a little
     philosophical divertissement." Neil Simon could have done
     better. The deepest failure is that when Miller deals with
     the first example of his dominant theme, the father-son
     conflict, he "fiddles and fumbles." When O'Neill was
     finally able to confront the same theme, he wrote his best
     play, Long Day's Journey Into Night.

36   _____. "Right Down the Middle." New Republic, 166 (May 27),
     22, 34.
     Review of Lincoln Center revival of The Crucible. It is
     still Miller's best play, though it is "thematically
     schizoid and its last act a moral-metaphysical drama."
     Miller is the most popular social dramatist of his time
     because he deals with received liberal ideas rather than
     dangerous ideas; except in The Crucible's last act, where
     he asks whether a man can rationally give his life for
     something he can be aware of only while he is alive, and
     whether his life has any foundation if there is nothing he
     will die for. Abridged: 1974.19.

37   KERR, WALTER. "Arthur Miller, Stuck with the Book." New York
     Times (December 10), sec. II, pp. 3, 5.
     The Creation of the World and Other Business fails be-
     cause Miller loses "control of the philosophical argument

1972

between God and Lucifer." Lucifer alone can prevent the murder of Abel, but he is also the only one who can motivate it. Since no resolution is possible, the evening "ends with a harangue and a whimper," despite commendable acting and Miller's "casually imagined, modestly whimsical teasing of Genesis."

38   _____. "'Staged Without Care or Kindness.'" New York Times (May 7), sec. II, p. 3.
        Review of Lincoln Center revival of The Crucible. Rather than concealing the play's defects, John Berry's production advertises them. Berry further fragmentizes the play, further melodramatizes it, and fails to make us believe in the community's belief in witches.

39   KROLL, JACK. "Double Trouble." Newsweek, 80 (December 11), 71.
        The Creation of the World and Other Business "deserves no comment or any attempt to unravel its stupefyingly boring muddle-headedness." Reprinted: 1972.44. Abridged: 1974.19.

40   LUMLEY, FREDERICK. "Broadway Cortege--Tennessee Williams and Arthur Miller," in his New Trends in 20th Century Drama. Fourth edition. New York: Oxford Univ. Press, pp. 137-38, 182-86, 194-99.
        Analyzes the plays through The Price. Miller progresses from the tragedy of the common man in the early plays to a preoccupation with intellectual guilt and the need for a moral confrontation with responsibility in the later ones. There is tragedy in modern man's inability to come to terms with himself. Expanded version of 1956.39.

41   MCLEAN, LYDIA. "A Weekend with the Arthur Millers." Vogue, 159 (March 15), 102-109.
        Account of life and activities of a typical weekend at Miller's Connecticut farm.

42   MCMAHON, HELEN. "Arthur Miller's Common Man: The Problem of the Realistic and the Mythic." Drama and Theater, 10 (Spring), 128-33.
        Traces recurrent myths in Miller's plays: the American Dream myth; the myth of the common man; and traditional Judeo-Christian myths. Miller's technical realism does not always "effect the coherence between the mythic and the realistic necessary to a complete dramatic experience."

1972

43   MANSKE, DWAIN E. "A Study of the Changing Family Roles in the
     Early Published and Unpublished Works of Arthur Miller, to
     Which is Appended a Catalogue of the Miller Collection at
     the University of Texas at Austin." Ph.D. dissertation,
     University of Texas at Austin, 1970. Dissertation Abstracts
     International, 32 (January), 4008A.
         Examines, in ten full-length plays and two novels of
     Miller's apprenticeship (1936-1949), the father-son rela-
     tionship, his true subject. The plots, however, avoid
     father-son confrontations, and the final scenes avoid the
     leading argument that corrupt fathers influence the world
     and especially their sons. Finally, in All My Sons and
     Salesman, Miller can see both brothers in each play as com-
     posites of good and evil.

44   MARLOWE, JOAN and BETTY BLAKE, eds. "The Creation of the
     World and Other Business." New York Theatre Critics'
     Reviews, 33 (December 1), 150-54.
         Reprints of New York critics' reviews: Gottfried
     (1972.24); Kalem (1972.33); Kroll (1972.39); Watt (1972.57);
     Watts (1972.58); Wilson (1972.64).

45   _____. "The Crucible." New York Theatre Critics' Reviews,
     33 (April 28), 296-98.
         Reprints of the New York critics' reviews: Gottfried
     (1972.25); Kalem (1972.34); Watt (1972.56); Watts (1972.59).

46   MESERVE, WALTER J. "Who Killed Willy Loman?," in The Merrill
     Studies in "Death of a Salesman." Edited by Walter J.
     Meserve. Columbus, Ohio: Charles E. Merrill, pp. v-ix.
         Willy Loman is not equipped for life in an adult society.
     His "superficially determined enthusiasms" and "equally
     disturbing gloominess" reveal his psychopathic tendencies.

47   _____, ed. The Merrill Studies in "Death of a Salesman."
     Columbus, Ohio: Charles E. Merrill, 99 pp.
         Reprints 1949.41; 1949.54; 1955.17; 1960.11; 1960.27;
     1962.6; 1963.12; 1963.16; 1964.56; 1965.1; 1965.27;
     1965.36; 1967.37; 1968.14.

48   MURRAY, EDWARD. "Arthur Miller," in his The Cinematic Imagi-
     nation. New York: Ungar, pp. 69-85.
         Though filmic as a play, the theatricalism of Death of
     a Salesman vitiated the film adaptation. The director,
     Laslo Banedek, failed to "replace Miller's theatrical styl-
     ization." Sentimentality, and the fact that Miller has too
     much respect for the word and too little for the "merely"

1972

visual, are the chief reasons for the failure of The Misfits
as film and cinema-novel. Abridged: 1976.19.

49 PAUL, RAJINDER. "Death of a Salesman in India," in The Merrill
Studies in "Death of a Salesman." Edited by Walter Meserve.
Columbus, Ohio: Charles E. Merrill, pp. 23-27.
An account of Indian productions of Death of a Salesman
in English, Hindi and Bengali. Miller is the best known
American dramatist in India, and Salesman is his most popu-
lar play, though he has had less influence on Indian play-
wrights than Williams and Albee. Miller's themes of guilt,
responsibility, family fealty and manhood find echoes in
India's male-dominated society, as does his streak of
Puritanism.

50 PROBST, LEONARD. "The Creation of the World and Other Business." New York Theater Critics' Reviews, 33 (December 1),
154.
Television review. Despite good acting, the play is
more "silly than significant." It seems made up of endless
rewrites, fragments, and attempts at humor, many of which
fail.

51 RAYMONT, HENRY. "U.S. Bars Cubans from Film Event." New York
Times (March 24), p. 8.
Miller and others protest State Department's refusal to
issue visas to four Cuban film directors to participate in
the First New York Festival of Cuban Films.

52 SANDERS, KEVIN. "The Creation of the World and Other Business."
New York Theater Critics' Reviews, 33 (December 1), 153-54.
Television review. Intended as a "dramatic cosmic
comedy," the play is "more like a Flintstones version of
the Book of Genesis." Though "well acted and imaginatively
staged," the play merely "restates in a novel, light-hearted
way" the familiar origins of the Judeo-Christian fear of
death, and the concept of sin, guilt, and all its attendant
sexual hangups. Humor is "obviously not Miller's forte."

53 _____. "The Crucible." New York Theater Critics' Reviews,
33 (April 28), 298.
Television review of revival of The Crucible. The play
dramatizes magnificently the terror of the Salem witch
hunts. Its "court scenes are still some of the most harrowing in the repertoire of modern drama."

54 SHEPHERD, ALLEN. "'What Comes Easier': The Short Stories of
Arthur Miller." Illinois Quarterly, 34 (February), 37-49.

The stories in I Don't Need You Any More are uneven and
undistinguished. They illustrate Miller's interests in the
fifteen years of their composition--his humanism, his dis-
pute with American values, his inquiry into personal
responsibility--as do his plays.

55 SIMON, JOHN. "Eloquence in Spite of Words." New York Maga-
    zine, 5 (May 15), 70.
        Review of Lincoln Center revival of The Crucible.
    Miller's best play "holds the stage with tooth and nail as
    good plays must." Proctor is an "Aristotelian hero complete
    with hamartia and a Freudian hero made incomplete by a sense
    of guilt." The play's main flaw is its "pidgin-Colonial"
    language. Abridged: 1974.19.

56 WATT, DOUGLAS. "Arthur Miller's Crucible Returns." New York
    Daily News (April 28).
        Review. John Berry's overwrought staging of a revival
    of The Crucible "shows all too clearly the seams in a play
    that has always been, at best, shrewd melodrama." Though
    "shrewdly written, playable and with some good confrontation
    scenes," the play is "contrived, full of bombast, and too
    pat." Reprinted: 1972.45.

57 _____. "Miller's Creation of the World is a Plodding Comedy-
    Drama." New York Daily News (December 1).
        Review. The Creation of the World and Other Business
    tries to be both serious and playful, but is neither. The
    "jesting is awkward and heavy-handed"; the "statements are
    preachy" and the "writing flat and mechanical." In trying
    to unravel an eternal mystery, the author becomes "merely
    perplexed and perplexing." Miller is at his best in deal-
    ing with the present or recent past. He should not toy
    with myth. Reprinted: 1972.44.

58 WATTS, RICHARD. "Arthur Miller's Creation Opens at Shubert
    Theater." New York Post (December 1).
        Review. Despite an excellent cast, admirable direction,
    an "unexpected vein of humor" and a good first act, The
    Creation of the World is "confused and confusing."
    Reprinted: 1972.44.

59 _____. "The Witch Hunt in Old Salem." New York Post (April
    28).
        Review. The revival of The Crucible shows the play is
    "powerful and effective in its own right" and striking in
    its "ability to recall memories of the McCarthy period."
    It is Miller's second best play. Reprinted: 1972.45.

1972

60 WEALES, GERALD. "All about Talk: Arthur Miller's The Price."
    Ohio Review, 13 (Winter), 74-84.
       Without denying that Miller's major theme in The Price
    is that "choice is dictated by responses to received atti-
    tudes," it can be argued that the play is "questioning the
    dramatic, social and therapeutic uses of talk." Our under-
    standing of it "hinges on the degree to which we admit
    there may be efficacy in conversation."

61 _____. "Clichés in the Garden." Commonweal, 97 (December   /
    22), 276.
       Review of New York opening of The Creation of the World
    and Other Business. Miller has finally turned to the
    "first, best sibling rivalry," but this is his worst play--
    "the dullest, the least dramatic, the most pretentious and
    the most vulgar reworking of the Biblical material this
    critic can recall."

62 WELCH, CHARLES A. "Guilt in Selected Plays of Arthur Miller:
    A Phenomenological Inquiry and Creative Response." Ph.D.
    dissertation, United States International University.
    Dissertation Abstracts International, 33 (September), 1031A.
       Analyzes guilt in the main characters of The Crucible,
    After the Fall and Incident at Vichy from the perspective
    of phenomenological psychology. Guilt in each case is
    specific, the character knows (or believes he knows) the
    reason for his sense of guilt, awareness of guilt is pain-
    ful to him, and the fundamental structure of guilt is the
    character's self-condemnation for failure to live up to his
    vision of self and/or his concept of morally responsible
    behavior.

63 WELLAND, DENNIS. "Death of a Salesman in England," in The
    Merrill Studies in "Death of a Salesman." Edited by
    Walter J. Meserve. Columbus, Ohio: Charles E. Merrill,
    pp. 8-17.
       Reviews notices and criticism of Death of a Salesman in
    England. The play met with less anti-American feeling than
    expected, but with a reluctance to recognize an American as
    a commanding dramatist of the 1940's and an uneasiness
    about its form and idiom similar to that felt in the United
    States.

64 WILSON, EDWIN. "Adam and Eve in the Garden." Wall Street
    Journal (December 4).
       Review. The Creation of the World and Other Business
    is three plays in one: the comic story of Creation, a
    parody of this, and a series of musings on the meaning of

good and evil. The parody is tasteless, the musings given
to "hollow profundities," but the original story is often
"fleshed out with great charm and insight." Had Miller
omitted the "other business," the play might have succeeded.
Reprinted: 1972.44.

1973

1 ANON. "5 in Various Fields Chosen for Awards." New York
   Times (May 4), p. 27.
      Miller receives an Albert Einstein Commemorative award
   from the Albert Einstein College of Medicine at Yeshiva
   University for his "extraordinary contributions to American
   letters and his devotion to cultural freedom."

2 BECKERMAN, BERNARD and HOWARD SIEGMAN, eds. On Stage. New
   York: Arno Press, pp. 275-76, 298-99, 344-45, 456-59.
      Reprints 1947.14; 1949.25; 1953.7; 1964.77.

3 BUCK, RICHARD M. "The Creation of the World and Other Business," in Library Journal Book Review. New York: Bowker,
   p. 609.
      Hardly funnier to read than to see, the play suggests
   Miller does not know how to laugh. If MacLeish in JB is
   guilty of "poetic pomposity," Miller's play is a "pathetic
   triviality."

4 CALTA, LOUIS. "News of the Stage." New York Times (September
   9), p. 58.
      Miller plans to attend spring rehearsals at the Univer-
   sity of Michigan of his The American Clock, a play begun
   in 1970 and "based partly on Studs Terkel's Hard Times."

5 _____. "News of the Stage." New York Times (November 4),
   p. 83.
      Miller grants permission for a revival of Death of a
   Salesman to Philadelphia Drama Guild after refusing for
   twenty-five years to allow any professional production of
   it in New York City or within 100 miles of Broadway. His
   refusal was based on his belief that "anything that could
   be classified as a revival would be reviewed as professional,
   whether it was warranted or not." Before the Drama Guild,
   no group had the "capacity to do the play."

6 CISMARU, ALFRED. "Before and After the Fall." Forum
   (Houston), 11 (Summer-Fall), 67-71.

1973

  After the Fall resembles Albert Camus' The Fall in
"title, situation, tone, mood, vocabulary and setting."
Miller has "not borrowed excessively or rehashed situations
long prevalent in postwar French literature." Rather, he
has combined "tendencies and aspects" of contemporary
French letters with his "deep tragic sense and profoundly
engaging style."

7 CLARITY, JAMES F. "Notes on People." New York Times (July
   31), p. 34.
       Miller is appointed adjunct professor-in-residence at
   the University of Michigan to "conduct informal seminars
   and advise the faculty on theater arts."

8 CORRIGAN, ROBERT W. "The Achievement of Arthur Miller," in
   The Theatre in Search of a Fix. Edited by Robert W.
   Corrigan. New York: Delacorte Press, pp. 325-47.
       Reprint of 1968.24.

9 _____. "Arthur Miller," in Contemporary Dramatists. Edited
   by James Vinson. New York: St. Martin's, 542-44.
       Excerpt from 1968.24.

10 DEEDY, JOHN. "Critics and the Bible." Commonweal, 97
   (January 5), 290.
       Quotes Miller's reaction to critics' panning of Creation
   of the World and Other Business. Criticism was often based
   on ignorance of the Bible, Miller argues, and, like After
   the Fall and Incident at Vichy, the play "needs to be produced again so that maybe [the critics] will discuss what
   the play is about."

11 FALB, LEWIS W. "Arthur Miller," in his American Drama in
   Paris, 1945-1970. Studies in Comparative Literature.
   Chapel Hill: University of North Carolina Press, pp. 37-50.
       Analyzes French reaction to Miller's plays produced in
   France. The French find that Miller "deals courageously,
   intelligently and compassionately with important social and
   moral issues" and applaud Miller's attempt to create a
   "drama that is actively involved with present realities
   that are neither totally subjective nor exclusively
   psychological."

12 GENT, GEORGE. "NBC Arranges Program Exchange with BBC." New
   York Times (June 27), p. 111.
       Miller has adapted After the Fall for a television
   production.

13   HAYMAN, RONALD. "Arthur Miller," in his <u>Playback 2</u>. London:
Davis-Poynter, pp. 7-22.
     An interview. Miller discourses on Ibsen, Beckett,
Brecht, American dialects, playwriting courses, critics,
naturalism, the reasons his plays appeal, self-destructive-
ness in Western society, and recent playwrights who confuse
journalism with theatre.

14   HEILMAN, ROBERT B. "Arthur Miller," in his <u>The Iceman, the
Arsonist, and the Troubled Agent</u>. Seattle: University of
Washington Press, pp. 142-61, 162-64.
     Though Miller's plays from <u>Salesman</u> to <u>After the Fall</u>
seemed to be moving from melodrama to tragedy, <u>The Price</u>
reverts to melodrama and to older themes. More than
O'Neill or Williams, Miller transcends and enlarges the
private.

15   HEWES, HENRY. "Arthur Miller's Cosmic Chuckles." <u>Saturday
Review of the Arts</u>, 1 (January), 57.
     <u>The Creation of the World and Other Business</u> is a
"leaden, unfunny play lacking even that hyperactive logic
characteristic of [Miller's] previous works." His failure
to fully exploit the comedy of Lucifer and God rational-
izing their actions perhaps stems from the same compulsion
to be serious that made him desert comedy in the second
half of <u>The Price</u>. It would be regrettable if Miller were
to "retreat from developing what seems to some of us the
most down-to-earth aspect of his talent."

16   HUGHES, CATHARINE. "<u>The Crucible</u>," in her <u>Plays, Politics,
and Polemics</u>. New York: Drama Book Specialist, pp. 15-25.
     On stage <u>The Crucible</u>'s "vitality, power and sense of
moral outrage communicate with an intensity that transcends
its numerous failings." There is too little moral outrage
in today's professional theatre.

17   KENDALL, ROBERT D. "A Rhetorical Study of Religious Drama as
a Form of Preaching." Ph.D. dissertation, University of
Minnesota. <u>Dissertation Abstracts International</u>, 34
(November), 2800A-01A.
     Applies the critical method of Kenneth Burke to <u>The
Crucible</u> to illustrate the similarity of its rhetorical
structures to those used by monolog preachers.

18   LENZ, HAROLD. "At Sixes and Sevens--A Modern Theatre Structure." <u>Forum</u> (Houston), 11 (Summer-Fall, 1973, Winter,
1974), 73-79.

1973

Like other modern European "morality plays," <u>Death of a
Salesman</u>'s characters lack separate identities, independent
imaginations, and a "creative impulse that would free them
from the mechanistic dream of a mechanistic success."

19   MCMAHON, HELEN M.   "Arthur Miller's Common Man: The Problem
of the Realistic and the Mythic."   Ph.D. dissertation,
Purdue University, 1972.   <u>Dissertation Abstracts Inter-
national</u>, 34 (July), 326A-27A.
Miller's plays typically use a topical or realistic
plot in which the "protagonist attempts to solve his immed-
iate contemporary problem, and a subordinate plot in which
he is moved by an unrecognized mythic force."   In the early
plays a failed father-figure sacrifices his life for sins
committed against family or society.   In the later plays a
second-generation figure (usually a son) is redeemed by a
substitute father-figure.   The Biblical pattern of the Fall
and Redemption is the "background to the character's private
life and the split in the drama is the failure to fully
articulate these archetypal roots."   <u>The Price</u> most success-
fully unites the topical or realistic with the mythical to
show that the mythic past has consequences in the present.

20   MAILER, NORMAN.   "The Jewish Princess," in his <u>Marilyn</u>.   New
York: Grosset & Dunlap, pp. 157-206, passim, 245.
Discusses Miller's marriage with Marilyn Monroe with
emphasis on their disintegrating relationship during the
filming of <u>The Misfits</u>.   The marriage was mutually destructive because after a "life in which her nerves had been
pulled by the imperatives of others," Monroe "had full need
to manipulate her talented slave," while in the "ambitious,
limited and small-minded" Miller the "instincts of a ser-
vant" came to fill the growing "vacuum in his own creative
force."   If Monroe had lived, <u>After the Fall</u> "might have
been her greatest role and Miller's greatest play."   The
play fails not because Miller cheapens Monroe's image, but
because "no production can offer the presence of Marilyn."

21   MUKERJI, NIRMAL.   "John Proctor's Tragic Predicament." <u>Punjab
University Research Bulletin</u>, 4 (April), 75-79.
The Crucible is the tragedy of one individual--John
Proctor--and his "heightened self-awareness adds to the
tragic dimensions of the play."   Unlike Willy Loman, Proctor
discovers himself and in dying "raises human nobility to
the level of tragic heroism."

22   RICHARDSON, JACK. "Arthur Miller's Eden." Commentary, 55
       (February), 83-85.
           Review of New York opening of The Creation of the World
       and Other Business. Miller is thanked for restoring in the
       critic "the desire to give a meretricious play no quarter."
       The play's faults illuminate faults in his previous plays
       that had escaped proper censure, especially the way "Miller
       has so often cheapened life through his readiness to under-
       stand it too quickly and to festoon it with gaudy pro-
       nouncements." Abridged: 1974.19.

23   RILEY, CAROLYN, ed. Contemporary Literary Criticism. Vol. 1.
       Detroit: Gale Research, pp. 215-19.
           Abridged versions of 1953.40; 1960.13; 1960.28; 1962.37;
       1964.20; 1964.36; 1965.16; 1965.53; 1967.34; 1967.35;
       1968.20; 1968.24; 1969.13.

24   ROTHENBERG, ALBERT and EUGENE D. SHAPIRO. "The Defense of
       Psychoanalysis in Literature: Long Day's Journey into
       Night and A View from the Bridge." Comparative Drama, 7
       (Spring) 65-67.
           A comparison of the characters' use of psychological
       defenses in the two plays. In Miller's play, Eddie and
       Katherine are the most defensive characters.

25   SHATZKY, JOEL. "The 'Reactive Image' and Miller's Death of
       a Salesman." Players Magazine, 48 (February-March), 104-10.
           The narrowness of American drama, attributable to a
       reactive (or helpless) image of modern man, is exemplified
       in Salesman. Since Miller's view of Willy, through the
       reactive image, "precludes his success on any level, the
       validity of the American dream is never really examined."

26   SLAVENSKY, SONIA W. "Suicide in the Plays of Arthur Miller:
       A View from Glory Mountain." Ph.D. dissertation, Loyola
       University of Chicago. Dissertation Abstracts Inter-
       national, 34 (October), 1936A.
           Miller's dependence on suicide for dramatic form in-
       creases through his career. Suicide in Miller is the
       "metaphorical embodiment of the psycho-social and cultural
       predicament of his hero's struggle to die honorably." Like
       Sophocles' and Euripides' heroes, Miller's heroes range
       from early suicidal protagonists to those who learn to
       suffer and endure. After the Fall marks the transition
       from suicide to endurance.

1973

27   STEINBECK, JOHN. "The Trial of Arthur Miller." <u>Esquire</u>, 80
      (October), 238-40.
            Reprint of 1957.41.

28   STEPHENS, SUZANNE. S. "The Dual Influence: A Dramaturgical
      Study of the Plays of Edward Albee and the Specific Dramatic
      Forms and Themes Which Influence Them." Ph.D. dissertation,
      Miami University, 1972. <u>Dissertation Abstracts Inter-
      national</u>, 34 (July), 342A.
            Chapter two examines the realist-expressionist plays of
      Miller and Tennessee Williams as one influence on Edward
      Albee's plays.

29   ZURCHER, CARL D. "An Analysis of Selected American Criticism
      of the Plays of Arthur Miller in the Light of His Own Com-
      mentary on Drama." Ph.D. dissertation, Purdue University.
      <u>Dissertation Abstracts International</u>, 35 (July), 619A-20A.
            Examines twenty-three newspaper, periodical, and book-
      length critics of Miller. Few critics recognize or under-
      stand his views of life and man; fewer still feel these
      views are intellectually profound. Miller is given more
      credit for fulfilling structural aims in his plays than for
      achieving his goals as a playwright. Some critics, insen-
      sitive to Miller's lofty aims, find the plays poor enter-
      tainment, while others expect greater intellectual depth or
      see the plays as polemics.

<u>1974</u>

1   ANON. "Arthur Miller," in <u>Current Biography Yearbook</u>. Edited
     by Charles Moritz. New York: H. W. Wilson, pp. 296-99.
            An enlarged version of 1948.1.

2   ANON. "P.E.N. Asks Amnesty for Jailed Writers." <u>New York
     Times</u> (January 6), p. 2.
            Miller and other members of P.E.N. propose to the United
     Nations an amnesty year for 380 writers who are imprisoned
     for "intellectual crimes."

3   BARNES, CLIVE. "Arthur Miller's <u>All My Sons</u>." <u>New York
     Times</u> (October 29), p. 32.
            Review of revival. <u>All My Sons</u> is dated, its "morality
     is too self-conscious and self-congratulatory," but it can
     still provide the kind of enjoyment gotten from a "vintage
     late-late show on television and a remembrance of times
     and plays past." It owes much to Ibsen, but whereas

1974

"Ibsen's world is one of people and true conflicts, All My Sons is a simplistic recruiting poster for black and white morality."

4   BRENNER, GARY. "To Have and Have Not as Classical Tragedy," in Hemingway in Our Time. Edited by Richard Astro and Jackson J. Benson. Corvallis: Oregon State University Press, p. 69.
     Harry Morgan in To Have and Have Not fulfills Miller's definition of the tragic flaw in "Tragedy and the Common Man," as well as his belief that the catastrophe must assert the hero's dignity by "positing a wrong or evil in his environment."

5   CALTA, LOUIS. "Roundabout Makes the RKO on 23rd Street Its Home." New York Times (September 10), p. 38.
     All My Sons will open Stage One, the new legitimate theater which the Roundabout Theater Company has created out of a former New York movie house. Miller hails this reversal of a historical trend as an "amazing and wonderful thing."

6   CORRIGAN, ROBERT W. "Arthur Miller Interview." Michigan Quarterly Review, 13 (Autumn), 401-405.
     Miller discusses the shift in his plays from tragedy in the modern idiom to spiritual explorations of guilt and responsibility, the structure of his plays, and his recollection that he was not concerned with tragic form when he wrote Death of a Salesman.

7   DITSKY, JOHN M. "All Irish Here: the 'Irishman' in Modern Drama." Dalhousie Review, 54 (Spring), 94-102.
     Though only two characters in A Memory of Two Mondays are literally Irish, there is a community of "shared sorrows and hurts that makes all of them 'Irish,' to an extent."

8   GUPTA, R. K. "Death of a Salesman and Miller's Concept of Tragedy." Kyushu American Literature (Fukuoka, Japan) 15: 10-19.
     The weaknesses of the play stem from Miller's inability to put his own workable theory of tragedy, enunciated in "Tragedy and the Common Man," into practice. The chief fault is that Willy Loman is not a sufficiently vital and impressive figure.

9   GUSSOW, MEL. "Arthur Miller Returns to Genesis for First Musical." New York Times (April 17), p. 37.

1974

Interview. Miller discusses <u>Up From Paradise</u>, a musical
version of <u>The Creation of the World and Other Business</u>.
"Musicalizing the play changed the whole form for the
better," the original Broadway production being "much too
heavy psychologically." Miller sees himself as "condensing
the play into verse," while Stanley Silverman puts it to
music.

10 HANSEN, CHADWICK. "The Metamorphosis of Tituba, or Why American Intellectuals Can't Tell an Indian Witch from a Negro."
<u>New England Quarterly</u>, 47 (March), 3-12.
In <u>The Crucible</u>, Miller makes Tituba into a Negress
practicing voodoo. Historically, she was probably Indian.

11 HEWES, HENRY. "On Broadway and on Campus." <u>Saturday Review/</u>
<u>World</u>, 1 (June 15), 44-45.
Review of <u>Up From Paradise</u>, a dramatic oratorio version
of <u>The Creation of the World and Other Business</u>. Stanley
Silverman's music and Miller's narration enhanced the production at the University of Michigan. "The new approach
is so successful that one wonders why Miller pulls back
from continuing in this fruitful vein."

12 HÖGEL, ROLF K. "The Manipulation of Time in Miller's <u>After</u>
<u>the Fall</u>." <u>Literatur in Wissenschaft und Unterricht</u>
(Kiel), 7: 115-21.
Through objective and subjective time and episodes linked
by common themes, "Miller manipulates time to represent the
protagonist's past, his present situation and his decision
about his future life as an interwoven psychic entity."

13 JACOBSON, IRVING F. "The Child as Guilty Witness." <u>Literature</u>
<u>and Psychology</u>, 24: 12-23.
"I Don't Need You Any More" is thematically central to
Miller's treatment of the family. It "stands to the rest
of his fiction as <u>Death of a Salesman</u> stands to the rest
of his plays." It is Miller's most extensive treatment of
childhood and the child's perception of the family, and
parallels in its descriptions of childhood the work of
Erich Neumann and Erik H. Erikson. Abridged: 1976.19.

14 ____. "The Fallen Family: A Study in the Work of Arthur
Miller." Ph.D. dissertation, University of California,
Los Angeles. <u>Dissertation Abstracts International</u>, 35
(October), 2271A-72A.
Miller's characters seek to return to primal security,
love and identity of the family through regression or

progression. Martin in "I Don't Need You Any More" fanta-
sizes about his early relationship with his mother, while
Chris Keller and Walter Franz form their own families to
reattain the lost primal state. Miller dwells on the
possibility that society might be made to function as a
family and be a "home," perhaps through military life or
political idealism and action. Actual family life in the
plays, however, is generally disastrous.

15   _____. "Christ, Pygmalion, and Hitler in After the Fall."
        Essays in Literature, 2 (August), 12-27.
           Quentin in After the Fall may be understood as a "con-
        flux of different selves, or different aspects of the self,
        some of them irreconcilable." In fact Quentin's self and
        sense of self lie at the core of the play.

16   KREBS, ALBIN. "Notes on People." New York Times (March 20),
        p. 33.
           Because his new play is still unfinished, Miller plans
        to stage "From the Creation" (based on The Creation of the
        World and Other Business) at the University of Michigan,
        which had planned to stage his new play this spring.

17   O'CONNOR, JOHN J. "Miller's After the Fall on NBC." New
        York Times (December 10), p. 91.
           While After the Fall remains an "egotistical abomin-
        ation" and "distressing failure," the television version
        is better than the original stage production as a result
        of Miller's reworking of the play.

18   OLIVER, EDITH. "Off Broadway." New Yorker, 50 (November 11),
        106-07.
           Review of New York revival of All My Sons. A poor
        production that does nothing for the "verbal ineptitude
        and dumb-cluck moral fervor that were to prove such a
        nuisance in Miller's later work."

19   RILEY, CAROLYN and BARBARA HARTE, eds. Contemporary Literary
        Criticism. Vol. 2. Detroit: Gale Research, pp. 278-80.
           Abridged versions of 1965.50; 1968.49; 1970.8; 1971.11;
        1972.36; 1972.39; 1972.55; 1973.22.

20   SCANLAN, THOMAS M. "The Domestication of Rip Van Winkle: Joe
        Jefferson's Play as Prologue to Modern American Drama."
        Virginia Quarterly Review, 50 (Winter), 51-62.
           Rip is seen as prefiguring the family plays of O'Neill,
        Miller and Williams. Jefferson's adaptation of Irving's
        story softens and sentimentalizes it and emphasizes the
        importance of family structure.

1974

21 VOGEL, DAN. "Willy Tyrannos," in his Three Masks of American
        Tragedy. Baton Rouge, La.: Louisiana State University
        Press, pp. 91-102.
            Argues that there is a "relationship between the Greek
        Tyrannos, Oedipus, and the American Everyman Willy Loman."
        Since it is not society's demands but what Willy thinks
        these are that makes the action, Willy's flaw--like that of
        Oedipus--is "self-delusion ironically induced by uncon-
        trollable external powers." Like Oedipus, Willy selects
        the wrong alternative, misinterprets his life as a tyrannos,
        and thereby becomes a tragic figure. Abridged: 1976.19.

                                1975

1   ANON. "Colleagues Pay Tribute." New York Times (December 8),
        p. 40.
            On the death of Thornton Wilder, Miller recalls that
        Wilder would often stop by for a stimulating post-mortem
        when a new Miller play opened in New Haven. He describes
        Wilder as a "very generous man. He was magnanimous, wise
        and worth listening to."

2   ANON. "25 Sign an Appeal to Ford on Spain." New York Times
        (November 21), p. 17.
            Cosigns letter to President Ford urging a "fundamental
        review of American policy toward Spain" in the post-Franco
        period.

3   ANON. "U.S. Urged to Guarantee Freedom to All Writers." New
        York Times (November 19), p. 25.
            Testifying with others before a U.S. government sub-
        committee, Miller argues that the internal affairs of other
        nations are subject to American scrutiny and pressure when
        they violate the Universal Declaration of Human Rights or
        the Declaration of Principles signed at Helsinki. Czech
        writers, however, are not awaiting American assistance
        because "the United States has a well-earned reputation for
        not caring a damn about these things."

4   ANON. "Writers and Actors Criticize UNESCO for Curb on
        Israel." New York Times (February 7), p. 3.
            Miller and others write letter to UNESCO attacking its
        resolutions directed against Israel. The resolutions would
        cut off cultural aid to Israel and deny it membership in
        any regional grouping.

5   BARNES, CLIVE. "Scott Puts Acting Magic in 'Salesman'" New
York Times (June 27), p. 26.
     Review of revival of Death of a Salesman with George C.
Scott as director and star. The play is as "dense, magnificent and meaningful as we all thought it was when it was
first produced soon after World War II," though perhaps it
is less representative of America today. "We may not be
more moral, but we are perhaps more knowing." Scott is
superb as Willy Loman, and his direction "sees the play
clear." Reprinted: 1975.28.

6   BEAUFORT, JOHN C. "Visions of America's Past-Recent."
Christian Science Monitor (June 27).
     Review of revival of Death of a Salesman. Stresses
continuing relevance of the play. Faults the production
for drab scenery, heavy-handed naturalism (in which the
literal predominates over illusion), the incipient madness
of George C. Scott's interpretation of Willy, and the use
of black actors as Willy's neighbors. Reprinted: 1975.28.

7   CLURMAN, HAROLD. "Theatre." Nation, 221 (July 19), 59-60.
     Reviews off-Broadway revival of Death of a Salesman.
The play is neither an "attack on the system, nor a caution-
ary tract," but a "depiction of people detached from
reality." Willy fails to possess his soul, though his
false dream is a "reaching toward something that might
nourish the hunger of his inmost being." The play has
power and stature because Willy's number is legion.
Abridged: 1976.19.

8   COOK, LARRY W. "The Function of Ben and Dave Singleman in
Death of a Salesman." Notes on Contemporary Literature, 5
(January), 7-9.
     Willy's inconsistent treatment of his sons stems from
the incompatibility of the two views of life represented
by Ben, the ruthless competitor, and Dave Singleman, the
well-liked successful individual. Willy's personal unsure-
ness comes from a vague realization that his basic beliefs
are contradictory. He passes this confusion on to his
sons.

9   CORRY, JOHN. "Arthur Miller and Others Contend Clock Absolves
Youth Convicted of Matricide." New York Times (December
16), pp. 1, 47.
     Conflicting accounts regarding the time the crime (see
1975.10) is alleged to have been committed warrant a new
trial, Miller and New York Times reporter argue.

1975

10   _____ . "Arthur Miller Turns Detective in Murder." <u>New York</u>
        <u>Times</u> (December 15), pp. 1, 46.
              Miller and the <u>New York Times</u> investigate conviction of
        a youth for matricide in 1973. A "compassionate man,"
        Miller dwells in his plays on the force of destiny, with
        the dead hand of the past reaching into the future. "The
        youth's past interested Miller; the conviction aroused his
        compassion." On the basis of a passed polygraph test and
        other indications of innocence, Miller will urge a new
        trial.

11   CUMMINGS, DOROTHY STACEY. "Major Themes in the Plays of
        Antonio Buero Vallejo and Arthur Miller." Ph.D. disserta-
        tion, University of Arkansas. <u>Dissertation Abstracts Inter-</u>
        <u>national</u>, 36 (December), 3221A-22A.
              Discusses similarities in themes and philosophical
        development between Miller and Buero. The "general move-
        ment in the plays of both is from the poverty theme to
        guilt and then to responsibility."

12   EPSTEIN, CHARLOTTE. "Was Linda Loman Willy's Downfall?" <u>New</u>
        <u>York Times</u> (July 20), sec. II, p. 5.
              Takes issue with Walter Goodman's view (<u>see</u> 1975.15)
        that Linda Loman is the "loving little woman behind the
        salesman," Willy Loman. Linda is actually "counter-
        productive and figures passively in the destruction of her
        family." She has no allegiance to Willy's myth of success
        and has done him harm throughout his career by refusing to
        confront him with the truth about himself. She thus "spurs
        him on to continuous frustration and failure."

13   FELDMAN, JACK. "The Plays of Arthur Miller: Theory and
        Practice." Ph.D. dissertation, University of Wisconsin,
        Madison. <u>Dissertation Abstracts International</u>, 36
        (September), 1172A.
              Examines Miller's theory of drama and his plays in the
        light of that theory. The plays through <u>The Price</u> are
        concerned with the alienation of man from society, while
        <u>The Creation of the World and Other Business</u> implies that
        any act that brings the individual and society together is
        good and any act that alienates the individual from society
        is bad. Despite Miller's belief that a play must show
        rather than tell, in both <u>All My Sons</u> and <u>The Price</u> the
        hero's important social decision occurs before the play
        begins.

14   GILL, BRENDAN. "A Painful Case." <u>New Yorker</u>, 51 (July 7),
        63.

Review of off-Broadway revival of Death of a Salesman.
Easier to admire than to like, the play's manipulation of
our emotions is skillful but unappealing because the principal emotion aroused is an easy, sentimental compassion.
The play has nothing to do with the realities of existence,
yet the audience (including Thomas Mann) wept because it is
Willy's fate never to know who he is, to be so obtuse as to
commit suicide through a misapprehension. Abridged:
1976.19.

15 GOODMAN, WALTER. "Miller's Salesman, Created in 1949, May
    Mean More to 1975." New York Times (June 15), sec. II,
    pp. 1, 5.
        In 1949, with the Depression over and World War II won,
    the seriousness with which Death of a Salesman was taken
    testified to its excellence as a play. In 1975, it is more
    appropriate to the state of a nation enduring the loss of
    an unnecessary, dishonorable war, economic insecurity
    (especially for salesmen), and disillusionment with
    technology.

16 GOTTFRIED, MARTIN. "Rebirth of the Salesman." New York Post
    (June 27).
        Review of revival of Death of a Salesman. Despite a
    mediocre production, the play and Scott's portrayal of
    Willy Loman "take hold almost at once and build to a climax
    of almost unbearable tragedy." The play represents "daz-
    zling craftsmanship and is one of the greatest plays ever
    written by an American; a major tragedy; a classic."
    Reprinted: 1975.28.

17 GRANDEL, HARTMUT. "Death of a Salesman: Tragedy or Social
    Drama?," in American Drama and Theater in the Twentieth
    Century. Edited by Alfred Weber and Siegfried Neuweiler.
    Göttingen: Vandenhoech and Ruprecht, pp. 204-22. (English
    summary, pp. 218-19.)
        The contradictions in Willy's character are the delib-
    erate effect of Miller's achievement in making Salesman
    both a tragedy and a social drama. Willy is both the
    "victim of a society that destroys him" and a hero because
    "his will insists on the formation and realization of a
    better world," the secret hope of all tragedy in Miller's
    view.

18 GROSS, BARRY. "All My Sons and the Larger Context." Modern
    Drama, 18 (March), 15-27.
        All My Sons fails because its point of view character
    (Chris) is adolescent, and because of the inadequacy of its

1975

insistently realistic mode for the "social relation Miller
requires the play to represent." Chris's fine speeches
delivered in his father's backyard "violate our sense of
suitability, of context." This is a failure in content as
well as technique. Joe Keller's real crime is his failure
to connect with the world, but Miller excludes Chris
Keller's vision of a future world just as rigorously as he
excludes Joe's past.

19 HEYEN, WILLIAM. "Arthur Miller's Death of a Salesman and
the American Dream," in American Drama and Theatre in the
Twentieth Century. Edited by Alfred Weber and Siegfried
Neuweiler. Göttingen: Vandenhoech and Ruprecht,
pp. 190-201.
  Discusses the "American rhythms, echoes, reverberations"
in Death of a Salesman. Miller's characters "search for
what will suffice," a "terrestrial morality" they can
justify in the absence of the old faiths. Willy's suicide
is a choice of "meaning over meaninglessness." Whether or
not sympathizing with Willy condemns one to his sort of
hell, one is "hurt for the American dream salesman who buys
his own dreams." Abridged: 1976.19.

20 ISHIZUKA, KOJI. "Two Memory Plays: Williams and Miller,"
in American Literature in the 1940's. Tokyo: American
Literature Society of Japan, pp. 208-12.
  Compares Williams' The Glass Menagerie and Death of a
Salesman as memory plays. Salesman is not a "social play
of indictment but the picture of the inside of a man's
head."

21 JACOBSON, IRVING. "Family Dreams in Death of a Salesman."
American Literature, 47 (May), 247-58.
  Willy's notion of success is related to his and Miller's
sense of the family. His family dream-ideals of past and
future are attempts to pressure reality outside the family
to conform to memory and imagination.

22 KALEM, T. E. "A Défi to Fate." Time, 106 (July 7), 43.
  Review of revival of Death of a Salesman. A "redoubt-
able revival of a masterwork of the American theater." Its
theme is that "failure is the only sin Americans will not
forgive." Scott's performance as Willy is one of "staggering impact." Reprinted: 1975.28.

23 KERR, WALTER. "This 'Salesman' Is More Man Than Myth." New
York Times (June 29), sec. II, pp. 1, 5.

Extensive analysis of George C. Scott's performance as
Willy in revival of <u>Death of a Salesman</u>. The principal
difference between Scott's and other interpretations of
Willy is that Scott does not see him as a once successful
salesman destroyed by the vacuousness of the American
Dream, but a man who "<u>always</u> had to compensate, to inflate
his indeterminate place in the scheme of things, to substitute for his sickened hollowness an equally hollow image
which only his adoring sons could possibly believe." In
Scott's production, the play becomes a "play of persons,
not of social prophesy or some archetypal proclamation of
an already failed American myth."

24   KROLL, JACK. "Triumph." <u>Newsweek</u>, 86 (July 7), 61.
      Review of off-Broadway revival of <u>Death of a Salesman</u>.
The play is a "great public ritualizing of some of our
deepest and deadliest contradictions." This production
makes clear that the play is not dated. The audience still
recognizes Willy, the "American as suicide who kills himself 365 times a year." George C. Scott's directing and
acting underscore the play's "most original intellectual
contribution, the identification of the spiritual bum as an
important American figure--the bum as failure and as decep-
tive success." Reprinted: 1975.28. Abridged: 1976.19.

25   LANNON, WILLIAM W. "The Rise and Rationale of Post World War
      II American Confessional Theater." <u>Connecticut Review</u>,
      8 (April), 73-81.
      <u>Death of a Salesman</u> is a typical example of the American
postwar confessional play. It evokes emotional involvement
on the part of the audience, and it implies confusion on
the part of the author, characters and audience regarding
the increasing gap between the American dream and the
American experience.

26   LOWENTHAL, LAWRENCE D. "Arthur Miller's <u>Incident at Vichy</u>:
      A Sartrean Interpretation." <u>Modern Drama</u>, 18 (March),
      29-41.
      <u>Incident at Vichy</u> is an "explicit dramatic rendition of
Jean-Paul Sartre's treatise on Jews, as well as a clear
structural example of Sartre's definition of the existential
'theatre of situation.'" Traces the Miller-Sartre affinity
in Miller's later plays. <u>Vichy</u> immediately recalls Sartre's
"The Wall" and <u>The Victors</u>. If Miller is now "pessimistic
about mankind, he is still optimistic about individual
man."

1975

27   MANOCCHIO, TONY and PATRICK ROBERTS. "The Loman Family," in
      Families Under Stress: A Psychological Interpretation.
      Boston: Routledge and Kegan Paul, pp. 129-68.
          Analyzes the Loman family in Death of a Salesman. Dis-
      cusses work roles, expectations, differentness, the model
      child, and fantasy. The secret of what Willy did in Boston
      destroys family relationships and Willy himself. Therapy
      may have helped Willy avoid destructive fantasies by focus-
      sing on the need to allow for differences, to share secrets,
      to allow for weaknesses.

28   MARLOWE, JOAN and BETTY BLAKE, eds. "Death of a Salesman."
      New York Theatre Critics' Reviews, 36 (September 15),
      pp. 221-25.
          Reprints New York critics' reviews: Barnes (1975.5);
      Beaufort (1975.6); Gottfried (1975.16); Kalem (1975.22);
      Kroll (1975.24); Sharp (1975.38); Watt (1975.42); Wilson
      (1975.43).

29   MILLER, ROBERT R. "Tragedy in Modern American Drama: The
      Psychological, Social, and Absurdist Conditions in Histor-
      ical Perspective." Ph.D. dissertation, Middle Tennessee
      State University. Dissertation Abstracts International,
      36 (December), 3717A.
          Discusses Miller's interest in the tragic experience of
      the common man as exemplified by Willy Loman.

30   ÖVERLAND, ORM. "The Action and Its Significance: Arthur
      Miller's Struggle with Dramatic Form." Modern Drama, 18
      (March), 1-14.
          Argues that the familiar debate over the real meaning
      of Miller's plays stems from the plays' conflicting themes
      or nonconcentric centers of interest: the emotional and
      the intellectual, the Freudian and the Marxian, the private
      and the social. The use of unrealistic and realistic modes
      of dramatic form are attempts to embody and reconcile these
      polarities. Miller's "distrust of the realistic drama as
      a usable medium was thus properly a distrust of the theater
      itself as a medium."

31   PROBST, LEONARD. "Death of a Salesman." New York Theater
      Critics' Reviews, 36 (September 15), 225.
          Review of revival of Salesman. The play has "gut-level
      meaning for America 1975" as well as 1949. It is the great
      American tragedy, the story of a failure, an Archie Bunker
      type, but George C. Scott plays the role of Willy "not so
      much defeated as defiant." He is a "memorable Willy Loman."

32 RODERICK, JOHN M. "Arthur Miller and American Mythology: The
    Dream as Life Force in Twentieth Century American Drama."
    Ph.D. dissertation, Brown University, 1974. Dissertation
    Abstracts International 35 (May), 7324A.
        Attempts to locate Miller within the central American
    mythology of the American Dream and to trace facets of the
    Dream myth through his dramatic canon. Miller's heroes are
    twentieth century Everymen or American Adams living after
    the Fall. Though Miller is usually regarded as a natural-
    istic playwright with a highly developed social conscience,
    mythic intent and archetypal echoes are present; and each
    hero needs what the Dream ideally represents: the beauty
    and dignity of the individual man.

33 SATA, MASUNORI. "Arthur Miller's Warning Concerning the
    American Dream," in American Literature in the 1940's.
    Tokyo: American Literature Society of Japan, pp. 219-25.
        Sees Biff Loman in Death of a Salesman as a fallen
    American Adam. In After the Fall the protagonist finally
    recognizes the original sin in himself and all other men.

34 SATO, SUSUMU. "The 'Awakening' Theme in Arthur Miller and
    Clifford Odets," in American Literature in the 1940's.
    Tokyo: American Literature Society of Japan, pp. 180-85.
        Differences in the social and personal awakenings of
    characters in the plays of Odets and Miller may reflect
    changes in the social climate between the 1930's and
    1940's, or differences in the playwrights' temperaments.

35 SCHUMACH, MURRAY. "Miller Still a 'Salesman' for a Changing
    Theater." New York Times (June 26), p. 32.
        Interview. Miller's opinions on politics, television,
    theater audiences. After one year's work he abandoned a
    play on the "big issue today, Big Brother." He admits he
    is not as much to the Left as he used to be. He is "sur-
    prised no one has written a cultural history of the American
    theater in terms of its relation to the nature of the
    audiences."

*36 SHARMA, P. P. "Making the World a Home: Arthur Miller's
    Major Thematic Concern." Rajasthan University Studies in
    English, 8: 62-71.

*37 _____. "Realism in Arthur Miller's Plays." Panjab Univer-
    sity Research Bulletin (Arts), 6: 1-11.

1975

38   SHARP, CHRISTOPHER. "Death of a Salesman." Women's Wear
        Daily (June 27).
             Review of revival of Death of a Salesman. George C.
        Scott's Willy "is so bizarre it seems he has only himself
        to blame for his crackup." He is too distinct an individual
        to be a universal failure. Scott aggrandizes the role at
        the expense of the play. Reprinted: 1975.28.

39   SHEPARD, RICHARD J. "Work Begins on City College Arts Hall."
        New York Times (May 13), p. 30.
             Miller participates in a symposium to mark groundbreaking
        ceremonies for a new performing arts center. "The best
        theaters, as far as buildings are concerned, are in univer-
        sities, but the people involved don't know what to do with
        them." There is too much emphasis on reproducing estab-
        lished successes rather than developing plays on local
        themes that might represent the various parts of the country,
        Miller believes.

40   SIMON, JOHN. "The Salesman Dies Again." New York Magazine,
        8 (July 7), 74.
             Review of off-Broadway revival of Death of a Salesman.
        The play is overrated, lacking poetry and clarity of
        thought. Though the subject is potentially tragic, Sales-
        man lacks tragic inevitability, fails to avert a melo-
        dramatic catastrophe, and reveals Miller as a victim of the
        obsessions he sets out to expose. George C. Scott's
        strength and violence are wrong for the role of Willy, as
        is his taking out (as director) the play's Jewishness.
        Abridged: 1976.19.

41   THIPPAVAJJALA, DUTTA RAMESH. "The Heroes of Arthur Miller."
        Ph.D. dissertation, University of Kansas, 1974. Disserta-
        tion Abstracts International, 36 (August), 894A-95A.
             Focusing on Miller's unpublished plays and early drafts
        of major plays, this study groups the plays according to
        two sources of conflict: the crisis of identity and the
        crisis of generativity. The two "major findings" are that
        the Miller hero in his "passionate struggle for identity
        reveals his sense of dignity" and that "his struggle for a
        viewpoint brings out the resources of his conscience, his
        responsibility." Thus the Miller hero is an index to
        Miller's moral vision.

42   WATT, DOUGLAS. "Scott in Miller's Salesman." New York Daily
        News (June 27).

Review of revival of <u>Death of a Salesman</u>. Analyzes the "technically spellbinding" performance of George C. Scott as Willy Loman, but faults his direction. The play envelops the audience in an atmosphere of defeat; but more than in Miller's other plays, "we are concerned with abuses to the soul." Reprinted: 1975.28.

43 WILSON, EDWIN. "Contrasting Views of American Life." <u>Wall Street Journal</u> (June 27).
Review of revival of <u>Death of a Salesman</u>. Compares and contrasts <u>Salesman</u> and <u>Our Town</u> and current productions of them. <u>Salesman</u> is meaningful to a generation "trying to recapture our sense of place and of the fitness of things." Reprinted: 1975.28.

1976

1 BARNES, CLIVE. Miller's 'Crucible' in Stratford." <u>New York Times</u> (June 17), p. 31.
Review of revival of <u>The Crucible</u>. The play is structurally, and perhaps emotionally, Miller's best. It is both a "clarion call for liberty and a soft-noted threnody for despair." Miller has "moral probity, social fearlessness, a conscience for humanity, and talks his mind on the stage--a genuine theatrical quality." If his mind is not that interesting, the "moral force behind it provides it with credibility." Miller's predictability is a source of strength for admirers and weakness for detractors. He is a "moralist who appears to applaud his morality." This is a "shallow spectacle, even with its social uses."

2 _____. "Plays by Williams and Miller Staged." <u>New York Times</u> (January 27), p. 26.
Review of revival of <u>A Memory of Two Mondays</u>. The play is "mawkish, sentimental and rambling." It is "long on characters but short on character." Reprinted: 1976.13.

3 BEAUFORT, JOHN. "Williams and Miller Revivals." <u>Christian Science Monitor</u> (February 4).
Review of revival of <u>A Memory of Two Mondays</u>. Though at times overwordy and sentimental, Miller's "affection registers strongly in these vignettes." Reprinted: 1976.13.

*4 BHATIA, S. K. "<u>Death of a Salesman</u> as a Social Document." <u>Banasthali Patrika</u>, 20: 45-49.

1976

5   GLUECK, GRACE. "Friends of Calder Honor Him." New York Times
(December 8), sec. D, p. 22.
     With three other friends of Alexander Calder, Miller
pays tribute on the death of the sculptor. Miller praises
his "commitment" in his statements on the Vietnam War, and
his "simple decency."

6   GOTTFRIED, MARTIN. "An Old Pair Get New Shine." New York
Post (January 27).
     Review of revival of A Memory of Two Mondays. Though it
"feels like a revival of a playwright gone by," the play is
an "extremely affecting and compassionate work" with a great
deal of honest feeling. Both its writing and construction
are excellent. It is not political or theoretical; it is
just human. Reprinted: 1976.13.

7   HAYASHI, TETSUMARO. An Index to Arthur Miller Criticism.
Second Edition. Metuchen, N.J.: Scarecrow, 151 pp.
     Expanded (by fifty percent) version of 1969.18. Includes
unpublished masters' theses, stresses secondary sources
(in English) through 1974, eliminates some errors in the
first edition, and keys entries to serialized numbers for
greater convenience.

8   JACOBSON, IRVING. "The Vestigial Jews on Mont Sant' Angelo."
Studies in Short Fiction, 13 (Fall), 507-12.
     Miller's short story "Monte Sant' Angelo" deals with
"man displaced from the enveloping context of the family"
but attempting to "feel at home in the larger world outside the family structure, reconstructing that earlier
state of satisfaction with later materials and experiences."

9   JENSEN, GEORGE H. Arthur Miller: A Bibliographical Checklist.
Columbia, South Carolina: J. Faust.
     A bibliography of primary sources that gives the complete
publishing history of all Miller's books, as well as illus-
trations of title pages.

10 KERR, WALTER. "Good Causes Can Make Bad Dramaturgy." New
York Times (June 27), sec. II, pp. 5, 22.
     Review of revival of The Crucible at Stratford, Connecti-
cut. The audience was amused, as was Kerr, at the unbeliev-
ability of the characters, especially the girls; they were
unbelievable because Miller could not believe in them as
characters. The audience, and Kerr, urged Proctor to sign
his confession because the "bullies were such obnoxious
frauds, because we were unable to credit Salem as Salem, or
an antiquated superstition as alive and truly menacing."

11   KNIGHT, MICHAEL. "Hearing to Open on Bid for New Matricide
        Trial." New York Times (January 15), p. 37.
            Hearings on a petition for a new trial for Peter Reilly,
        convicted of matricide in 1973 (see 1975.10), are held.
        Miller has attempted to help prove the youth's innocence,
        setting aside plans to write a play about the case.

12   _____. "Reilly Freed in Mother's Murder." New York Times
        (November 25), pp. 1, 26.
            New evidence is sufficient to persuade Judge Simon S.
        Cohen to dismiss the case against Peter Reilly, convicted
        of matricide in 1973 (see 1975.10). Miller calls for an
        investigation on the grounds that there was a miscarriage
        of justice at the original trial. Miller had hired a pri-
        vate detective who uncovered much of the new evidence.

13   MARLOWE, JOAN and BETTY BLAKE, eds. "A Memory of Two Mondays."
        New York Theatre Critics' Reviews, 37 (January 26), 382-85.
            Reprints New York critics' reviews: Barnes (1976.2);
        Beaufort (1976.3); Gottfried (1976.6); Sharp (1976.20);
        Watt (1976.23); Wilson (1976.24).

14   MARTIN, ROBERT A. and RICHARD D. MEYER. "Arthur Miller on
        Plays and Playwriting." Modern Drama, 19 (December),
        375-84.
            Question and answer session with students at the Univer-
        sity of Michigan in the spring of 1974. Miller discourses
        on intentions and methods in his plays, origins of View
        from the Bridge, motives of John Proctor, film adaptations
        of plays, Eugene O'Neill, social problems and unrest in the
        United States, and the family as a subject for drama.

15   MILLER, JEANNE-MARIE A. "Odets, Miller and Communism."
        College Language Association Journal, 19 (June), 484-93.
            Like Clifford Odets, Miller is concerned with social
        issues, possesses a "bold and sensitive social conscience,"
        and dramatizes social currents in an attempt to deliver a
        warning to the American people. Discusses the McCarthyite
        background of The Crucible and its critical reception.

16   O'CONNOR, PETER. "The Wasteland of Thomas Pynchon's V."
        College Literature, 3: 49-55.
            In the light of Eliot's The Wasteland and Joyce's
        Ulysses, questions Miller's view (New York Magazine,
        December 30, 1974) that 1949 was the last year of a common
        assumption of cultural unity in Western society.

1976

17   PRADHAN, NARINDAR S. "Arthur Miller and the Pursuit of Guilt,"
      in Studies in American Literature: Essays in Honour of
      William Mulder. Edited by Jagdish Chander and Narindar S.
      Pradhan. Delhi: Oxford, pp. 28-42.
           In All My Sons, Death of a Salesman and A View from the
      Bridge, guilt is individual and psychological, but in The
      Crucible, After the Fall and Incident at Vichy Miller
      believes that evil is universal and that there is a need
      for instinctual and moral guilt in the face of it.

18   PROBST, LEONARD. "A Memory of Two Mondays." New York Theatre
      Critics' Reviews, 37 (January), 385.
           Brief comment on revival of A Memory of Two Mondays.
      The play is a "sometimes funny, sometimes forced social
      document."

19   RILEY, CAROLYN and P. C. MENDELSON, eds. Contemporary Literary
      Criticism. Vol. 6. Detroit: Gale Research, pp. 326-37.
           Reprints (abridged) of: 1960.8; 1964.30; 1964.31;
      1967.36; 1968.17; 1968.26; 1970.9; 1971.23; 1972.48;
      1974.13; 1974.21; 1975.7; 1975.14; 1975.19; 1975.24;
      1975.40.

20   SHARP, CHRISTOPHER. "Miller and Williams at the Phoenix."
      Women's Wear Daily (January 28).
           Review of revival of A Memory of Two Mondays. The good
      use Miller makes of the large number of actors on stage is
      remarkable. The play resembles recent David Storey plays
      in its lack of plot, creation of personality in a group,
      and ongoing revelations of individual character flaws.
      Reprinted: 1976.13.

21   SHENKER, ISRAEL. "Jewish Cultural Arts: The Big Debate."
      New York Times (January 13), p. 42.
           Speaking at a panel on Jewish cultural arts, Miller
      admits he has "never been able to find where [my ethnic
      identity] leaves off and my American nature begins." He
      believes that what Jewish writers have in common is that
      they "seem to be dancing on the edge of a precipice."

22   THOMPSON, JOHN L. "Self-Realization in the Major Plays of
      Arthur Miller." Ph.D. dissertation, University of Nebraska,
      Lincoln, 1975. Dissertation Abstracts International, 36
      (June), 8065A-66A.
           Analyzes the degree of self-realization experienced by
      the main characters of the plays through The Price. As a

social playwright, Miller is almost didactically preoccupied
with teaching his audiences social responsibility. This
responsibility comes from self-knowledge and social
awareness.

23   WATT, DOUGLAS. "Depression Duet." New York Daily News
        (January 27).
            Review of revival of A Memory of Two Mondays. An "oddly
        affectionate piece" for Miller, the play is less popular
        than A View from the Bridge, for which it was originally
        the curtain raiser, but a better play. Reprinted: 1976.13.

24   WILSON, EDWIN. "Revival Nights on Broadway." Wall Street
        Journal (February 2).
            Review of revival of A Memory of Two Mondays. Though
        its lack of emphasis on plot is uncharacteristic of Miller
        and its length is excessive, the play "vividly depicts a
        time and place which are very much a part of the American
        scene and have come back to haunt us again in recent years."
        It is a "hard-edged Chekhovian piece." Reprinted: 1976.13.

25   WONZONG, RANDY L. "A Structural Analysis of Arthur Miller's
        Major Plays." Ph.D. dissertation, Northwestern University,
        1975. Dissertation Abstracts International, 36 (June),
        7736A.
            Though several scenes in Miller are theatrical and
        dramatically effective, and the developing action often
        skillfully constructed, he fails to "develop enough success-
        ful structural devices to combine developing action and
        overall theme into a compelling, unified whole." In forc-
        ing his characters into contact with the play's theme, he
        resorts to "manipulations and shifts of focus which make
        the concluding action in his plays seem arbitrary and
        artificial."

1977

1   ANON. "Appeal Sent by Writers and Artists." New York Times
        (February 15), p. 3.
            Miller supports a petition in the form of a letter to
        Gustav Husak, the Czechoslovak leader, protesting the
        recent arrests of dissidents in "contravention of the
        Helsinki accords."

2   ANON. "Arthur Miller Sees Insecurity." New York Times
        (January 11), p. 15.

1977

Miller protests the arrest of a friend, Czech writer
Pavel Kohout. The arrest means that the Czech regime feels
"insecure enough to indulge itself in open terror against
any writer who persists in expressing his personal truths
rather than using his art to justify Soviet strategic
interests."

3   ANON. "In the Country." Booklist, 73 (April 1), 1138.
        Brief review of Miller's text accompanying Inge Morath's
    photography. Miller's twenty-five years in Connecticut
    have mellowed him. A fondness for this isolated territory,
    threatened by developers and alien life styles, has softened
    the urban personality of earlier years.

4   ANON. "In the Country." Kirkus Reviews, 45 (March 15),
    344.
        Brief review of Miller's text accompanying Inge Morath's
    photographs. The text is "rambling and free-associating,"
    though Miller is aware of his "city limits and literary
    orientation" in providing a "gentle history of the changes
    he has witnessed since land became real estate."

5   ANON. "New Play by Miller Is Faulted in Washington." New
    York Times (May 3), p. 50.
        Summarizes mostly unfavorable reviews of opening of The
    Archbishop's Ceiling in Washington, D. C. Miller describes
    the play as "a dramatic meditation on the impact of immense
    state power upon human identity and the common concept of
    what is real and illusory in a group of writers living in a
    small European capital today." Tentative plans have been
    made to present the play in New York in the fall, after
    some reworking.

6   ANON. "The Theater Essays of Arthur Miller." Kirkus Reviews,
    45 (December 1), 1308.
        Review. Miller's hopes, quarrels, and worries all pro-
    ceed from his controversial credo: that since the theatre
    is a place where "an adult who wants to live can find plays
    that will heighten our awareness of what living in our time
    involves," its challenge "is still the Elizabethan one,
    the public address on the street corner," and a "drama
    rises in intensity and stature in proportion to the weight
    of its application to all manner of men." In this book one
    finds what is missing in today's theatre.

7   BROYARD, ANATOLE. "A Calder on Every Lawn?" New York Times
    (February 10), p. 37.

Review of In the Country, by Miller, with photographs
by Inge Morath. Agrees with Miller's assertion that the
current nostalgia for rural life is a mistaken conviction
that "here was the last stronghold of a vanished individualism." Rural life was always dominated by communal
needs. But the nostalgia is a "yearning for the vanished
communal feeling," Broyard argues.

8 BRUSTEIN, ROBERT. "Drama in the Age of Einstein." New York
   Times (August 7), sec. II, pp. 1, 22.
       Miller's dramatic premises come from the age of Newton,
   whereas those of post-modern playwrights came from the age
   of Einstein. As contrasted with the post-moderns, Miller
   believes that "the action A precedes the consequence B,
   which leads inevitably to the catastrophe C." Analyzes
   All My Sons and Death of a Salesman to show that Miller's
   "single purpose is to identify the guilt, establish the
   responsibility of various protagonists and bring about a
   moral showdown," especially between father and son, even
   if this means sacrificing credibility. Compares Miller
   with David Rabe.

9 COE, RICHARD L. "Arthur Miller's 'Ceiling.'" Washington Post
   (May 2), sec. B, pp. 1, 7.
       Review of Washington opening of The Archbishop's Ceiling.
   Miller's police state atmosphere contributes to the theme
   that to "transplant a writer from his roots, however con-
   stricting the regime around him, can kill the writer's
   gift"; but Miller's use of bugging as a technical device
   "forces him into purely technical choices which belabor his
   moral concerns." The play does not really begin until
   Act II, includes unnecessary characters, and clearly needs
   more work.

10 FRANKEL, HASKEL. "When Respect Is Fatal." New York Times
   (March 13), sec. xxiii, p. 8.
       Review of Hartman Theater Company (Stamford, Connecticut)
   revival of Death of a Salesman. The production is boring,
   not so much because of touches of age in the play, such as
   a son's being ruined for life by catching his father in
   the act of philandering, but because "we think when we
   should be feeling." If there is a tragic figure in the
   play, it is Biff rather than Willy.

11 GUSSOW, MEL. "'Salesman' Given in Stamford." New York Times
   (March 5), p. 10.

207

1977

> Review of revival of <u>Death of a Salesman</u> by Hartman
> Theater Company in Stamford, Connecticut. The play must
> have "sizable acting and authoritative direction" if it is
> to retain its "tragic dimensions." This production has
> neither. The play is too often "pushed into sentimentality
> and even self-parody," two areas it should avoid.

12   JOHNSTON, ALBERT H. "<u>In the Country</u>." <u>Publisher's Weekly</u>,
>   211 (January 24), 321.
>   Review. Miller's "muted, thoughtful and sometimes witty
> and amusing stories of life among New Englanders" lend
> resonance to Inge Morath's photographs.

13   LASK, THOMAS. "Equity Theater <u>Crucible</u> Focuses on Failing
>   Sense of Community." <u>New York Times</u> (December 10), p. 16.
>   Review of revival of <u>The Crucible</u>. Director David
> William Kitchen has "given us the play without the porten-
> tousness and hot-house didacticism that marked the first
> production." Though Miller is prolix, the play has been
> stripped down so that it becomes "flexible and supple with
> moments of genuine power and beauty."

14   MCKAY, CHARLES E. "The Themes of Awareness, Self-Knowledge
>   and Love in Arthur Miller's Major Dramatic Works." Ph.D.
>   dissertation, University of Mississippi, 1976. <u>Disserta-
>   tion Abstracts International</u>, 37 (January), 4356A.
>   Whereas love is a destructive force in the plays through
> <u>After the Fall</u>, it becomes increasingly affirmative in the
> later plays. In <u>The Creation of the World and Other Busi-
> ness</u> love and instinct are seen as attributes of God.
> Miller has come to reject awareness and self-knowledge as a
> basis for conduct and morality, and to believe that man is
> both good and evil, and most God-like when acting instinc-
> tively from love.

15   MASSIE, ALLAN. "Land of Lost Content." <u>Times Literary Sup-
>   plement</u> (June 17), p. 722.
>   Review of <u>In the Country</u>. Miller's ruminative and at
> times despairing text deals with the "decay of the indig-
> enous, almost self-sufficient farming community." The
> book evokes a "lost Eden, a simpler, innocent world where
> the American dream, the Protestant ethic, were
> unchallenged."

16   OTNESS, HAROLD T. "<u>In the Country</u>." <u>Library Journal</u>, 102
>   (March 15), 722.

Inge Morath's photographs are lovely and provocative,
but Miller's text makes the book much more than coffee-
table nostalgia. Miller's twelve impressionistic sketches
are marked by sadness and quiet desperation rather than
sermonizing or rage. A book for libraries "trying to document the changes taking place in our society."

1978

1   ANON. "The Theater Essays of Arthur Miller." Booklist, 74
    (February 15), 971.
        Brief review. Whatever the topic of discussion, Miller's
    views form a "serious and consistent assessment of the thea-
    ter's nature and aims."

2   BRATER, ENOCH. "The Theater Essays of Arthur Miller." New
    Republic, 178 (May 6), 32.
        Review. The essays afford the opportunity to compare
    the realism of Miller's early plays with the new realism of
    the American theatre. Miller does not merely render "iso-
    lated pieces of experience, but succeeds in theatricalizing
    experience itself." His realism is not merely a way of
    saying something; he has something to say as well. And his
    "old-fashioned humanism, so desperately struggling to make
    a comeback when so many of us are reluctant to take any
    stand at all," distinguishes him from the present gener-
    ation of American playwrights.

3   GOLD, RONALD L. "A Comparative Analysis of Arthur Miller's
    Death of a Salesman by Means of Dramatic Criticism and the
    Sereno and Bodaken Trans-per Model." Ph.D. dissertation,
    University of Southern California, 1977. Dissertation
    Abstracts International, 38 (April) 5800A-5801A.
        Applies communication theory as well as dramatic criteria
    to Death of a Salesman and concludes that it is a psycho-
    logical rather than a sociological play. Argues that
    applying dramatic criteria only would not "highlight this
    fact."

4   HAVENER, W. MICHAEL. "The Theater Essays of Arthur Miller."
    Library Journal, 103 (March 1), 582.
        Review. The collection provides "valuable insights into
    Miller's plays and contemporary drama," though the omission
    of pieces like "Subsidized Theater" (1947) and Miller's
    comments on the autobiographical controversy surrounding
    After the Fall is regrettable.

1978

5 JOHNSTON, ALBERT H. "The Theater Essays of Arthur Miller."
   Publisher's Weekly, 213 (January 2), 60.
        Review. The essays and interviews "speak cogently and
   eloquently to the problems of the contemporary theater and
   to the ills of our society." Miller seems to disavow, in
   his foreword, the search for a tragic mode--an attitude
   that perhaps bears on what some consider his decline as a
   playwright.

6 MARTIN, ROBERT A. "Introduction," in The Theater Essays of
   Arthur Miller. Edited by Robert A Martin. New York:
   Viking, pp. xv-xxxix.
        Surveys Miller's career as playwright and critic of the
   theatre. Argues that Miller matured as a dramatic critic
   in the 1950's partly because of the turmoil in his private
   and public life, and that his theatre essays "may well
   represent the single most important statement of critical
   principles to appear in England and America by a major
   playwright since the Prefaces of George Bernard Shaw."

7 SCHLUETER, JUNE. "The Theater Essays of Arthur Miller."
   Bestsellers, 37 (February), 345.
        Review. Though scattered comments do "illuminate modern
   drama in general and Miller in particular," the book lacks
   a thesis and any evidence of a "maturing playwright's
   vision." Miller's views are a professional's rather than
   a literary critic's, and the prefaces, helpful as such, are
   incomplete in isolation.

8 SULLIVAN, JACK. "The Theater Essays of Arthur Miller."
   Saturday Review, 5 (April 1), 36.
        Review. The later essays have more focus and sophisti-
   cation than the earlier ones, though it is startling to
   find the author of Death of a Salesman complaining about
   the cult of defeat and alienation in contemporary drama.
   Miller's foreword is especially impressive in its attack
   on the modern obsession with irony and the "stylized re-
   duction of human suffering to a groan and a cough."

Index

Abirached, Robert, 1965.1
Adamczewski, Zygmunt, 1963.1
Adler, Henry, 1960.1; 1962.2
After the Fall, 1964.2-6, 11,
    14, 15, 17, 18, 20, 21, 23-
    27, 30-34, 36, 38, 40, 42,
    45, 47, 50, 53, 54, 58, 61,
    63, 64, 67, 69-71, 73, 77,
    81; 1965.7, 15, 20, 22, 23,
    28, 29, 31-34, 38, 44, 46,
    50, 59; 1966.5, 6, 9, 13,
    17, 18, 20, 24; 1967.9, 12,
    14, 20, 35, 40, 41; 1968.13,
    16, 58; 1969.13, 22, 24, 38;
    1970.6, 15, 21; 1971.27;
    1972.7, 62; 1973.6, 10, 14,
    20, 26; 1974.12, 15; 1975.33;
    1976.17; 1977.14; 1978.4;
--foreign productions, 1965.33;
    1966.1, 8; 1967.4;
--television production,
    1973.12; 1974.17
Albee, Edward, compared with
    Miller, 1968.42; 1972.8
Allen, Harold van, 1964.1
Allenby, Peggy, actress, 1950.4
All My Sons, 1947.1-6, 8, 9, 11-
    16, 18-20, 22-34, 36-44;
    1948.3-13; 1949.22, 63, 64,
    67, 71; 1950.16; 1951.12;
    1952.8; 1953.42; 1955.29;
    1958.12; 1959.19, 28;
    1960.2; 1961.10, 13, 22;
    1962.39; 1964.1, 37, 44, 82;
    1967.15, 36; 1968.13;
    1970.21; 1971.22, 39, 44;

    1972.7, 43; 1974.3, 5, 14,
    18; 1975.13, 18; 1976.17;
    1977.8;
--film, 1948.3, 4, 6, 8, 11, 12;
--London production, 1947.29;
    1948.5, 7, 13
Allsop, Kenneth, 1959.1
Alpert, Hollis, 1951.1; 1961.1
American Bar Association,
    1953.10, 36
American Clock, The, 1973.4
American Committee for Cultural
    Freedom, 1956.1, 2, 26
American Jewish Committee,
    1962.32
Anderson, Robert, 1971.1
Angell, Roger, 1961.2
Archbishop's Ceiling, The,
    1977.5, 9
Archer, Eugene, 1961.11
Arendt, Hannah, influence on
    Miller, 1964.75; 1965.12
Arts and Humanities Act, 1965.10,
    28
Ashley, Franklin B., 1971.3
Atkinson, Brooks, 1947.12-15;
    1949.25-27; 1950.4-6;
    1951.7; 1953.7-10; 1955.9-11;
    1957.22; 1958.7, 8; 1959.6;
    1960.5; 1971.4
Aughtry, Charles E., 1963.4
awards, 1947.5, 20; 1949.5-8,
    11-13, 15, 16, 36, 57, 84;
    1956.6; 1958.1, 20; 1959.3,
    5; 1968.29; 1970.1; 1971.2;
    1973.1

Index

--compared with Miller, 1964.12;
   1968.37
Douglass, James W., 1963.7
Downer, Alan S., 1949.46;
   1951.12; 1961.17, 18;
   1968.25
dramaturgy, 1957.43; 1958.25;
   1959.24; 1960.13; 1961.50;
   1962.29; 1963.15; 1964.60,
   65; 1965.15; 1967.34, 36;
   1968.50, 1973.29; 1975.30;
   1976.25
Driver, Tom F., 1960.13; 1964.23;
   1970.8
Drury, Allen, 1956.27, 28
Dudek, Louis, 1961.19
Duffield, Marcus, 1945.6
Dunnock, Mildred, actress,
   1949.36, 52, 69; 1966.16;
   1970.8
Duprey, Richard A., 1961.20
Dusenburg, Winifred L., 1960.14

Eaton, Walter P., 1947.24;
   1949.47
Edwards, John, 1961.21
Eisenstatt, Martha T., 1962.11
Eisinger, Chester E., 1970.9
Eliot, T. S., 1958.17; 1967.13;
   1976.16;
--compared with Miller, 1949.9;
   1962.20; 1963.6
Emerson, Ralph Waldo, romanticism
   of, 1965.57
Emery, Fred, 1972.16
Enemy of the People, An, 1950.5,
   7, 9-11, 13, 15, 17; 1951.2-
   4, 7, 8, 10, 12, 13, 17, 18,
   20, 21, 23, 25; 1953.15;
   1959.6, 14, 18; 1968.16;
   1971.5, 10, 16, 18, 21, 25,
   26, 30-32, 40, 41;
--See also Henrik Ibsen
Epstein, Arthur D., 1965.19;
   1970.10
Epstein, Charlotte, 1975.12
Epstein, Leslie, 1965.20
Ericson, Raymond, 1967.17
Erikson, Erik H., influence on
   Miller, 1974.13

Esslin, Martin, 1965.21
Esslinger, Pat, 1972.17
Esterow, Milton, 1962.12
Evans, Richard I., 1969.14

Falb, Lewis W., 1973.11
Fallaci, Oriana, 1965.22
Farnsworth, T. A., 1961.22
Farrell, Isolde, 1955.18
Farrell, James T., 1956.29
Fast, Howard, 1955.19
Feldman, Jack, 1975.13
Fellini, Federico, compared with
   Miller, 1966.9
Fender, Stephen, 1967.18
Ferguson, Francis, 1965.23
Feron, James, 1965.24
Ferres, John H., 1972.18, 19
Ferris, Oliver H.P., 1969.15
Fields, B. S., 1972.20
Findlater, Richard, 1957.27
Fisher, William J., 1952.3
Flanagan, James K., 1970.11
Fleming, Peter, 1948.7; 1949.48
Fleming, William P., 1972.21
Focus, 1944.1; 1945.2-5, 7, 8,
   10-12; 1946.1-3; 1948.2;
   1962.32; 1967.21
Foster, Richard J., 1961.23
Frank, Stanley, 1966.10
Frankel, Haskel, 1977.10
Freedley, George, 1947.25;
   1949.49; 1953.18, 19, 26;
   1956.30, 31; 1961.24;
   1964.24; 1965.25
Freedman, Morris, 1967.19;
   1971.12
French, Philip, 1967.20
"From the Creation," 1974.16
Fromm, Erich, influence on
   Miller, 1965.12
Fruchter, Norm, 1962.13
Fuller, A. Howard, 1949.50
Funke, Lewis, 1953.20; 1958.14;
   1964.25; 1969.15; 1971.13, 14

Gable, Clark, actor, 1961.47
Gabriel, Gilbert W., 1949.51
Ganz, Arthur, 1963.9; 1964.26
Gardner, R. H., 1965.26

215

Nathan, George Jean, 1945.9;
 1947.37; 1949.67, 68;
 1951.21; 1953.26, 34, 35;
 1960.22; 1967.26
National Institute of Arts and
 Letters, 1958.20; 1959.3;
 1972.15
Nazis, 1964.29, 39, 79, 80;
 1965.6, 49
Nelson, Benjamin, 1968.42;
 1970.8, 17
Neumann, Erich, 1974.13
Newman, Edwin, 1971.32
Newman, Paul, actor, 1964.78;
 1968.1
Newman, William J., 1958.24
New York City Youth Board,
 1955.6-8, 12, 21-23; 1965.30
Nichols, Lewis, 1944.10; 1965.42
Nietzsche, Friedrich, compared
 with Miller, 1966.6
Nightingale, Benedict, 1969.26
Nolan, Paul T., 1966.20
North, Alex, 1949.76
Nourse, Joan T., 1965.43, 44
Novick, Julius, 1964.60; 1971.33
Nyren, Dorothy, 1960.23

Oberg, Arthur K., 1967.37
O'Connor, Frank, 1956.42
O'Connor, John J., 1974.17
O'Connor, Peter, 1976.16
Odets, Clifford, compared to
 Miller, 1949.29; 1955.13,
 19; 1964.68; 1975.34;
 1976.15
Oliver, Edith, 1965.45; 1974.18
Olivier, Sir Lawrence, 1956.16;
 1965.21, 24, 41, 52, 58
O'Neill, Eugene, 1947.20, 31;
 1949.69; 1956.41; 1959.4;
 1963.13; 1964.58; 1966.8,
 19; 1969.22; 1971.11;
 1974.20; 1976.14;
--compared with Miller, 1949.54;
 1958.6; 1959.12; 1963.6;
 1965.15; 1968.37, 47;
 1971.37; 1972.35; 1973.14, 24
Osborne, John, 1958.6;
--compared to Miller, 1965.55

Otness, Harold T., 1977.16
Otten, Charlotte F., 1963.19
Överland, Orm, 1975.30

Palmer, Tony, 1968.43
Parker, Brian, 1966.21
Parks, Larry, investigation by
 HUAC, 1957.24
Parradine, Thomas E., 1954.2
Partridge, C. J., 1969.27;
 1971.34
Paul, Rajinder, 1972.49
Payne, Darwin R., 1956.43
Pellegrin, Raymond, 1962.22
P.E.N., 1965.8, 9, 42; 1966.3;
 1967.5, 38; 1968.46; 1969.8,
 31; 1974.2
Peterson, Ralph, 1944.11
Phelan, Kappo, 1947.38; 1949.69
Philadelphia Drama Guild, 1973.5
Phillips, John, 1965.46
Pinsker, Sanford, 1971.35
"Poets for Peace," 1967.31
Ponti, Carlo, 1964.78
Popkin, Henry, 1960.24; 1961.43;
 1964.61, 62; 1965.47-49
Porter, Thomas E., 1969.28
Pradhan, Narindar S., 1976.17
Price, The, 1968.4, 6, 7, 9, 12,
 16-23, 25, 28-30, 32-34, 36-
 41, 43-45, 47-49, 52, 53,
 55-57; 1969.4, 12, 19, 39;
 1970.6, 10, 14, 16, 17, 24;
 1971.9, 14, 28, 44; 1972.7,
 40, 60; 1973.14, 15, 19;
 1975.13; 1976.22;
--London production, 1969.3, 26,
 34;
--published version, 1968.3;
--television production, 1971.19,
 33
Price, Jonathan, 1964.63
Prideaux, Tom, 1964.64
Prince and the Show Girl, The,
 1956.16, 22
Probst, Leonard, 1972.50;
 1975.31; 1976.18
"Prophecy, The," 1970.21
Prudhow, John, 1962.29

Quasimodo, Salvatore, 1964.65
Quigly, Isabel, 1957.39; 1961.44

Rahv, Philip, 1965.50; 1969.29
Raines, Mary, 1968.44, 45
Ranald, Margaret Loftus, 1965.51
Raphael, D. D., 1960.25
Rascoe, Burton, 1944.12
Raskin, A. H., 1953.36
Rattigan, Terence, compared with
    Miller, 1961.22
Rauh, Joseph L., 1957.7, 20, 30
Raymond, Harry, 1953.37
Raymont, Henry, 1967.38; 1968.46;
    1969.30, 31; 1971.36;
    1972.51
Reade, Charles, 1945.4
Reason Why, The, 1969.16
Reeve, F. D., 1970.18
Reilly, Peter, Miller's defense
    of, 1975.9, 10; 1976.11, 12
Reno, Raymond H., 1969.32
Rice, Elmer, compared with
    Miller, 1961.36; 1963.6
Richardson, Jack, 1968.47;
    1973.22
Riley, Carolyn, 1973.23; 1974.19;
    1976.19
Robards, Jason, actor, 1964.81
Roberts, Hanley, 1952.4
Roberts, James L., 1964.66
Roberts, Patrick, 1975.27
Robinson, Edward C., actor,
    1948.6
Robotham, John S., 1970.19, 20
Roderick, John M., 1975.32
Rogoff, Gordon, 1964.67
Rolo, Charles, 1961.45
Rosenberg, Ethel and Julius,
    1955.19
Ross, George, 1951.22
Ross, Jean L., 1945.10, 11
Rossellini, Renzo, composer,
    1961.6; 1967.17, 28
Rossellini, Roberto, producer,
    1961.6
Rosten, Norman, screenwriter,
    1962.2, 30
Roth, Martin, 1966.22
Rothenberg, Albert, 1973.24
Rothkopf, Carol Z., 1964.13

Rothman, Stanley, 1953.38
Rouleau, Raymond, director,
    1955.35; 1958.13
Rovere, Richard H., 1956.44;
    1957.40; 1962.31; 1963.20
Rowe, Kenneth Thorpe, 1960.26
Russia, 1956.1, 25; 1957.1;
    1961.11; 1969.17, 31, 33, 35;
    1970.13, 18, 19
--See also Soviet Union
Ryan, Robert, actor, 1969.16

S., F., 1949.70; 1965.52
Saisselin, Rémy G., 1960.27
Salisbury, Harrison E., 1969.33
Samachson, Dorothy and Joseph,
    1954.9
Sanders, Kevin, 1972.52, 53
Sargeant, Winthrop, 1963.21
Saroyan, William, 1952.3;
--compared with Miller, 1949.82;
    1955.13;
--influence on Miller, 1944.10
Sartre, Jean-Paul, 1955.34;
    1956.14; 1971.23;
--compared to Miller, 1960.27;
    1967.33; 1970.14; 1975.26
--screenwriter, 1957.45; 1958.13,
    18, 22; 1959.2, 13, 17, 22,
    25
Sata, Masunori, 1975.33
Satu, Susumu, 1975.34
Scanlan, Thomas M., 1971.37;
    1974.20
Schlueter, June, 1978.7
Schneider, Daniel E., 1949.71;
    1950.16
Schraepen, Edmond, 1970.21
Schumach, Murray, 1949.72;
    1975.35
Schwartz, Harry, 1956.45
de Schweinitz, George, 1960.11
Scott, George C., actor, 1971.19;
    1975.5, 6, 16, 22-24, 31, 38,
    40, 42
Seager, Allan, 1959.20
Selz, Jean, 1955.35
Seiger, Marvin L., 1952.9
Shakespeare, William, 1958.9,
    18; 1964.12
Shanley, John P., 1962.32